AN INTRODUCTION TO
THE STUDY OF EDUCATION

EXPLORATION SERIES IN EDUCATION

UNDER THE ADVISORY EDITORSHIP OF

JOHN GUY FOWLKES

3RD EDITION

AN INTRODUCTION TO THE STUDY OF EDUCATION

Revised by
JAMES E. FRASIER
College of Education
Arizona State University

HARPER & ROW, PUBLISHERS
NEW YORK, EVANSTON, AND LONDON

AN INTRODUCTION TO THE STUDY OF EDUCATION, 3RD EDITION
Copyright © 1951, 1956 by Harper & Row, Publishers, Incorporated
Copyright © 1965 by James E. Frasier

C-1

Library of Congress Catalog Card Number: 65–11702

To Jean
and
Janet, Doug, Curt, and Tom

CONTENTS

PART III/THE TEACHER AND AMERICAN EDUCATION

Introduction

Critical Issues in American Education

EDITOR'S INTRODUCTION

The principle of a free educational opportunity was established in the United States as a result of two laws passed by the State of Massachusetts in the seventeenth century, the Act of 1642 and "The Old Deluder Act" of 1647. In keeping with the spirit of these statutes the American public has continued to express over the years abiding faith in our system of public education.

Today, the citizens of local communities are showing even more interest in the support and operation of their school systems. They are also recognizing the importance of teachers as the major determining factor in the quality of both elementary and secondary school programs. Teachers are regarded now as professional workers and are recognized as valuable members of their communities. As a result many young men and women are turning to teaching because of the personal satisfaction such recognition brings.

This volume will prove valuable both for teachers already committed to the profession and for students who are still contemplating teaching as a career. It is, in fact, pointed at helping these students in deciding about the critical question of vocation. It will further aid the student in learning how present-day education developed and how the intimate and essential interrelationship between education and our society operates.

This work is the third edition of a book written by George Willard Frasier and published in 1951. The second edition was published in 1956. These first two editions were used by many students throughout the country, and it is in answer to a demand that the third edition appears. The author of this edition, Dr. James Frasier, is the nephew of the late George Willard Frasier and has himself won distinction in the field of education.

JOHN GUY FOWLKES

PREFACE

In the past ten years there has been significant evidence which suggests that teacher education has matured beyond its normal school-oriented past and is moving into its rightful place among the professions. Interdisciplinary studies of teacher education programs such as those conducted by TEPS (the National Education Association group concerned with these programs), the advent of a national basis for the accreditation of teacher preparation institutions, and the rapid disappearance of sub-baccalaureate teacher certification provide valid evidence that teacher education has "come of age." Now it is the responsibility of teacher education students and teachers to take advantage of the increased opportunities the new perspective of teacher preparation affords. As T. M. Stinnett[1] has noted: "The chief task of education in the future is to upgrade drastically the intellectual and technical competence of our teachers." The intent of this third edition of An Introduction To The Study Of Education is to contribute positively to the upgrading process.

In preparing the third edition of this already widely accepted textbook every attempt has been made to maintain the vitality and appeal of the original and revised editions which made them so attractive to students. Pedantry would be completely out of character in an introductory book. However, in view of the time lapse since the publication of the revised edition, the great changes in education noted above, and the significantly increased calibre of teacher education students, a major rewriting and reorganization of the content was required. Obvious information has been deleted, unnecessary repetition of ideas eliminated, and the style of writing upgraded.

The book is still primarily addressed to undergraduate classes in professional education. It is hoped, however, that the addition of new provocative material together with a more sophisticated approach to the entire volume will also make it valuable as a resource for certain graduate courses as well as interested lay persons. The "Critical Issues" statements which introduce each of the major sections of the book should help all readers focus their attention on the crux of the content.

Although it is impossible to acknowledge everyone who has contributed,

[1] G. K. Hodenfield and T. M. Stinnett, *The Education of Teachers,* Englewood Cliffs, New Jersey, Prentice-Hall, 1961, p. 135.

either directly or indirectly, to the production of this book, the special contributions made by certain persons and groups should be noted.

First, I wish to express gratitude to my late uncle, George W. Frasier. To thousands of educators he was a friend, teacher, college president, and leader. To me he was also confidant, model, and inspiration. The current edition stems from the base of his earlier works and, but for his untimely death several years ago, would have been jointly authored by him.

Deep thanks is owed the many students at Arizona State University and Oklahoma State University who used this material in its formulative stages and whose numerous comments and criticisms proved invaluable.

To the typists, proofreaders, and other secretarial personnel goes further thanks.

Any credit is gratefully shared with those noted above plus my own teachers, colleagues, and friends. Shortcomings can all be credited to me.

J. E. FRASIER

Tempe, Arizona

PART I

The Foundations of American Education

INTRODUCTION

"In this world of ours, we are fundamentally in a race between education and catastrophe; either we will have sufficient knowledge with which to solve our national and international problems, or the catastrophe of an unwelcome tyranny is bound to overcome us in our ignorance. That's why our free public school system is the great hope of our future preparedness, and really, the hope of the free world." The foregoing statement made, not by a renowned educator, but by a military leader, General Omar N. Bradley, is synoptic of the basic premise of this textbook.

Our free public school system as a vital institution did not just "happen." American public education as it exists today rests upon foundations of great significance. We will examine some of the underlying ideas and review the backgrounds of the important people and incidents contributing to our emerging modern school system.

Education is an important aspect of freedom, one with which the Americans should concern themselves. A summary, even if brief, of where education has been, what important problems it has faced, how it fits into a democratic social order, and where it must go in the future is of great importance to all citizens of the United States—such a summary is prerequisite for anyone contemplating the profession of teaching. It is to be hoped that all fine students, those with keenest intellect and personality, will become intrigued with the story of American education so that they cannot resist a career in teaching as a life's work!

———————————————

CRITICAL ISSUES
IN AMERICAN EDUCATION

Each of the statements listed below is representative of opinion concerning American education today. Most of them indicate a position on issues that are closely related to the topics discussed in Part I of the text. It should be interesting for you to consider your own beliefs before you continue reading this section of the book, and then again near the end of this portion of the course.

These are not true-false statements. They are opinions, and you should react with your own opinion. A scale is suggested which you may want to use to check your beliefs, or, you may want to devise a scale of your own. If you will react to these statements both before and after working with the material, you may discover that your opinion has changed with regard to some of the issues; in other cases your study will probably serve to strengthen your original position. Whichever way, it is important for you to build a set of intelligent, defensible beliefs, and to know *why* you believe what you do.

What's Your Opinion?

React to each of the numbered statements below, in one of the following ways:

I am in full agreement—(AA)*

I agree, with some reservations—(A)

I agree, but only slightly more than I disagree—(a)

I disagree, but only slightly more than I agree—(d)

I disagree, but with some reservations—(D)

I am in total disagreement—(DD)

I have no opinion at this time—(N)

1. Our schools have put great emphasis upon individual success, but they have done so with due consideration for the common good.
2. Effective instruction results when the teacher aims primarily to prepare the child for adult life.
3. Courses in science and mathematics are necessary and effective mental disciplines for all students.
4. The school should instill obedience because it is a condition of the highest type of leadership that "he who would command must first learn to obey."
5. Education should work towards producing a curriculum the individual can draw upon when the need arises in life experiences.

* If you want to keep a record of your opinions, you should note the number of the statement and the symbol which indicates your reaction in your notebook.

6. The school should strive to develop in its pupils the hardy and rugged individualism that characterized early American life.

7. Rigorous control of learning by adults gives children the moral stamina and fiber on which self-control is built.

8. Emphasis should be placed upon the special method of teaching a subject rather than upon improving the learning process.

9. Education can be best achieved by emphasizing the organized subject matter of the regular school curriculum, rather than by wasting time on the problems young people have here and now.

10. The wise teacher keeps classroom discussion away from controversial questions.

11. Each community should be free to order its own education without interference from a state board of education or state department of education.

12. The pupil profits to the degree that the materials of instruction are presented to him in logical organization.

13. The increasing use of scientific method in education will ultimately lead to the abandonment of philosophy of education.

14. In the interest of social stability, the new generation must be brought into conformity with the enduring beliefs and institutions of our national civilization.

15. The finer aspects of culture are best pursued for their own sake, and should be kept separate from matters of practical or vocational development.

16. Adult life changes so rapidly that it cannot be used for setting standards for the education of children.

17. As a rule, drill should be introduced only in situations where pupils feel a genuine need for it.

18. To think of motive as a part of the act performed is truer than to think of motive as behind and impelling the act to be performed.

19. It is more true to say that the self is the habits acquired by the individual in the course of his life than to say that the self must be there to acquire the habits.

20. In general, schools today are better than schools 50 years ago.

21. Federal aid to education will surely lead to undesirable federal control of local education.

22. Systems of uniform standards for education, on a nation-wide basis, would be an improvement in our educational system.

An officer of the student council speaks to enthusiastically interested parents about student government. (Hays from Monkmeyer)

Left: Some communities stimulate interest in schools through panel discussions. A student, two teachers, and a parent discuss "Educational Decisions." (Seattle School District)

Parents meet to discuss health and nutrition problems among children of minority groups in a large city school. Intensive remedial reading instruction is also given in these sessions. (Arthur Leipzig, Ford Foundation)

Left: Parents and teachers plan together during a meeting of the Joint Committee of the NEA and the National Congress of Parents and Teachers. (National Education Association)

The PTA involves itself in many school activities. The furnishings in this school library were donated by the PTA. (*Seattle School District*)

Below: PTA interest goes so far that a father permits himself to become involved in a school concert. (*Two bottom photos, National Congress of Parents and Teachers*)

An active PTA is always the best liaison between school and community.

Chapter 1 / WHAT WE EXPECT FROM OUR SCHOOLS

OUR SCHOOLS

In America the schools belong to the people! The statement is simple to make and disarmingly easy to repeat. All of us have heard and have repeated ideas, sometimes with a shallow glibness, which refer to *our* schools. They are *our* schools, in the real sense of the word, but Americans cannot afford to be glib or complacent about such ownership. As American citizens, one of our most valuable possessions is a free, tax-supported, nonsectarian, state-controlled public school system. Each citizen has the responsibility of understanding the rights and duties that such a possession carries with it.

The responsibility of members of the teaching profession goes further and is of far greater concern. In addition to sharing the common burden of ownership with all other citizens, it is imperative that teachers realize the many implications of the fact that our schools *do* belong to the people. It is also necessary that all professional educators understand how the unique relationships among teachers, pupils, parents, and all citizens must function if our system of education is to operate at an optimum level. Obviously no one textbook can include the many aspects of these relationships. Only a number of education classes together with courses in economics, sociology, and political science can provide sufficient information bearing upon the obligations of citizens to their schools and schools to their many publics. However, the principle underlying the proper relationship is apparent without further study—the most desirable relationships between schools and citizens are two-way relationships.

Perhaps the most commonly observed effect of a democratic, two-way relationship between schools and citizens is the right, which each exercises, to make demands upon the other. Educators have the right to expect that citizens will maintain interest in schools and follow intelligent courses of action with regard to the problems of education. Citizens, in turn, have the right to make demands on their schools, and the demands of individual citizens and groups of citizens are constantly being heard.

Citizens' demands vary from specific to general: from ideas which apply to one phase of the program to those which are concerned with education generally, from temporary reactions of criticism or condonement to long-range plans for concerted action on issues. The exact nature of the requests which each citizen makes is determined in large part by the image he holds of what constitutes the proper function of schools in society, and because the average citizen's image of the "best" school is seldom clear or precise, it has a degree of central stability but is constantly being revised. Therefore the demands made by citizens undergo constant change, and educators must strive continuously to remain cognizant of the best expectations held for schools by parents, pupils, and by people generally.

FUNDAMENTAL CRITICISM OF EDUCATION

In a publication entitled, *The Great Debate: Our Schools in Crisis,* the authors have written the following introduction:

Throughout the length and breadth of our land public education is being debated as never before. Most of the discussion has to do with fundamental issues and some of it is well reasoned and pointed. A considerable portion is much more emotionally charged than it is reflective. All of what is being said and written seems to indicate that our schools are indeed in a period of crisis.

The gravity of the situation cannot be overestimated. If we fail to educate the present and immediately future generations appropriately and well, we may lose the current conflict with the Soviet powers and cease to be free to educate and live as we see fit. This is the grim prospect before us.

In the final analysis, laymen more than educators will determine the educational issues that now confront us. . . .[1]

This statement well describes the current place of schools in society. It seems obvious that a period of readjustment is now taking place, and that tomorrow's schools are being shaped by today's criticisms. As the quotation noted, some of today's criticisms are emotional in nature: some are based on half-truths and atypical examples; a few are totally lacking in intellectual honesty. These kinds of criticisms have always been made and do not merit consideration or deserve answers.

There have been some fundamental criticisms and denials of the values of education, however, and our schools' future will be determined largely by the way in which these are resolved. Although the criticisms demand attention, they cannot, of course, be discussed in a few pages. Rather, an attempt will be made to introduce the ideas and issues of greatest concern.

Environment and Heredity

One fundamental denial of the value of schools and education is that as environmental factors they are subordinate to heredity as a factor in cultural development. This argument received some impetus from an unthinking acceptance of the fact that there are individual differences among people. The first intelligence tests, and the theory of a normal curve of ability—some high, some average, some low—together with an earlier belief in the constancy of the "IQ" seemed to indicate that ability was totally inborn. From this basic belief came a deterministic philosophy that those of low IQs were to be "hewers of wood and drawers of water"; not much could be done for them anyway. This idea was expanded to the point where some supposedly thinking persons reached the conclusion that education was largely superfluous. Later research has shown this to be untrue. It probably is true that heredity sets the outer limits of man's ability, but within these limits education can make a truly significant difference. Various studies have shown that a person's measured ability can be altered as much as 20 points by an improved environment. It could also be noted that even if the great majority of our cultural leadership does come from a few highly gifted persons, progress in a democratic society also demands intelligent followers capable of understanding.

The significant thing is that man's biological inheritance is set and unalterable from the moment of conception, but environment improved by education opens up untold possibilities of what can be done, in and out of

---

[1] Winfield Scott, Clyde Hill, and Hobert Burns, *The Great Debate: Our Schools in Crisis,* Englewood Cliffs, N.J., Prentice-Hall, 1959, p. iii.

school. This nation cannot really seek and practice democratic education on the hypothesis that all can be educated unless it believes that giving every person a chance at prolonged schooling will result in high levels of competence for all in some field or another. The positive thing in modern psychology is that people can do things better than they do them. Education is the process, school is the agency, and the teacher is the expert guide to improve people's competence. Our history of education shows that we have improved, and most important is the fact that as we do improve greater improvement becomes possible.

Current Criticisms

No institution as vital as the public school can ever be free from criticism, and since the end of World War II attacks on the public schools have increased significantly in number and intensity. The educator cannot ignore such criticism, and it is evidence that the American people are acutely aware of the importance of their school system. People do not criticize a social institution they consider to be unimportant. Indeed, the seemingly endless stream of criticism of today's schools is perhaps the greatest proof that Americans still maintain their traditional interest in education.

Many strictures of varying kinds are being made. The central charge underlying all of them is that the schools are failing to fulfill the role the critics conceive as the proper one. The critics, however, do not agree with one another. Whatever the curricular issue the school offerings are too limited for some or too broad, while others maintain they include the wrong things. It is alleged that schools teach fudge-making, not science; fly-casting instead of mathematics; auto-driving in place of English. Simultaneously, others are saying that the school program lacks practicality and offers little or nothing to the terminal student. Others insist that the school should concern itself with general education, and leave vocational education to on-the-job training. Some wish to de-emphasize attempts at direct college-preparatory courses. One needs only to pick up a daily paper or current magazine to find examples of these and other criticisms and suggestions.

Confusion and Mediocrity

The American school system has been criticized by some for what they term a state of confusion and an almost total loss of perspective as to what constitutes the basic purpose of education. According to these critics the basic purpose of education is to teach students to use their minds and this, they hold, has been sacrificed for job training and "life adjustment" education. The "fundamentals" such as reading, writing, and arithmetic have been squeezed out along with the equally important mathematics, sciences, and foreign languages. With these fundamentals being taught only to a small group, say these critics, we are lowering rather than raising our intellectual level.

It is argued further that the public schools are geared for the average or below-average student, and must be adapted for the gifted child. The opposite situation should apply, they feel. Schools are also charged with dodging the problem of the slow learner by accepting him as the "norm" rather than as the below-average student which he is. Thus, it is alleged, instructors tend to teach on the lower level, and such a process hinders the progress of the above-average pupils by allowing them to set their own laggardly pace.

The facts of the situation do not support these criticisms. The truth is that more, as well as a greater percentage of pupils, are following academically rigorous curricula than ever before. Brown and Oburn[2] recently reported on the research findings of a massive survey on offerings and enrollments in science and mathematics courses in American public high schools. They note that total enrollments in science rose 58.6 percent in the period from 1948–1949 to 1958–1959 to a new high total of 4,670,000 pupils; that the rate of increase in the period 1956 to 1958 was much greater for chemistry and physics than for general science and biology; and that, for the first time since 1900, the percent of pupils enrolled in physics has shown an increase.

This survey also revealed that less than 10 percent of the schools enrolling twelfth-grade pupils fail to include chemistry or physics and that these schools enrolled only 3.3 percent of all twelfth-grade pupils in the country. Most significantly of all perhaps, they note:

Although the population age group has increased 22 per cent during the past decade and the total public school enrollment 45 per cent, the science enrollment has increased 59 per cent and the mathematics enrollment 73 per cent.[3]

The 1961–1962 Biennial Survey of Education also included a significant documentation of the fact that public schools are teaching more and more of the academically orientated courses. In a survey of suburban school systems, where the greatest concentration of college preparatory students are found, it was noted that approximately 99 percent offer chemistry, 98 percent include physics, 95 percent solid geometry, and 96 percent trigonometry.[4] The educational needs of these students require these offerings, and, as it always has, the American public school system is ready to meet these needs.

Progress in Reverse

It has been charged that 50 years ago a high school diploma meant something, now it is merely a certificate of attendance. The diploma, it is said, formerly indicated a certain degree of skill in the subjects of mathematics, foreign languages, English, history, and science. Today, say these critics, the

---

[2] Kenneth Brown and Ellsworth Oburn, "Offerings and Enrollments in Science and Mathematics in Public High Schools," U.S. Department of Health, Education, and Welfare Bulletin, no. 5, 1961, p. 21.

[3] *Ibid.*

[4] "Statistics of Local School Systems," *The Biennial Survey of Education, 1961–62,* U.S. Department of Health, Education, and Welfare Bulletin, p. 38.

diploma means nothing at all in terms of real intellectual understanding. The consensus of the critics' opinion is: "things are not as good as they used to be." Few of them would appreciate the sense of the humorist's rejoinder: "and they probably never were." But no generation has been satisfied with its schools, and the past is easily glorified. Aristotle decried the state of youth and student lack of motivation in his day; Horace Mann left a lucrative law practice to devote his life to education because he became convinced that the schools of the nineteenth century were "in a low and backward state."

It is not true that schools offer less than formerly: a study of the history of education will reveal that schools have more than kept pace with the rest of society. The data concerning offerings and enrollments given earlier in the chapter offer evidence to support this position, but it seems important to note here again the enrollments in some of the courses the critics claim have been neglected in the 50-year period from 1900 to 1950 as an example of specific trends in school curricula. In 1900 approximately 400,000 pupils were enrolled in science and mathematics courses. Fifty years later, while the population of the country approximately doubled, the number of high school students taking science courses had increased by 600 percent, and class enrollments in mathematics have grown by 900 percent.[5] These figures become even more significant in view of the fact that during the same period the American high school changed from a totally college preparatory-orientated institution to a comprehensive school designed to serve all youth of high school age.

Our schools face a task which is far more complicated than that of "keeping up." The students in school today must be prepared to take their place in the adult society of tomorrow. The form and paraphernalia, the names of the courses, and the size and nature of their diploma are among the least significant of the factors which determine the quality of their education, however-much familiar trappings might appeal to unclear memories.

The Grass Is Greener . . .

Another favorite platform of negative criticism of American education has been the use of unfavorable comparison. It has been said that more than one-third of the Russian students attending a 10-year school pass an examination at age 17 that few American high school twelfth-grade graduates could pass; and that only a rare and occasional American graduate could make a passing mark on the European secondary school-leaving exam. One critic has claimed that a *European student covers much more critical material* (italics added) in 10 years than an American student covers in 12 years.

The character of such statements as the foregoing truly is fallacious. Such claims are not substantiated because their comparative nature seldom makes the gathering of empirical evidence at all possible. It seems logical to ask: Does a generalized "European" student exist? What material is "critical"? On

[5] Brown and Oburn, *op. cit.*

what basis can it be predetermined that "only a rare and occasional American graduate could pass the European secondary school-leaving exam"? Is there an examination commonly given to all European students? The position of the critic seems impossible to defend.

The glaring weakness of criticism of America by its comparison with Europe lies in the fact that just as the United States is different from Europe, the schools of the United States must reflect the unique nature of this country. Dr. James B. Conant, after an intensive study of American schools, noted this fact when he said:

Our free society is unlike that of any other country. Therefore, it is not strange that our educational system—and its problems—should also be unique.

First, our educational ideals reflect the history of our nation; unlike European countries, we have never been divided by a class system based on conqueror and conquered. We believe, uniquely, in equality of opportunity for all youth, irrespective of the economic status of the family. Our system of education must provide for a side diversity of talents and vocational goals.

. . . Clearly, unlike any other nation, we in the United States are committed to a system of education that, at both the high school and college levels, must provide for a wide variety of abilities and vocational aims.[6]

Criticisms of Teacher Education and Certification

Teacher education and the state teacher certification requirements to which it is closely related have also been the subject of strong attack. In the main, teacher education has been criticized for emphasizing the methodology of teaching to the neglect of subject matter. It has also been charged that laws and regulations for the certification of teachers have tended to produce poorly prepared candidates. Much of the trouble here has stemmed from the all too common fallacy of expecting yes-or-no, left-*vs*-right answers to complex problems. Those concerned with teacher education point out that teaching methods as opposed to teaching content is a foolish oversimplification. Yet many persons who attack professional education, view content and method as opposite ends of one pole. Daniel Tanner, writing in *The Atlantic Monthly*, puts it this way:

Does the nuclear physicist ignore the scientific method in his research work? Of course not. Teaching is a science and an art. It must be far more than drillwork in facts and skills. The teacher must be concerned with both content and process.

It would be dangerous for society to license a medical doctor as a brain surgeon simply because he gave evidence of knowing the theory of brain surgery practice. Yet some people argue that any person who manages to secure a bachelor's degree be given the privilege of walking into the classroom of our nation and taking control of the minds of our children.[7]

[6] James B. Conant, *The American High School Today*, New York, McGraw-Hill, 1959, p. 15.
[7] Daniel Tanner, "The Case for Certification," *The Atlantic Monthly*, vol. 202, no. 1, July, 1958, p. 35.

All can agree in the wisdom of having only high-caliber men and women admitted to teacher preparation, and having only those who successfully complete a rigorous training program certificated to teach. This can be accomplished by strengthening the entire program; it can be defeated by senseless attacks on one part or another.

CITIZENS ARE STUDYING THEIR SCHOOLS

All criticism of America's schools in the past few years has not been negative. Indeed, the overall effect of it may prove to be the greatest boon in the relatively short history of American education. When the statements of the critic permeated not only the scholarly journals but also appeared in magazines aimed primarily towards general consumption, large numbers of citizens became awakened to the importance of their schools. Disturbed by what they read and heard, people in increasing numbers began to take an active interest in their schools. They realized the necessity of clarifying their idea of what constitutes a good school system. A moving factor in the burst of local self-study, which began about 1950 and continues at a high level today, was the National Citizens Commission for the Public Schools. The NCCPS was organized in 1949 by a group of prominent Americans who were deeply interested in public education and who noted and decried widespread public apathy towards schools. The National Citizens Commission saw its function as a catalyst in local self-study and action. It did not engage in making surveys and recommendations to local schools, or in drawing conclusions. Rather, it provided encouragement and specific suggestions to citizens who wanted to study school problems at the local level.

There is little doubt that the Commission fulfilled its function and that it reached its objective of spurring local interest and study of schools and their problems. In May, 1949, shortly after they began their work, the national organization reported that only 17 local citizens councils for education could be identified in the United States. In April, 1950, there were 175, and by mid-1955, 2,500 local and state committees were in regular communication with the national group. Even more significant was the fact that by 1955 an estimated 7,500 additional local groups were so well under way that they were operating totally on their own.[8] It is probable that today more than 300,000 people are working with local citizens groups studying their schools.

The maintenance of open two-way communication between schools and citizens depends on more than merely a desire to cooperate. Much factual information must be available before an intelligent attack on problems and issues of mutual concern can be made. Difficult problems in school-citizen rapport usually occur when school personnel are only partially aware of what citizens want, or when the citizen makes demands which are vague or

[8] David Dreiman, *How to Get Better Schools*, New York, Harper & Row, 1956, p. 77 n.

are made without regard to the problems involved in fulfilling the request. Some sort of organized, coordinated effort is needed to achieve the level of school-citizen relationship desired. A local school advisory council has served as a functional vehicle for such successful study and action.

RELATED READINGS

Hannah, Paul R., *Education: An Instrument of National Goals,* New York, Mc-Graw-Hill, 1962.

Kimball, Solon T., and James E. McClellan, Jr., *Education and the New America,* New York, Random House, 1962.

Mayer, Frederick, *Man, Morals, and Education,* New Haven, College and University Press Services, 1962.

Thelen, Herbert A., *Education and the Human Quest,* New York, Harper & Row, 1960.

The officers and Board of Directors of the New York State Citizens Committee for the Public Schools, Inc. meet in special session with its membership. This independent non-profit service organization helps local citizens in New York and in other states to improve their schools through study and action. (*New York State Citizens Committee for the Public Schools, Inc.*)

The school building is often used for various community purposes. Here, adult students arrive for evening classes.

Improvement in the community through education: these earnest students are taking advantage of a state adult education program to make up missed schooling. (*Wide World*)

Left: One of the best ways of communicating student progress is face-to-face, as in this parent-teacher conference. (*Two upper left photos, Seattle School District*)

Business takes an interest in a community school. These school children in the board room of a savings bank are about to receive awards for Christmas decorations on the windows of local merchants. Parents and teachers look on. (*West Side Savings Bank, New York City*)

A music teacher explains to a teachers' meeting at an elementary school the how and why of her teaching—an important part of being professional.

Below: An evening may find parents and students coming together at the school to hear the orchestra and glee club. (*Both photos, Hays from Monkmeyer*)

Chapter 2 / EDUCATION AND SOCIETY

SCHOOLS AND COMMUNITIES

Local responsibility for schools is traditional in the United States. In 1642 the Colonial Legislature of Massachusetts enacted legislation that recognized the township as the primary unit for schools, a pattern which has remained basic in American education. The relationship between a single schools system and its community is a complex and varied one that is also very direct. It is not difficult to recognize a school system and a community that understand and appreciate each other. In such communities school bond issues are acted upon favorably, teachers' salaries are relatively high, proper buildings, equipment, and facilities are provided for. It is in these towns that teachers tend to remain until retirement, buy homes, and work in many types of community projects. Good schools and teachers and good communities are vital to one another, and both are aware of the fact.

The Teacher and the Community

To a significant degree the image of the schools in any community is determined by the relationships that are built between the citizens of the community and the teaching staff. As a teacher works in and for some community he adds a facet to the image. It is important, therefore, that each teacher understand the aims, ambitions, and dreams of his community so that the schools, as personified by the teachers, will be thought of as a major contributor to the worth of the community.

Teachers must remember that the schools belong to the people of the community. Except in a few cases public school buildings are planned and paid for by the citizens of the school district, and the largest portion of the continuing support of American schools comes from local sources. A school is one important way in which a community can express itself. If a town wants a good school and is interested in working and paying for it, the teachers have a highly potential school in which to work.

A teacher works with the most important ingredient of a community—the people who live there—and so his human relationships are of utmost importance. The successful teacher does not go into a community as a missionary intending to make radical changes, nor does he remain aloof from the community. He sees himself as one more alert, intelligent citizen whose major contribution to the community is to offer leadership in the area for which he has special preparation—education.

The Child and the Community

Teaching would be simple, and teachers would have little difficulty in evincing a popular image in the community, if all children were alike. But children are born uniquely different from one another and become more different as they grow up in varying environments. Most sociologists recognize at least six socioeconomic classes even in our democratic society, ranging from low to very high; the corresponding levels of environment have a great effect on the individual members.

No one can understand a child until he understands the child's community and what it has done to and for him. Some children are reared in homes with a high cultural level, others in barren surroundings. Some are wanted and loved; others never receive love or affection. These things condition the learning process as it occurs in school.

Social behavior is learned behavior and all environments educate. Social behavior is learned in the home, on the street, in movies, watching television, and playing baseball in a vacant lot. Everything with which the individual comes into contact is a "teacher," and children bring many significant behavioral patterns with them to school. Language affords a good example. A bilingual community presents a different problem to teachers in English classes than a community where the home language is also English. In addition to knowing and appreciating the general wishes of the community, the success of a teacher is closely related to how well he understands individual children and their varying environments.

The Teacher and the Public

Good teaching is best public relations for schools. The teacher's reputation in a community is determined largely by the children and their parents. If the teacher is doing a good job, the children are happy and bring home a positive attitude toward the teachers and the school to their parents, who transmit this feeling to their friends. When a citizen says, "We have a fine school system," he usually means that he is pleased with the type of teaching his children or his neighbors' children are receiving. But if the pupils come from school unhappy and reflect a negative attitude, parents soon form the generalization that the schools in their community are not very good. Thus upon the classroom teacher rests most of the responsibility for good community relationships. No amount of planned public relations programs can offset a poor teacher, nor will the parent of a child who is pleased with his teacher be readily susceptible to unfair criticisms of the school.

The Individual Teacher in the Community

It has been known for a long time that if a school administrator or teacher approximates the ideal image people have of them, they will be judged "effective." Conversely, the educator is thought of as "ineffective" in proportion to the degree he varies from this ideal image. Although these facts are generally accepted and commonly heard, they represent a badly oversimplified concept of a complex set of relationships. Recently, however, significant attempts have been made to analyze empirically some of the facets relative to the image of the teacher and school administrator in the community.

Much of this research has been in the realm of what is called "role theory." Although these research projects have taken various forms, a common approach to role theory is evident in most of them. In most cases role theory is assumed to deal with the patterns of behavior or other characteristics common to a certain class or groups of persons (teachers, for example) and with the variety of reasoning processes through which the members of this group and the citizens of the community arrive at their concept of the proper role of such a group.

A group of research associates at Oklahoma State University, under the leadership of Dr. Robert Sweitzer, recently conducted a role theory project involving teachers and school administrators in the state of Oklahoma. This study, under the auspices of the Oklahoma Commission on Educational Administration, asked school personnel and citizens to indicate in their opinion the relative importance of certain qualifications as determiners of success for a school administrator or school teacher. The findings of this study lend credence to the thesis that different groups hold varying images of the ideal school teacher and school administrator:

> Different groups tend to place different degrees of importance on some of the same qualifications. For example, while most Oklahoma superintendents and teachers indicated that the most important qualification of school administrators was "secondary school teaching experience," other school administrators and citizens felt that "ability to see the whole picture" was most important. . . . It is interesting to note that teachers and citizens placed much more importance on "high intelligence" than school administrators did.
>
> These findings suggest that different groups have different ideas of what to look for when seeking an effective school administrator. Superintendents and principals don't agree entirely among themselves as to what are the most crucial qualifications that result in success. . . .
>
> A different standard seems to be used in deciding if a person is a good or poor teacher. Competency in classroom instruction and directing pupil learning on the part of the teacher are felt to be most important.[1]

In addition to the specific competencies of the type discussed above, the teacher in the community who helps build a favorable image of himself, and therefore of the total school system, also exemplifies a number of important personal traits.

1. He is proud of his job.   This is of prime importance. The teacher who does not believe that teaching is the greatest profession in the world should not try to be a teacher. Numerous surveys have been made in which students list the qualities they admire in their favorite teachers. Almost without exception the statement, "He likes to teach" is one of the attributes most often mentioned. Good teachers do not teach because it is a way to make a living; to them it is a way of life.

2. He is ethical and professional.   Every member of any profession shares the responsibility for improving the services which his group offers, and one rewarding way of proceeding in a program of improvement is to study and criticize current practices. However the place to air grievances, to attack prevailing philosophies, to discuss weaknesses and failures is within the profession through professional procedures. Certain college professors, publicists, journalists, and others have found a ready market for articles consisting of scathing criticisms of the public schools. Other teachers have used the tea party, the bridge club, and the public meeting as a place to air their grievances. These are not the proper channels or approaches for criticism and improvement. The most common result of them is chaos.

3. He enjoys working with people.   No one works with people more than

[1] Robert E. Sweitzer and Richard Jungers, "Images in the Mirror," *The Oklahoma Teacher,* vol. 43, no. 5, January, 1962, p. 11.

the teacher; therefore no one needs skill in human relations more than a teacher. Teachers should remember that children react to tolerance, humor, sympathy, and mutual respect in the same way as adults. To the good teacher each pupil is important; each must be studied and understood. The teaching methods and materials taught must be suited to individual needs. To some people children are just problems, and how to live with them through the day without shaking them is the main question! Such an attitude is unworthy of anyone who works with children. The pupil who said of his teacher, "He was a friend to all of us" was conscious of the greatest asset a teacher can have.

Teachers, too, are human. They have the same strengths and weaknesses as other people. There was a time when teachers were expected to behave as extra-human beings. The June, 1960, issue of the *Phi Delta Kappan* re-reported that an Idaho woman teacher's contract in 1923 included the following restrictions:

1. Do not loiter in ice cream parlors.
2. Do not keep company with men.
3. Do not leave town without permission.
4. Do not dye hair or use face powder, mascara or lipstick.
5. Wear at least two petticoats.

This cloistered idea of the proper role for a teacher no longer holds true. Today's teacher can expect to be accepted as another professional citizen of the community, and his mode of living is similar to the other professionals.

4. He is part of his community. One major aim of modern education is the development of good citizens. How can a teacher teach good citizenship without being a good citizen himself? To exercise his citizenship, a teacher must become an integral part of the community in many ways, and joining local civic groups is a common practice of the community-minded teacher.

The community also serves as a laboratory for the teacher. Field trips into the community taken as a special part of a lesson is familiar procedure to all teachers. The science class goes to a pond to study animal life, or to a park to study trees. The social studies class visits the city hall to discover at first-hand how the city government is organized and operated. Children and teachers often visit farms, factories, radio stations, newspaper plants, and other places, as a part of their educational program.

Some schools set aside a special day called "Business-Industry Education Day." Schools are dismissed while the teachers spend the day visiting at a place of business or industry. The purpose of this activity is to give teachers greater insight into the commercial aspects of the community and to help them understand how and on what a community operates. In the majority of instances the business and industrial leaders spend a day visiting in the schools at some later time.

The teacher's primary contact with his community is through the parents

of school children. A teacher must keep in close contact with parents to en-
sure proper cooperation with them. Many years ago parents were invited to
school only on the closing day of the term. On this day the children "spoke
pieces" and sang songs for them. It was a special performance designed primarily to impress the parents; it was not meant to give an indication of the
actual learning experiences of the year. The modern teacher is anxious for
parents to see the children at work and school visitation is encouraged at any
time. To reach parents who cannot or will not come to school, teachers use
numerous devices. One teacher, proud of her art program, encouraged her
pupils to set up their easels on busy community corners. Citizens paused to
admire their unruffled excellence, and saw art education in action. Displays
in department store windows, newspaper stories of school happenings, and
concerts are other examples of presenting the school to the parents.

The ever-present report card is also a vehicle for parent-teacher communication. Sometimes it is a source of friction. In some schools the problem
of reporting the child's actual progress and achievement in school is met by
supplementing the cold, impersonal "grade" on a card with an accompanying
letter discussing the child's progress. Some teachers send examples of the
pupil's work with the card. In other schools the report card has been abandoned entirely in favor of parent-teacher conferences. Often the report to
parents, whatever form it takes, is the only tie between the teacher and the
parents. It is bad, therefore, to make it an instrument of friction when it
might be made into a friendly aid to mutual understanding.

Finally, there is no better way for a teacher to demonstrate his interest in
his community than to help in a campaign to strengthen and maintain good
schools. Not only is it his duty as a citizen, but his position in the schools
makes him especially cognizant of the needs of the school. Whenever a
teacher works and talks honestly and intelligently to help the people of the
community to have good schools, he makes friends for himself and his
schools.

The Community and School Administration

Under the American plan of local responsibility for public education, the
school district is the legal administrative unit of education and the board of
education is the legal agency through which the state educational plan is
carried out. The major responsibility of the board of education is to operate
a school system, under state law, which will minister to the needs of the
local community. In a later chapter, on the legal and financial foundations of
education, the specific legal functions of the board of education will be discussed more fully.

In the context of the social relationships of the school system it is significant to note that the school board is the liaison between the professional staff
and the lay persons of the community, and as such serves to interpret each
to the other. The professional personnel are obligated to plan a program of

education which is in keeping with the best educational theory and practice. The citizens of the community are obligated to be interested in their schools and to arrive at considered decisions concerning the kind of educational program they desire for the community. The most important point of contact between these two functions is at the superintendent-school board level. There are many ways in which a school board acts as the spokesman for the community to the school staff, and for the school staff to the community. Sometimes a board member is elected because a segment of the population is unsatisfied with existing programs or procedures and wants to make its opinion known. In many cases the ever-present problem of school finances represents an issue in school board elections. Also, school board members are in the best position to inform the public of the rationale behind a proposed change of program or a decision not to change.

In the final analysis it is the general public, not the professional educator, which determines the level and quality of the local school system. It is the citizen, acting through his vote and his representative (board member), who approves or vetoes the program proposed by the educator. The future of any school system rests on how well the citizens regard their schools.

COMMUNITY-SCHOOL ORGANIZATIONS

Parent-Teacher Associations

The most important organization that includes the teachers and administrators of the schools and the parents of the community is the Parent-Teacher Association. The PTA is without doubt the most effective means now available for creating and maintaining good school-community relationships by bringing together the parents and the teachers of the children in an organization dedicated to the betterment of the educational program.

The National Congress of Parents and Teachers is composed of affiliated local Parent-Teacher Association units in most school districts. It is difficult to understand how any school district would attempt to operate without such an organization. The growth of the Parent-Teacher Association has been phenomenal in recent years.

Whenever there is an educational problem to solve, the Parent-Teacher Association is always active. Most school board elections find PTA taking a lively part. Often this group makes a study of all candidates, drawing up a list of their qualifications. When bonds are to be voted upon, the school board can depend upon the PTA to take part in the campaign. On election day the PTA members often help in getting the voters to the polls.

The PTA usually sponsors monthly meetings at the school building. Such meetings often feature discussions concerning the problems of the school. The fact that the problems are usually social as well as educational gives teachers an opportunity to meet parents. Principal and teachers also have a chance to acquaint parents with the program of the school and with the teaching methods that are used. No school should attempt a program without the active cooperation of a functioning Parent-Teacher Association.

It is interesting to note that most PTA groups are organized around elementary or junior high schools, seldom with senior high schools. There is no particular reason why this should be true. Certainly, a senior high school, too, needs to keep in touch with the community.

Community Councils

Many communities have more or less informal organizations for parents and community leaders, usually district-wide in scope. These are often called "Community Councils" or "Citizens' Advisory Councils." Such councils, if well-constituted, are the focal point for many community-school activities. They usually are active in studying the educational program of the schools and in making recommendations to the administrators and to the board. Some councils are organized to do a specific job, such as making a study of the school-building needs of the community, while others are more general in nature and are organized on a continuing basis.

Although these local councils are organized and operated on the local level and serve to achieve local purposes, many of them have been affiliated with the National Citizens Commission for the Public Schools. The NCCPS[2] has served as catalyst and resource-center for thousands of community councils.

The School as a Community Center

A good school becomes the center of its community. The school building is one of the dominant architectural features of any community; it is also the focal point of educational activity in its area. The importance of schools to their communities becomes apparent during the time a new school building is being conceived and constructed. As a recent publication of the American Association of Administrators noted:

> Of all the activities in which the American people engage as they live and work together in local communities, counties, and states, perhaps none expresses in material form, so many aspects of our culture as school-building construction.[3]

The American concept of the proper role of the school in a community has broadened greatly in recent years. The school building is no longer a nine to four, Monday through Friday, Labor Day to Memorial Day servant of the community, if indeed it ever was. A community-centered school is the meeting place for youth groups, parent groups, and community organizations.

[2] Interested students should read more concerning this fascinating organization. David Drieman's book, *How to Get Better Schools* (New York, Harper & Row, 1956), would be an excellent starting place.

[3] *Planning American School Buildings,* American Association of School Administrators, School Building Commission, Washington, D.C., 1960, p. 1.

Many schools, often in cooperation with municipal government, offer programs in recreational and special areas. These attract as many "students" to the school after four o'clock as the compulsory attendance laws require in the school during the regular schedule. Such activities as dancing, arts and crafts, swimming, remedial and enrichment courses, and ceramics are typical of these voluntary programs. The community school also operates during the summer vacation period, when activities ranging from hobby interests to personal-use typing and advanced mathematics are taught.

Today's schools are indeed a vital part of their communities. The report quoted earlier states it this way:

> With a look toward the future, the school building reflects the ambitions, the hopes, the aspirations, and the dreams of a people that is struggling to move forward and upward to a way of life that is better and richer, fuller and more rewarding than that which it now knows.[4]

SCHOOLS AND SOCIETY

Teachers, schools, and communities also have relationships which transcend local boundaries. Each town is in a much larger community—it is part of a state, a region, a nation. The schools are also part of a larger community. In this instance the larger community can be called "society."

Sociologists often define society as: "an enduring, cooperating, social group, so functioning as to maintain itself and perpetuate the species." This definition is an especially important one for students interested in education and schools. A look at the implications of the definition show why. Society is described as an enduring social group whose chief aim is self-perpetuation. How does a society perpetuate itself? What is the role of the school in this process of maintenance?

Societies perpetuate themselves chiefly through their institutions. A society establishes such institutions as it deems necessary, charges each with a definite responsibility, and tends to support them so long as they fulfill their function satisfactorily.

Religious groups are good examples of social institutions. American moral and spiritual beliefs did not spring from out of nowhere, and the fact that religious beliefs are handed from generation to generation is no accident. To be sure, many parents begin and continue to be active in the religious education of their children. But society also establishes and supports denominational groups, church groups and societies, and specially trained persons who are primarily concerned with the perpetuation of our American moral and spiritual heritage.

There are also other social institutions of importance. The family unit is one, civic and fraternal groups are other examples. Each has its unique contribution to make. What our society is today, and what it will be tomorrow, is

---

[4] *Ibid.*, p. 1.

determined at least partially by the nature and strength of our social institutions.

This discussion is primarily concerned with one social institution—the school. It should be noted that the words "school" and "education" are not synonymous. "Education" denotes a much bigger concept than the word "school." Education occurs in many places, under diverse circumstances. No one's education begins the day he first enters a school; some of man's most basic and important learning experiences occur before the age of two. Nor does education end when formal schooling is completed. The statement, "You are never too old to learn" is a truism. Even during the time of our lives when we are enrolled in school, a great deal of our education occurs outside the jurisdiction of the school. Schools are relatively recent social institutions, education is an ancient responsibility.

Education Out of School

Education is as old as civilization. In the earliest days, however, it was unorganized and on an individual basis; it was also extremely practical. Before the establishment of schools, boys and girls were taught by their parents to perform the tasks that all adults must face in order to live. Self-preservation was the basis of all learning. The boy learned from his father and the older men of the tribe how to hunt, fight, and take part in tribal worship and government. The girl was taught by her mother and by the older women of the tribe. Learning and doing were not separated—rather, the young learned by doing under the supervision of the elder members of the tribe.

The aim of education in primitive society was the same as its aim in any society—it enabled children to become acceptable members of the culture of which they were a part. Each primitive group attempted to bring up its children in the image of their elders. Thus when the children were adults they could continue the culture in its existing pattern. Because of the limited amount of things which the elders knew, the scope of the learning was limited. The ultimate goal was for each generation to master the things which the preceding ones knew. This type of education tended to produce a static society, one that could not last.

Education in Modern Society

Primitive education was very practical in its time and served primitive society well. But neither learning nor society can remain static for long. Modern society is dynamic. Technology and scientific endeavor have made prime changes in our way of life. Today's discoveries and inventions make yesterday's newest ideas obsolete. It is no longer enough for education to transmit the culture of preceding generations intact because the culture is no longer static.

In addition to being dynamic, society has also become compartmentalized. Each man performs a more specialized duty for the other members of society, who in turn render the products of their specialized labor. Schools are one example. Primitive man taught his own sons (just as he saw to all their needs), but as his own life became more specialized, man turned to others whose speciality was teaching. Perhaps the most important advancement that led to the establishment of schools was the development of writing. When this took place man was able to record the folklore of his tribe and write out significant documents dealing with religion and government. Children could then be taught to write and read the things that had been written, and since this was most efficiently done in an organized manner, teachers were eventually designated for the specialized job of teaching the young.

A great amount of thought and effort has been necessary to effect the change from the rudimentary society-school relationship described above to today's complex approach to education and schools. Nor have the changes occurred automatically or been effected easily.

THE BATTLE FOR FREE SCHOOLS

Most Americans are aware of the necessity of a free, tax-supported, state-controlled, nonsectarian public school system. The United States has had such a system of education for many years, and it is easy to become complacent about it. Educators need to remind themselves that as schools are established by society, so they can be eliminated by society. Our democratic society is complex and is affected by many forces, some of which are not favorably inclined toward schools. Ellwood P. Cubberley in his history of education[5] points out that seven great battles had to be won before free, tax-supported, nonsectarian, state-controlled public schools became a reality.

1. *The battle for tax support.* The early schools were supported by tuition, gifts, lotteries, land grants, and a host of other devices. The struggle to establish an orderly system of public taxation for schools was a long and bitter one. It involved the idea that education was necessary to a democratic society and that property should be taxed to supply schools for all children.

2. *The battle to eliminate the pauper-school idea.* The pauper-school idea was brought from England, where it was the accepted plan for educating the poor. All who could pay for education sent their children to private schools; only paupers sent their children to the free schools. In fact, in Pennsylvania and in several other states these schools were actually called "pauper schools."

In 1834 the legislature of Pennsylvania passed an act which proposed to extend to the whole state the free system of education that had been established in Philadelphia. There was an almost instant reaction from the taxpayers of Pennsylvania who would have to support the free schools. In the election the following fall the issue before the voters was "free public schools" to replace the pauper-schools so long existing in the state. When

[5] E. P. Cubberley, *A History of Education,* Boston, Houghton Mifflin, 1920, p. 676.

the legislature assembled the next winter a bill was introduced to repeal the public school act. It was entitled "An act making provision for the education of the poor, gratis."

The proposed new law passed the Senate by a 2 to 1 vote. Then it was taken up by the House. The enemies of free public education claimed a clear majority in the House. It seemed to be only a matter of a vote.

At this point there arose in the House of Representatives a passionate believer in the equality of men and free public education. Thaddeus Stevens gave one of the greatest speeches ever made by a friend of public education. He was against the repeal of the public-school act. He was opposed to the repassage of the pauper-school act.

The repealing act is, in my opinion (said Stevens), of a most hateful and degrading character. It is a re-enactment of the pauper law of 1809. It proposed that the assessors shall take a census and make a record of the poor. This shall be revised and a new record made by the county commissioners, so that the names of those who have had the misfortune to be poor men's children shall be forever preserved in the archives of the county. The teacher, too, is to keep in his school a pauper book and register the names and attendance of poor scholars; thus pointing out and recording their poverty in the midst of their companions. Sir, hereditary distinctions of rank are sufficiently odious; but that which is founded on poverty is infinitely more so. Such a law should be entitled, "An act for branding and marking the poor, so that they may be known from the rich and proud.[6]

The act was not passed.

3. *The battle to make the schools entirely free.* Even after taxation for schools had become accepted practice the schools were not entirely free. If there were not sufficient funds to run a school, the deficiency was charged against the parents of the children attending it. The "rates," as they were called both here and in England, were abolished by law in Pennsylvania in 1834 and in other states at a later date.

4. *The battle to establish state supervision.* Described in a later chapter are the circumstances surrounding the establishment of a state board of education in Massachusetts and later in Connecticut and Rhode Island, and the work of Horace Mann and Henry Barnard in attempting to set up state systems of public education under suitable state supervision.

5. *The battle to eliminate sectarianism.* The battle to separate public education from sectarian influences was long and bitter. The early schools were closely aligned with religion and with church organizations. The schools in New England, for example, were established largely for religious purposes; in the middle colonies most of the education was directly connected with churches; in the South the Church of England was predominant in directing the schools. Later, Roman Catholics became more numerous in

[6] James Albert Woodburn, *The Life of Thaddeus Stevens,* Indianapolis, Bobbs-Merrill, 1913, p. 44.

some states and their interest in establishing parochial schools continued the pattern of church domination of secular education.

In the early days of public education, school funds were often divided between the public schools and the schools conducted privately and by religious groups. This became a complicated problem with the appearance of so many different religious groups all desiring to direct the education of the young. The very multiplicity of church groups was probably the most important factor leading to the separation of the church and public education. There was also a growing feeling that a democratic form of government demanded an educated citizenry and that the schools should be an instrument of the democratic state.

The problem was resolved by the complete separation of public education and religious groups. State after state wrote into its constitution a provision which prohibited the use of public funds for any schools not public in nature.

In spite of the fact that this was supposedly settled a great many years ago, the problem still exists. Bills before the Congress to appropriate federal funds for public education have always been blocked by those who maintained that the funds should be used for certain services provided by private and parochial schools. The problem will probably continue to confront educators for some time to come.

6. *The battle to extend the system upward.* In the chapter on secondary education the development of high schools in America will be discussed. Long after free public schools were available at the elementary level, secondary education was largely a private matter. The Latin grammar schools and the later academies were mostly private. Even those that were semipublic still charged tuition. The battle for free public high schools was won about a century ago. With the acceptance of the idea that taxes could be levied to build and maintain schools on the secondary level, these schools developed rapidly and now are universal throughout the nation.

7. *Addition of the state university to crown the system.* George Washington made several pleas to the Congress to establish a national university. He argued that American boys should not have to go to Europe for a higher education. He thought that a national university bringing together boys from all the states would add to the country's solidarity. In his will, Washington left several shares of stock to be used to found such an institution, but it was never established.

When our nation was created, all the colleges were private and had been established largely for religious purposes. It was the influence of these colleges that had much to do with defeating Washington's plan for a national university. Instead of a national university, state universities have been established quite generally in the United States. Here again it was necessary to establish the principle that property might be taxed to raise funds to build, equip, and maintain colleges and universities as part of the total pattern of free public education.

We are still fighting the battle for free public education in America. It is centered currently on educational equality. The states vary greatly in their ability to support education. If all Americans are to have an equal opportunity for education, funds must be provided on a national basis.

TRANSMITTING OUR DEMOCRATIC CULTURE

The relationship between schools and modern, dynamic society is not as direct and simple as it was between primitive society and its schools. Yet even in modern times each school system takes its aims and objectives from the culture of which it is a part; thus the schools in Russia differ from those in England or America. American society expresses itself in a great many ways. One most important way is in the education of its children. Why should we tax ourselves to build schoolhouses and maintain a system of free public schools? The answer lies in our desire to develop adult citizens who will be something they would not be if there were no schools. We have faith, in America, that education is necessary to build and maintain democracy. We also believe that children will develop into more useful citizens if they have the advantages of an education. Every parent wishes his child to have the best possible education so that he will be equipped to make the best possible job of living.

Since the earliest days of our nation, our leaders have had faith in education. Thomas Jefferson wrote to the Virginia legislature on January 6, 1818: "Well-directed education improves the morals, enlarges the mind, enlightens the councils, instructs the industry, and advances the power, the prosperity, and the happiness of the nation."[7]

RELATED READINGS

Clark, Burton R., *Educating the Expert Society,* San Francisco, Chandler Publishing Company, 1962.

Harris, Raymond P., *American Education: Facts, Fancies, and Folklore,* New York, Random House, 1961.

Kallenbach, W. Warren, and Harold M. Hodges, Jr., Eds., *Education and Society,* Englewood Cliffs, N.J., Merrill, 1963.

Mason, Robert E., *Educational Ideals in American Society,* Englewood Cliffs, N.J., Allyn and Bacon, 1960.

Thayer, V. T., *The Role of the School in American Society,* New York, Dodd, Mead, 1960.

[7] John C. Henderson, *Thomas Jefferson's Views on Public Education,* New York, Putnam, 1890, p. 39.

These portions of two sides of a Greek vase showing scholars studying are indicative of the importance of the humanities, especially music and literature, in the education of the young Grecian. (*Staatliche Museen, Berlin*)

Roman school bas relief. (*Marburg-Art Reference Bureau*)

The schools of Comenius' time emphasized memory, attention, punishment. With such a foreboding atmosphere, little wonder the boy at the door seems reluctant to enter.

Above right: Portion of a schoolmaster's sign, Basel—1516. (*Oeffentliche Kunstsammlung, Basel*)

Erasmus gives a lesson to young Charles V as the royal court observes. The influence of the master teacher is great.

Chapter 3 / HISTORICAL FOUNDATIONS OF AMERICAN EDUCATION

EUROPEAN BACKGROUNDS OF AMERICAN EDUCATION

Historically American education is an extension of the educational patterns of western Europe (especially that of Great Britain), just as originally American civilization was an extension of western European culture. Our forefathers were born into western European culture, and crossing the Atlantic ocean did not make radical changes in their patterns of living. In a very real sense, the institutions of the American colonies and later of the nation were built upon European foundations. It is true that the patterns have gradually changed in form and content, but even today there is a marked similarity between American culture and European culture, and between American schools and European schools.

The American colonists wanted their older culture patterns to change in a number of ways. Primarily, they wished to have the religious freedom that had been denied them in the countries from which they came. Political liberty was another major objective they sought. The legal traditions of their old countries did not make provision for the people to be governed by statutes passed by lawmakers of their choice and enforced by magistrates of their own selection. It is significant to remember that the liberties most desired were not secured immediately. In fact, the Bill of Rights, which embodies the freedoms most sought by the new-world settlers, was not added to our Constitution until 1791, approximately 170 years after the original settlement at Plymouth, Massachusetts.

Achieving democratic patterns in education has also been an evolutionary process. It is important to note that democratic schools as the right of all children were not part of the new life envisioned by the new Americans. They were ready to fight for religious and political freedoms, but they did not seem interested in including children in the democratic pattern. Our early schools, from elementary schools through the Latin grammar school to the university, were patterned after those the settlers had left behind. It is true that the colonists did expand the elementary-school program to include a larger proportion of the population, but even the extended program followed the pattern, in materials and methods of teaching, that was common in Europe. In fact they used the same books and curricula and often imported the teachers from England and France. It was more than two centuries after the settlement of New England that the movement for democratic schools in a democratic society gained noticeable momentum.

The modern cultural pattern had its beginnings in the dawning of civilization—European culture was a product of all that had preceded it—and it has gradually developed since that time. The threads of that growth are many and complex. The history of education in our world, only one facet of the cultural pattern, is a thrilling story, but it is too complex to review here. Our text is concerned with the development of free, universal, public education in the United States, and this chapter is limited in scope to a summary of only those ideas and persons of significant influence on public education in America. Thus it is limited to mention of our western heritage and to review of some significant antecedents of European culture.

GREEK EDUCATION

The earliest civilization having direct bearing on the educational pattern of Europe and later of America belonged to ancient Greece: to the citizens of Sparta and Athens. A study of the educational pattern of each of the two city-states is of particular interest today because across the modern world educational systems are still following in the general pattern of each. Politically Sparta exemplified the monistic culture of a dictatorship; Athens, with its more pluralistic society, strove towards a concept of democracy. Their beliefs about the proper functions of education and schools were also conflicting.

Education in Sparta

Education was of great importance to Sparta: its constitution reads more like a description of a military academy than an outline for a government. The life and interests of the individual were absolutely subservient to the public welfare. Every detail of conduct was carefully regulated, and even what little there was left of private and domestic life was utilized for the preservation of the state.

Spartan education, in a word, was concerned chiefly with the welfare of the state and, since welfare was thought of in terms of military superiority, it followed that Sparta was most interested in the development of warriors. Because of the supremacy of the state, the individual citizen was of importance only when he added to the military strength of his city; schools, of course, were organized in a manner reflecting the pervading objective of military superiority. The educational aims of Sparta later became those of Bismarck's Prussia, of Germany under Hitler, Italy during the time of Mussolini. In fact, in any dictatorial society all values are subjugated to the aim of the ruling class, group, or party.

In Sparta the city-state provided for the complete control of the training of the children by a system known as the "Spartan Agoge." The chief rulers had general authority over education, and every year a special educational officer was chosen from the highest leaders to supervise the training of the young. His authority was absolute. Under this superintendent were various types of assistants, including a number of official "whip-bearers," whose duty it was to administer punishment.

Spartan training, or *agoge*, began at birth. The newborn infant received a bath in wine on the theory that such a bath would kill the feeble but invigorate the healthy. Because children were the property of the state, the infant was immediately taken to the public council chamber. There the elders of the group decided whether it was worthy of being reared; if delicate or deformed, they decreed that the infant must be exposed on the mountain until death.

When the boys reached the age of 7 they were handed over to the state teachers who supervised their training until they emerged into full citizenship at 30 years of age. This period of training was not financed by the state; each citizen had to supply provisions for his sons. The boys were organized into bands or companies (of 64 students each) and were subjected to strict military discipline. The bravest and most prudent of the group was chosen as a leader; the entire group was placed in charge of a young man just above 20 years of age.

The program of living was designed to inure the boys to hardship and to prepare them to endure the severities of the life of a soldier. They slept on beds of reeds, without blankets, winter and summer. They wore only a tunic throughout the year, and always went barefooted. Their hair was clipped, so as to harden their heads to bear the heat of the summer and the cold of winter. The food was purposely kept in short supply, to teach them to bear hunger and to encourage resourcefulness in foraging for themselves.

At the age of 18 the young men were ready to take over the training of a group of youths of ages 7 to 18, who were embarked on the same program of barracks life. At age 20 the young men took the oath of loyalty to Sparta, and continued with their military training until they were 30. They became full citizens of Sparta, when they reached this age, and took their seats in the public assembly.

As is true in contemporary monistic cultures, the educational program of Sparta laid heavy emphasis on mind-training and memorization. The young men were taught to recite the laws of the state to music, and to sing from memory the grave and dignified chants of the old Doric style. Yet, as is also true in modern dictatorships, general intellectual education was considered unimportant.

The lack of intellectual training was the dark side of Spartan culture. Spartans had no interest in letters and taught neither reading nor writing. . . . The bare elements of mental arithmetic were acquired, but even for this they had little use. Of the great themes of human thought—history, geography, astronomy—we hear nothing. The drama was never admitted at Sparta. Rhetoric, studied so fervently in other parts of the Greek world, was frowned upon at Sparta. . . .[1]

Although in Spartan culture women were considered the equal and companion of men, and not their inferior, the education of girls was severely restricted. The main function of women was to bear children, and they were given gymnastic training, notably dance, to make them strong and capable of producing more acceptable children. No attempt was made to provide additional experience, and even the simplest home arts were ignored to a degree that Spartan women were noted for their lack of interest in the home.

Spartan education achieved its aims: Individuality was crushed out. Its people looked with disdain on others whose schools were not orientated militarily; and so did Sparta develop military men, but not a poet, philosopher, or artist, of note.

Spartans were exclusive, narrow, and arrogant. Their system was the resurgence of the primitive; all the more interesting because it synchronized with the birth of the higher civilization with which it stood in direct contradiction.[2]

[1] Frederick Eby and Charles Arrowood, *The History and Philosophy of Education, Ancient and Medieval*, Englewood Cliffs, N.J., Prentice-Hall, 1940, p. 211.
[2] *Ibid.*, p. 241.

Education in Athens

The Greeks have made use of two terms to express education, *agoge* and *paideia*. (Both have influenced English words denoting teaching and learning: for example, "pedagoge" and "pedagogy.") *Agoge*, bearing the root idea of leading, discipline, oversight, applied especially to the type of education in Sparta. *Paideia* derived from *pais* meaning "child," usually signified the child's sport or play and formed the basis of Athenian education. Athenian culture was the result of the natural evolution of the activities of the play spirit and the outgrowth of child interest in songs and stories. Their culture contained no repressive educational traditions or prejudices, and, because a society mirrors itself more perfectly in its educational system than in any other social institution, the rearing of the child—both in and out of "school"—was natural. His growth in body and mind was as unhampered as the growth of the culture itself. Thus Athenian education, in sharp contrast to that in Sparta, can be characterized by the word "humanism."

Athenian boys started to school at about age six in a school far more adaptable to individual progress than most of our contemporary school systems. Artificial grading and grouping were de-emphasized, and music and literary education were given by individual rather than group instruction. The Athenian curriculum emphasized gymnastics and music, with the emphasis being shifted from one to the other in accordance with the growing capacities and needs of the child.

Gymnastics was offered for its military value, but also for its intrinsic value in building a strong body to house an alert mind. The greatest value of gymnastic training lay in its effect upon the moral life and sense of sportsmanship. All games and contests among the Athenians were played according to elaborate rules and "good form." It is significant to note that it is from Athens that our modern Olympic games come.

To the Athenian, music included all those arts that made for beauty and happiness as opposed to the drudgery of life. It began with melody, rhythm, poetry, dancing; later on, all literary instruction such as reading, writing, arithmetic, the learning of laws, the sciences and philosophy grew from a harmonic base.

It is obvious that Athenian educational patterns were designed to produce the well-rounded individual. According to Eby and Arrowood:

> Education to the Athenians was a fine art, ranking with ceramics, sculpture, and oratory. The materials which they molded into form were different in each case, but the ends they sought were all alike—the products of the one idealizing, artistic spirit. Through a harmonious unfolding of the capacities of the individual, they aimed to produce a beautiful unity, a perfect human. . . . The old Athenian education produced the heroes of Marathon, and Salamis, and such men as Phidias, Pericles, Socrates, Plato, and all the other brilliant artists and thinkers of fifth-century culture. This artistic process of cultivating the native powers of the child in a harmony of personality is the true and original humanism.[3]

[3] *Ibid.*, p. 285.

Table 1 provides summary comparison of education in Sparta and Athens, and has many implications for the modern monistic-pluralistic cleavages in conflicting contemporary societies.

TABLE 1. COMPARISON OF EDUCATIONAL PROGRAMS IN ATHENS AND SPARTA

Basis of comparison	Athens	Sparta
Purpose of education	To develop citizens	To develop soldiers
Type of development	Moral, social, and civic	Physical and military
Greatest emphasis	The individual	The state
Education, 7 to 16	In two private schools—physical education and music	In public barracks organized militarily and operated by state
By whom taught	Teachers—each boy accompanied at all times by slave called a pedagogue	Older boys and military personnel
Education, 16 to 18	Gymnasium—a public school—and civic training in assemblies and courts	Continued military life in barracks
Education, 18 to 20	Military training	Continued in barracks as captains over younger boys
After 20	Participation in community life	Army service from 20 to 30; citizenship at 30
Higher education	University of Athens; philosophy and rhetoric	None
Outcome of education	Philosophers, poets, scholars	Soldiers
Place in history	Great influence on philosophy and education throughout history	Little or no influence

ROMAN EDUCATION

The part played by Rome in the development of western culture is well-known, and admittedly great. Some students of education, however, have tended to depreciate the value of Roman contribution to educational history because Rome borrowed much of the pattern of its educational system from Greece, and added little that was novel. The truth is that Rome, in possession of most of the civilized world, was the teacher as well as the conqueror of the nations destined to become the centers of later western civilization. Imposing her language, political institutions, ethical code, arts, and approaches to living, Rome was notably a transmitter of culture.

Although Rome was for many years officially dedicated to stamping out Christianity, it was principally because Roman influence spread across Europe to the British Isles that the Judeo-Christian heritage spread to northern and western Europe. The ancient Christian church of Rome adopted Latin as its language of worship and (more significantly, here) also used classical Latin as the language of instruction in its schools. As Christianity spread among the Roman people, the church schools developed in influence and popularity. In 391 A.D. Christianity became the official state religion of Rome, and about a century later the Emperor Justinian ordered the closing of all other schools.

Finally, the Roman Catholic Church was the only group left to preserve the culture, learning, and education of Greece and Rome during the Dark Ages when education was at its lowest ebb in history. The Germanic tribes that overthrew the Roman Empire were simple, illiterate, barbaric people. Rather than fostering education and culture, they destroyed as far as possible all the culture of the newly conquered territory. During these times learning was found only in the Christian centers. It was not until the Middle Ages that there was a revival in learning and a new interest in education.

EDUCATION DURING THE RENAISSANCE

The countries contributing the most to the educational ideals and patterns of the United States were those in central Europe and the British Isles. Most of the men and movements discussed here belong to that part of the world.

It is necessary to go back to the latter part of the fifteenth century to find the beginnings of modern education. In the period of awakening called the "Renaissance," ancient learning was rediscovered and education took on new life. Along with it went a determined revolt against the narrowness of the culture of the Middle Ages; the development of a new literature, architecture, and art; and the beginning of scientific endeavor.

The revival of learning came first in Italy; from there it spread northward over Europe and the British Isles. Academies were founded for literary study in most important Italian cities, and libraries were established. There was much interest in Greek culture. Florence, which took the lead, in 1348 established a university for the promotion of the new learning.

The movement appeared much later in northern Europe than in Italy. It first became an important factor in educational, religious, and literary fields in the Netherlands. It was here that middle-class merchants had become wealthy through trade, and that much of the educational pattern that was to spread widely in Europe and England was first developed. It was here that Erasmus was born and contributed his first important work.

ERASMUS

Desiderius Erasmus (1469?–1536) was perhaps the most famous man of letters and the most eminent educational theorist of the early sixteenth century. He was probably born in Rotterdam about 1469 and was educated first in his home country and later at the University of Paris and in Italy. He was ordained a priest of the Roman Catholic Church. His greatest influence on our American educational pattern came from his work in England, where he went during the reign of Henry VIII and remained for four years. There he assisted in the refounding of St. Paul's School, and taught Greek and divinity in Cambridge. More than anyone else he was responsible for the humanistic pattern of the curriculum at St. Paul's. This movement gave rise to many of the academies in England which later became the pattern for similar schools in America.

Erasmus wrote many books, particularly in the field of educational theory. His theories of education were far ahead of his time: he believed in universal education, condemned corporal punishment, and advocated the study of Latin and Greek. He believed that the teacher should not spend his time teaching too many rules of syntax—that a language was learned not by memorizing rules but by daily intercourse with those who could speak it.

The humanities as we know them today came into the educational pattern during this period. There developed two conceptions of the humanities. One was the narrow humanism which tempered the study of Latin with some attention to Greek in order to develop an elegant literary style. The broader conception called for the study of classical literature for a better understanding of the pursuits and activities proper to mankind. It required the study of all subjects dealing with man as a human personality. This broader conception of humanism was the forerunner of the present emphasis in education on the social studies, political economy, government, economics, sociology, psychology, and education. Unfortunately, narrow humanism too often dominated the schools during the revival of learning, and as time went on, many schools became more narrowly humanistic.

IMPORTANCE OF PRINTING

In discussing Erasmus, and later Luther, it is important to note the development of printing. Nothing that happened in this period was of greater importance. Prior to the invention of printing with movable type there were very few books, and these were hand-written. It was impossible for an ordinary person to own a Bible or a book of any kind. All teaching had to be done by word of mouth.

Printing with movable type had been in use in China for some centuries before it was invented in Europe, but the European who invented movable type had no information concerning printing in China, so he was an independent inventor. The time, the place, the exact date, and the inventor are all clouded in mystery, but this great event took place in central Europe, probably in Holland or Germany, about 1440. The inventor could have been Gutenberg, a German printer. It is known that he printed the earliest books of which copies remain. Gutenberg printed his first Bible in 1456, and from Holland and Germany printing rapidly spead to other countries.

For the first time in the history of the Christian religion Bibles were now available in some number. The reaction of church authorities was mixed: some welcomed the Bibles, others forbade their use by laymen.

Printing was well developed in central Europe before Luther was born, but it became one of the most powerful agencies for the dissemination of the doctrines of Luther and his followers. If movable type had not been invented, the Reformation might have been delayed for many years or might have had a very different outcome.

MARTIN LUTHER

Martin Luther (1483–1546) was born on November 10, 1483, at Eisleben, Germany, to a family of the free peasant class.

At the desire of his father, Luther began the study of law in 1503. However, two months later he entered a monastery—no one knows just why. His decision may have been the result of a vow he took, during a violent thunderstorm, to become a monk. Having entered upon his religious career he devoted his life to it with great seriousness.

This discussion is concerned only with Luther's influence on education, hence it will not deal with his pestuous career in the service of the church. Luther finally broke with the Catholic Church and in October, 1517, nailed his famous theses to the door of the church at Wittenberg. From then on he was an outcast so far as the established church was concerned.

It must be remembered that Germany had no lack of schools in Luther's time. By 1500 Germany boasted 13 universities and a great many lower schools, some of them very good.

The German people were extremely religious at the time of the Reformation. The Bible was a favorite book among the common people, and when it was made more easily available through printing its use became more general. What, then, did the Reformation have to do with the development of public schools? In the first place Luther placed a great stress upon the dignity of the individual. In his treatise on "The Christian Liberty" he wrote: "Nor are we only kings and the freest of all men, but also priests forever, a dignity far higher than kingship, because by that priesthood we are worthy to appear before God, to pray for others, and to teach one another mutually the things which are God."[4]

Secondly, Luther taught that the Bible was the ultimate source of religious truth, which made education a necessity. Man now had a reason for education. If he was to be his own priest and if the Bible was to be his guide, then he could not fulfill his life's mission unless he was able to read. This

[4] F. V. N. Painter, *Luther on Education*, Philadelphia, Lutheran Publication Society, 1889.

led to a great spread in education. Furthermore, Luther wrote many sermons, treatises, books, and pamphlets giving his religious views which were read by the multitudes as soon as they had learned to read.

Even before the coming of Luther a large number of Bibles and many other books had been printed in German, and these could now be read by more and more people. The student of education should not conclude that the Protestant Reformation was all Luther and all in Germany. Many other famous men, in many different countries, were a part of the Reformation. The groups they represented differed in numerous points of doctrine, but they did agree on the dignity of the individual, the importance of the Bible, and the need of universal education. It must not be concluded, however, that free public education sprang into being at this time, for this was not the case. Luther never did separate education from the church. Even the Puritans, after they had set up schools and churches in New England, always thought of them as a part of the same plan—in fact the weekday school and the Sunday church were usually held in the same building.

A great many different movements grew out of the Reformation—the various protestant denominations were one result. These were developed in various countries under various important leaders. One small group, developed in Moravia, was fundamentalist so far as beliefs were concerned. Its members believed in a literal interpretation of the Bible. They were an interesting and very devout group, but they would not be mentioned at this time if it were not for an outstanding bishop of the church who was the first great modern in educational thinking. His name was John Amos Comenius.

COMENIUS

John Amos Comenius (1592–1671) was born at Nivnitz in Moravia. He attended the village school and at the age of 15 entered the grammar school at Prerau. The schools of the day were very poor and Comenius was dissatisfied with them. He moved on to the University of Herborn to study when he was 18.

Four years later, after one year at Heidelberg, he returned to his native country, planning to be ordained a minister in the Moravian Brotherhood. However, this was not possible until he was 24, so he turned to teaching and became master of the school of the Moravian Brotherhood at Prerau. He became interested in education and wrote his first book, a textbook on grammar.

He entered the ministry at a time when there was a great struggle between the Protestants and the Catholics in Moravia. His home was twice plundered; his books and manuscripts were burned, and his wife and children were killed. The Moravian Brotherhood was driven into exile in Poland in 1628.

Comenius, who became a bishop in his church, lived for 79 years, mostly in exile. He gave all his thought and energy to the advancement of mankind through religion and education. He chose to be a priest but spent most of his life as an educator and wrote a great many books in both fields.

While in exile he was in charge of a school at Lissa, Poland. Here he worked out much of his educational program and wrote his great work on method. He subsequently went to Sweden to help reform the schools there. Later he worked in England, then went back to Sweden for eight years, thence to Hungary, and finally to Amsterdam where he completed his life's work.

Cotton Mather reported in 1702 that Comenius was offered the presidency of Harvard College, in 1654. Henry Dunster had resigned as president and Comenius was suggested as a successor. But Comenius did not accept the offer, and Cotton Mather noted, "But the solicitations of the Swedish Ambassador, diverting him another way, that Incomparable Moravian became not an American Citizen."[5] Much research has been done in an attempt to establish the truth of this report. No one has been able to uncover anything to substantiate this story published by Cotton Mather, and historians of Harvard seem to agree that the incident never happened.

Comenius was without doubt the greatest educator of his century. In fact, many of his ideas are incorporated in our present educational system. He proposed a grading system based on the growth and development of children. His plan called for a single-track educational program; it applied to the boys and girls of all classes. He rejected the idea of one school system for upper-class children and another and poorer one for the children of the lower classes. His plan was democratic.

Comenius wrote in the *Great Didactic*, "Everyone ought to receive a universal education and this at school." He was much ahead of his time in this respect. Although the single-track plan of education is basic to any democratic conception of education, it is just now being tried for the first time in most of central Europe.

The most important educational proposal made by Comenius concerned the organization of a school system. He proposed four levels of education. Each stage was to be a different kind of school, and each school was to be six years in length. Roughly the divisions corresponded to his conception of the four periods in the life of a growing child.

There should be a mother's school, in the home, for children from birth to age 6. There should be a vernacular school in every village for all children from 6 to 12. There should be a gymnasium in every city for children from 12 to 18. The gymnasium was to be followed by six years at the university. These divisions correspond quite closely to the present-day organization of education in America.

The child's mother was to be his teacher for the first six years. She would teach the child the beginnings of knowledge that would be useful to him

[5] Will S. Monroe, *Comenius*, New York, Scribner, 1900, p. 78.

during his life. Comenius put great emphasis on the teaching of objects and the development of the senses. Children were to be made acquainted with such things as water, earth, air, fire, rain, stones, iron, and plants to prepare them for the later study of the natural sciences. In the same manner the mother was to teach the children about the sun, moon, stars, mountains, valleys, and plains. Seeing, hearing, tasting, and touching were avenues through which children were to make contact with many natural things. Comenius wrote a book for the mothers called *School of Infancy,* in which he told them what to teach. He also prepared a picture book called *Orbis Pictus* for the children, to help them understand things that were not in their own physical environment. This type of book represented a new idea in education. The children asked questions which the mother answered, and they answered questions she asked, thus laying the foundation for reasoning.

Comenius had great faith in mothers, a faith that was not shared by most contemporary educators. He envisioned a mother who was well-educated and all-wise, but because there were few mothers of that kind, the first step in his educational pattern was not a great success. The nursery school is an outgrowth of the idea so well expressed by Comenius, but it depends upon specially prepared teachers instead of mothers for most of the teaching.

At the time of Comenius there were schools for the poor in which they were taught in the vernacular of the region. The children of more well-to-do parents were sent to schools where the language of instruction was Latin. Comenius considered this a bad plan. He thought that all children of all the people should go through the six years of elementary education together, for this would be good for the social development of all the classes. Moreover, he thought that using the vernacular in teaching those who were to be the country's leaders was valuable to them.

The subjects of the vernacular school were about the same as those taught in the early elementary schools in America. Comenius worked out a system of teaching whereby the pupils were grouped in six different classes. They studied the same subjects in each class but every year they went more deeply into each subject.

The third 6-year period was to be spent in the gymnasium or Latin school. Here again Comenius proposed the gradation used in the vernacular school. However, the offerings of this type of school were very ambitious, for here students were to achieve universal wisdom. They were to learn four different languages and get a suitable grounding in all the sciences and arts. He thought it best to approach the teaching of language by having the students read familiar material; grammar was to be taught later.

Comenius set down his educational beliefs in a book called the *Great Didactic.* Much of what he wrote is very modern even today. He believed that education should follow nature, and that it should proceed from the simple to the more difficult. Far from believing that proper education is circumscribed rote learning, he felt that children should learn to do by doing.

He also put much emphasis on the teaching of practical things; he wished to eliminate all useless materials. He made a plea for gentle discipline in place of the brutal methods that were common in his time.

In spite of his pioneer work, education was little changed for centuries. Those with whom Comenius worked soon forgot both him and his educational philosophy. Not until much later did he take his place as a frontier thinker in education. Most of his plans in this field have influenced education in our time.

It is interesting to note progress and development in any field. One is impressed by the gap between the aspirations and ideals of the frontier thinkers and the achievement of their programs. Many of Comenius' ideals have not as yet been attained in the countries where he lived and worked.

A great many Moravians migrated to America in the eighteenth century. One group founded a community named Salem. It is now a part of Winston-Salem, North Carolina. Here they built the kind of houses they were familiar with in Moravia. They set up their church and organized a type of cooperative living.

ROUSSEAU

Jean Jacques Rousseau (1712–1778), a political as well as an educational pioneer, rebelled against the religious, educational, social, and governmental conditions of his time. He attempted to circumvent the artificiality in religion and education and to curb the exploitation by government prevalent in France.

Rousseau's writings had great political influence. His book *The Social Contract* became the bible of the French Revolution. His influence was also felt in America; Jefferson and other American leaders knew and believed in his political teachings. In fact much that was written at the time of the American Revolution found its source in Rousseau's ideas. Rousseau believed that men were not bound to submit to a government against their own will. He advocated the overthrow of the existing autocratic government in France and the establishment of a republic. He believed in universal suffrage based on "liberty, fraternity, and equality." He was the prophet of both the American and the French revolutions.

In the field of education Rousseau's ideas were just as radical. He protested against the stern, unreal, artificial schools of his time, in which little boys were treated as small men. Education was meaningless, the methods were stiff and unnatural. There was excessive emphasis on religious instruction and book education. Like Comenius more than a century before, Rousseau preached the substitution of life amid nature, childish problems, ways, and sports.

Rousseau believed that education was the remedy for the ills of society and that in the processes of education the child should be the center of gravity. The nature of the child should determine the nature of the teaching rather than a logical order of subject matter suited only to an adult mind. According to Rousseau, the child was to be considered a child and taught as a child rather than as a miniature adult. His chief concern was to provide the child with real, vital, concrete experience.

Rousseau's educational program was concerned with the child's physical and mental life.

> Do not suffer the child to be restrained by caps, bands, and swaddling-clothes; but let him have gowns flowing and loose, and which leave all his limbs at liberty, not so heavy as to hinder his movement, nor so warm as to prevent him from feeling the impression of the air. By keeping them dressed and within-doors, children in cities are suffocated. . . . I repeat it, the education of man begins at birth. Before he can speak, before he can understand, he is already instructing himself.[6]

Much of Rousseau's educational teaching is contained in his famous book *Emile*, which became as important in education as his *Social Contract* was in the world of politics. "All is good as it comes from the hand of the Creator; all degenerates under the hands of man." This is the opening sentence in *Emile*, a book in which Rousseau described the education of a boy, whom he called Emile, from birth to maturity. No one reading it now would take it as a serious discussion of the philosophy of education. It is a book of protest, its suggestions are extreme, but it contains a great many of the truths that are now commonly accepted by those who advocate modern and progressive schools.

Rousseau believed that we should treat the child instead of subject matter. He taught that present life is more important in teaching than a life to come later, and that authority should be replaced by reason. Education should take place through the senses rather than the memory; therefore, he felt that physical activity and health were of great importance. Education at each age should be suited to the activities normal for that age. Teachers should make use of the natural interests of children in education. All these statements are in keeping with good educational practice in America today.

Rousseau's writings may seem to the reader today to be filled with suggestions that are crude and impractical. However, when considered in the light of the conditions that prevailed in his time, these writings are of the greatest significance. *Emile* created interest in educational reform in France. Its influence soon spread to Germany and to other European countries. The torch of educational reform along humane and democratic lines that had been lighted by Comenius was rekindled by Rousseau and handed by him to the many men who were to follow him, both in Europe and in America. In particular, a young man in Switzerland by the name of Pestalozzi was greatly influenced and inspired by *Emile*: he picked up the torch and carried it much farther ahead.

---

[6] Jean Jacques Rousseau, *Emile*, New York, Appleton-Century-Crofts, 1898, p. 25.

PESTALOZZI

Johann Heinrich Pestalozzi (1746–1827) was born in Zurich, Switzerland. As a young man he came under the influence of the teachings of Rousseau. Pestalozzi first tried out Rousseau's method of teaching on his own children, and discovered many shortcomings. In 1774 he established a school on his farm: 50 abandoned children were his pupils. Combining work on the farm with study of the ordinary subjects in the elementary curriculum, the children learned to make cheese while they learned to read. The school was conducted for two years and, when the family funds were exhausted, it was closed. But Pestalozzi still held to a firm belief in the power of education. He also saw many answers to the pressing educational problems of his day. In Europe at the close of World War II there were many orphan children needing homes and education, and a school was established in honor of Pestalozzi. Most of the money was raised in Switzerland and the school was built in the Swiss Alps. The school for orphans that Pestalozzi established lasted only two years but the new Pestalozzi School seems to be a permanent organization.

Locke and Rousseau took into account only the difficulty of dealing with one pupil. Their method was to shut up their solitary pupil, away from the contaminating influences of the world, to provide him with a tutor who was a marvel of discretion and wisdom, and to show how under these circumstances they might work their ideal of education.

Pestalozzi sought to reform education on more generous lines. He aimed at the regeneration of mankind. He lived for years among beggars, in order to learn "how to make beggars live like men." He dealt with the poor and outcast, and strove by means of education to give these neglected children self-respect and to raise them from moral degradation.[7]

After closing his school Pestalozzi turned his attention to writing. His most famous book, *Leonard and Gertrude,* was written at this time. The great success of this book made him an important figure. It is an unusually interesting novel, concerned with Swiss peasant life and practical home education, and it makes good reading even today.

Pestalozzi's many teaching positions took him from one place to another. For six months he had charge of a village school where he taught 169 orphans. His last and most important position was as director of the institute he established at Yverdon and conducted for 20 years. Here, he demonstrated with children the methods that were to make him famous.

His institute became so well-known that it attracted the interest of prominent friends of education from all over Europe. Teachers came from other countries to learn his methods, and ruling monarchs came to learn what they could do to provide better schools in their countries. Froebel, Herbart, and

---

[7] Catherine I. Dodd, *Introduction to the Herbartian Principles of Teaching,* London, Swam, Sonnenschein and Company, 1898.

Sheldon, all of whom will be discussed later, came to Pestalozzi as students. Froebel remained for two years as a student and teacher. Herbart, the eminent German psychologist, visited the institute and was much impressed by what he saw. Recognizing that what the movement needed was an educational psychology, he returned to Germany and developed not only a psychology but a method of teaching.

Pestalozzi set forth his educational beliefs in a book called *How Gertrude Teaches Her Children*. This is his book of methods. Pestalozzi begins his teaching with nature and the five senses. But he does not trust nature as Rousseau did.

> Even at the infant's cradle we must begin to take the training of our race out of the hands of blind, sportive Nature, and put it into the hands of that better power which the experience of ages has taught us to abstract from the eternal laws of our nature.[8]

> The most essential point from which I start is this:—Sense-impression of Nature is the only true foundation of human instruction, because it is the only true foundation of human knowledge.[9]

> All instruction of man is then only the art of helping Nature to develop in her own way; and this art rests essentially on the relation and harmony between the impressions received by the child and the exact degree of his developed powers. It is also necessary in the impressions that are brought to the child by instruction that there should be a sequence, so that beginning and progress should keep pace with the beginning and progress of the powers to be developed in the child.[10]

Pestalozzi also wrote a guide for teaching spelling, and another for teaching reading. Although he is well-known for his writings, perhaps his greatest contribution to education is embodied in the lives of those whom he taught.

Comenius worked out, in some detail, a system of education. Herbart developed detailed methods of presenting subject matter. Pestalozzi did neither. His contribution was largely his philosophy of education and the relationship of teacher to child. The best statement of his ideas was made by Pestalozzi himself when he contrasted, for his followers, the methods of the usual schoolmaster and those he recommended.

> The teacher starts usually from objects, you from the child himself. The teacher connects his instruction with what he knows, in order to teach the child; you know in the presence of your child nothing else than himself and connect everything with his instincts and impulses. The teacher has a form of instruction to which he subjects the child; you subject your course of instruction to the child and surrender it to him, when you teach, as you surrender yourself to him. With the teacher, everything comes from the understanding, with you all gushes out from

---

[8] Johann Heinrich Pestalozzi, *How Gertrude Teaches Her Children*, Syracuse, N.Y., C. W. Bardeen, 1898, p. 249.

[9] *Ibid.*, p. 316.

[10] *Ibid.*, p. 58.

ÉMILE,
OU
DE L'ÉDUCATION.

Par J. J. ROUSSEAU,
Citoyen de Genève.

Sanabilibus ægrotamus malis ; ipſaque nos in reſtum
natura genitos, ſi emendari velimus, juvat.
Sen : de irâ. L. II. c. 13.

TOME PREMIER.

A LA HAYE,
Chez JEAN NÉAULME, Libraire.

M. DCC. LXII.
Avec Privilége de Noſſeign. les Etats de Hollande
& de Weſtfriſe.

Frontis and title page for
Emile. (*Rare Book Room,*
New York Public Library)

When a children's village, dedicated to helping youth
whose lives had been shattered by World War II, was
established in Trogan, Switzerland, in 1945, it was most
appropriately named "The Pestalozzi Children's Village."
(*Swiss National Tourist Office*)

No one loved children more than Pestalozzi, and the reaction of
these Swiss orphans shows they were aware of the fact.

The Moravian people brought
their religion, their schools,
their houses, and their way
of life to America. This street
is in the Old Salem resto-
ration in North Carolina.
(*Old Salem, Inc., Winston-*
Salem, North Carolina)

the fullness of heart. The child is childlike toward you, because you behave motherlike toward him; the more you are motherlike, the more childlike he is.[11]

To understand why this was a revolutionary doctrine at that time, it is necessary to be familiar with the kind of schools that were prevalent for the poorer classes. In the usual school, subject matter, most of it useless and uninteresting, was predominant. The schools were conducted in unsanitary and largely unequipped buildings. The methods of teaching were chiefly assignment, recitation, and punishment. The children were beaten much and taught little, there was no feeling of friendship between teacher and pupils.

The teaching method of Pestalozzi spread first to Prussia. The king of Prussia, becoming very much interested in the new education, wished to visit Pestalozzi. When he arrived, Pestalozzi, although ill, insisted on being taken to see the king. As he was being lifted into his coach, he fainted, whereupon his friends urged him to give up his intended visit. But Pestalozzi said, "Let me go; for if by my humble intercession, I shall only cause a single Prussian child to receive better instruction, I shall be satisfied."

Pestalozzian schools were established in large numbers in Prussia. The new teaching methods spread largely from Prussia (instead of directly from Pestalozzi) to other European countries, and to England, and later to the United States.

In 1843 Horace Mann visited the schools of Europe and reported on his trip in his seventh annual report as secretary of the Massachusetts State Board of Education. The most interesting part of this report had to do with his observations on the schools of Prussia. Here Mr. Mann discovered what he thought to be the best type of elementary education he had seen on his trip. He was enthusiastic in his praise of the schools that had been set up by the followers of Pestalozzi. In these schools there was perfect harmony between teachers and pupils. The children were happy, no force or bribes were necessary to obtain the desired results. The report was widely read in America.

The schools in Oswego, New York, comprised the first public-school system in America to adopt the Pestalozzian method. The superintendent of schools, E. A. Sheldon, was dissatisfied with the methods in use. He was looking about for something better. He found it in the Normal and Training School at Toronto, Canada, which he visited in 1859. On his return to Oswego, Mr. Sheldon obtained from England the plans for the new type of education and introduced it into the Oswego schools. The teachers met once a week to learn about the new method and to ask questions. The experiment was so successful that soon people were coming from a distance to find out about the Pestalozzian method.

Because of the great popularity of the new method of teaching and the

[11] Quoted by Tadaus Misawa, *Modern Educators and Their Ideals,* New York, Appleton-Century-Crofts, 1909, p. 127.

desire on the part of so many people to study it, the Oswego Normal School, a state institution, was set up in 1865 under the direction of Mr. Sheldon. The spread of Pestalozzi's teachings in America stemmed in large part from this normal school, which became nationally important almost immediately. Teachers came to it from more than half the states in the Union. Normal schools as far west as San Francisco obtained teachers from Oswego so that they too might learn about and teach the new method.

So the influence of Pestalozzi spread. He took the torch from Rousseau and carried it far in his lifetime. With it he kindled torches for Herbart, Froebel, and a host of other educators to carry forward.

FROEBEL

Friedrich Froebel (1782–1852) was the son of a pious, poor, orthodox Lutheran minister who never understood the dreamy, troublesome child. His mother died when he was an infant. His father married again, but his step-mother was unkind to him. A mother's love and a happy home life thus denied him, he left home to live with an uncle. He attended the village school but was not a successful pupil, so he apprenticed to a forester. It was in the forest that he developed his lifelong love of nature. There also he attained some of the sense of the unity of nature that was to pervade his philosophy. Froebel studied at Jena, the foremost university in Germany, with little success. His university career ended in disgrace when he was jailed for two months for a very small debt that he could not pay. The circumstances of Froebel's early childhood and his experiences in the forest give us a key not only to his whole life pattern but also to his educational philosophy.

The most important thing that happened to him was the opportunity to work with Pestalozzi at Yverdon. In him Froebel found a kindred soul. He understood Pestalozzi's passion for little children and desire to build an education that would be a part of life. Froebel remained at Yverdon for two years, first as a pupil and later as a teacher. His educational philosophy was profoundly affected by Rousseau and Comenius as well as by Pestalozzi.

In 1837 Froebel opened his first kindergarten in Blankenburg. This type of school was his greatest contribution to education. He was influenced, no doubt, by the plans for a mothers' school advocated so ably by Comenius. But mostly the kindergarten was a result of his passionate love for little children and his desire to do something for them. Pestalozzi's teachings and his own unhappy childhood also contributed to Froebel's wish to make life better for them.

Froebel said that the object of the kindergarten was

. . . to give the children employment in agreement with their whole nature, to strengthen their bodies, to exercise their senses, to engage their awakening minds, and through their senses to bring them acquaintance with nature and their fellow creatures; it is especially to guide aright the heart and the affections, and to lead them to the original ground of all life, to unity with themselves.[12]

This statement is a bit vague. Froebel's desire for unity, which is found in all his writings, is not always clear. His philosophy is filled with religious mysticism. Whatever he said about his philosophy, we know him best by what he actually did for the education of the little children.

Froebel devoted the last years of his life to his kindergarten, and established a special school for kindergarten teachers. The rapid spread of the kindergarten movement over the educational world was due largely to the teachers who received their inspiration and the preparation for their work directly from Froebel and then went to other countries to establish these institutions.

Only in its home country, Germany, did the kindergarten movement die. The Prussian government under Bismarck desired to stamp out everything that looked like democracy. The kindergarten was, of course, almost pure democracy, so kindergartens were forbidden by edict of the Prussian government. Froebel, it is said, died of a broken heart.

Froebel's two main principles were self-activity and social participation. Music, supervised play, handwork, dramatics, dancing, drawing, group work, singing, and many other activities in the modern school were part of the school for little children planned so well by Froebel more than a century ago.

Froebel set down his educational beliefs in a book entitled *The Education of Man*. He wrote a great many other books in this field, including *Songs for Mother and Nursery*, a songbook for little children.

HERBART

Johann Friedrich Herbart (1776–1841) was a German professor and a contemporary of both Pestalozzi and Froebel. He was a very different type of individual, however. He was born into the important professional class and was given an excellent education, graduating from the University of Jena. He spent most of his life as a university professor of philosophy and education. Herbart was first of all a scholar, he did not share with Pestalozzi and Froebel their passionate desire to help the poor and needy. He established the first demonstration school in connection with a university, and taught a small selected group of children. His teaching and writing were done at the Universities of Gottingen and Konigsberg.

Herbart based his educational theories upon ethics and psychology, and he emphasized at the outset that the one supreme aim of education is the development of moral character. He rejected the theory of the mind's division into "faculties," and believed that the mind functions as a unit. For many years Herbart was hailed as the father of modern psychology and

[12] Ross L. Finney, *A Brief History of the American Public Schools*, New York, Macmillan, 1925, p. 99.

modern method. However, his concepts were not of great lasting value; on them have been built a much more usable psychology and theory of method. It should be said, nonetheless, that Herbart was the first to take teaching methods out of the realm of the accidental and build a scientific approach to classroom problems.

Herbart worked out a scheme to make teaching an orderly and scientific process. The scheme included five formal steps: (1) preparation, a review of related material that had been previously learned; (2) presentation, in which the teacher presented the new material to be learned; (3) comparison, in which the new facts were organized under the teacher's direction in preparation for the development of any general truth that should be arrived at in comparing the old and the new; (4) conclusion, a generalization from the old and new facts presented (this was the climax of the lesson); and (5) application, of the general principles learned. This final step was added later by the followers of Herbart.

It is apparent that the above plan involves the process of inductive thinking. Herbart's mistake was in assuming that all teaching could be made to fit this pattern. Those who followed his plan soon found that teaching in accordance with it was often sterile, formal, and not of any great value. From the standpoint of modern educational philosophy, the plan's greatest fault is that it is always text problems that the children are solving. Life and learning are seldom made up in such handy packages.

Herbart's real influence came after his death. Many of his followers carried on the work in German universities, particularly at Jena. The most important of these "Herbartians" was Dr. Wilhelm Rein, professor of pedagogics at Jena. Herbartianism spread far beyond Germany. It had great influence in England. Many American educators studied with Rein, at Jena. Enthusiastic Herbartians on their return to America organized the National Herbartian Society in 1895. In 1902 the name was changed to the National Society for the Study of Education. This is still a very important educational organization in America.

THE BEGINNINGS OF EDUCATION IN AMERICA

During colonial days education was scattered, fragmentary, and largely unsatisfactory. Each group of settlers brought with them not only their language, customs, and religion, but also their ideas of education. Thus many very different patterns of education were attempted in the various colonies. Three of these patterns are important: those in (1) the southern colonies, (2) New England, and (3) the middle colonies.

The Southern Colonies

The southern colonies developed their own peculiar kind of education based on their English background. Virginia and the other southern colonies were largely settled by Englishmen, most of whom came from the ruling class. They brought the English ideas of class with them. The colonists settled on large tracts of land and developed great plantations, and an aristocratic society. The owning and ruling class hired tutors to teach their children until they were old enough to be sent to England to complete their education. The work on the plantations was done by slaves, indentured servants, and convicts brought over from England. The children of these groups received no education. The Virginians were simply following the pattern of the mother country, for in England the official position at the time was that the laborers should be kept ignorant as well as poor; the business of the poor was to work, not to think. The southern colonists believed in authority—the authority of the Church of England over religious affairs, the authority of the owners over those who worked. It was the royalist pattern so common in England and in other European countries at the time. No organized attempt to promote public education in the South was made during colonial days.

It should be noted that one lone voice was raised in Virginia for general education, it was the voice of Thomas Jefferson. But no other effort followed Jefferson's, hence Virginia had to wait until the middle of the nineteenth century for the establishment of anything resembling a school system.

New England

While aristocratic Englishmen were planting their class system and their ancient ideas of man's relationship in Virginia, other Englishmen were establishing a far different type of colony farther north, on the rockbound coast of what was to be called New England. To this place came men with a dream of freedom and a desire to make a new kind of society in the New World. They left class system behind them, for it had no part in their plans. They left England and her autocratic civil government to establish a colony where men would be free to govern themselves. One would expect such a group to establish something new in education, and they did. They established that education was universal, and taxed themselves to pay the bill. Both ideas were different from those held in the mother country. Nevertheless, they patterned their schools after those they had known; their Latin grammar schools and universities were all faithful copies of similar schools in England.

The ideas of education held by the settlers of New England grew more out of religious than out of political considerations. The Puritans believed that the Bible was the guide of life and that the right to read and interpret it was a test of religious liberty. It was very necessary, therefore, that every person should learn to read the Bible for himself. The Pilgrims in Massachusetts, the Quakers in Rhode Island and Pennsylvania, the Dutch in New Amsterdam, the Swedes in Delaware, and the Germans in Pennsylvania were all motivated by the desire to read the Bible. This great religious urge led to the establishment of schools.

Whereas the South developed an educational pattern based upon the tutorial plan in the home, in New England the educational center was the community. The wealth of the community was taxed to pay the bill. In the South the poorer classes were disregarded; in New England education was for all since it was motivated by the desire to read the Bible. There was no question of religious freedom in the New England schools because the early colonists settled among groups with the same religion. Hence the public school in a Massachusetts town could teach the children to read and write at the same time that it taught them the faith of their fathers.

The Middle Colonies

In the middle colonies we find a different plan of education. They too were motivated by a desire to read the Bible. However, their schools were organized by the churches and not by the local civil government.

The situation in the middle colonies is well stated by Cubberley in his *Public Education in the United States.*

In New England the Puritan-Calvinist had had a complete monopoly of both Church and State. Into the Middle Colonies, best represented by New Jersey and Pennsylvania, there had come a mixture of peoples representing different Protestant faiths, and no such monopoly was possible there.

Unlike New England, though, no sect was in a majority. Church control by each denomination was, as a result, considered to be most satisfactory, and hence no appeal to the state was made by the churches for assistance in carrying out their religious purposes. The clergymen usually were the teachers in the parochial schools established until a regular schoolmaster could be had, while private pay schools were opened in a few of the larger towns. These, as were the church services, were conducted in the language of the different immigrants. Girls were educated as well as boys, the emphasis being placed on reading, writing, counting, and religion, rather than upon any form of higher training.

The result was the development in Pennsylvania, and to some extent in the other Middle Colonies as well, of a policy of depending upon Church and private effort for educational advantages. As a consequence, the provision for education, aside from certain rudimentary and religious instruction thought necessary for religious purposes, and aside from the apprenticing of orphans and children of the very poor, was left largely for those who could pay for the privilege.[13]

The tax-supported school came out of the New England colonies, the private institution-supported school was a product largely of the South, while the middle colonies developed private church-supported schools. It required two centuries for universal, free, nonsectarian, tax-supported education to become the national pattern.

EDUCATION IN THE YOUNG NATION

In 1776, when Thomas Jefferson wrote the Declaration of Independence declaring that all men were created free and equal, there was no equality

[13] E. P. Cubberley, *Public Education in the United States,* Boston, Houghton Mifflin, 1934, pp. 20–21.

of education and no general freedom of educational opportunities in the new nation. It became one of the great tasks for the new nation to develop an adequate plan for public education.

When this nation was established, Pestalozzi was conducting his important educational experiments in Switzerland, and men from many lands were journeying to his school to sit at his feet. Rousseau was just completing his great work in France as the philosopher of the French and American revolutions. These two men had a profound influence on the educational thinking of our country. Froebel and Herbart came later—both of them were born at about the time our nation came into being.

Thomas Jefferson

A great liberal, Thomas Jefferson (1743–1826) was born in Virginia and lived there on a large estate—except for the years he was away in public service—until his death.

Jefferson had great faith in democracy and in the rights of the common man. It naturally followed that he had great interest in public education. He believed that man was created to govern himself. He also believed that education was necessary in a democracy, for how could man govern himself if he could not understand the economic and political problems around him? In a letter to George Washington, Thomas Jefferson wrote on January 4, 1786: "It is an axiom in my mind, that our liberty can never be safe but in the hands of the people themselves, and that, too, of the people with a certain degree of instruction."

In 1779, while a member of the Virginia legislature, Jefferson introduced a bill providing for free public education in his state. This bill, which he called "A Bill for the More General Diffusion of Knowledge," was the first definite proposal in America for the establishment of a state system of public schools. It is amazing that such a plan should have been proposed by a southern planter in Virginia, a state that believed not at all in free or public education: if the proposal had been made in Massachusetts it would not have been so startling. But Jefferson's fellow planters who made up the legislative body in Virginia would have none of this educational plan. It remained for other states to establish public-school systems, and in fact it was not until 1860 that any public educational system was adopted in Virginia. Jefferson did live to see the University of Virginia established, but his plan for separating the state from the church had no success.

In the light of what is now known about state systems of public schools, it is interesting to examine Jefferson's plan. The counties of Virginia were to be divided into hundredths (these divisions correspond to the school districts of today) and the qualified voters were to elect three county aldermen who were to build, have charge of, and maintain schools where both boys and girls were to be educated. The plan provided that all children should have three years of elementary education free. If children attended the elementary school for a longer time, their parents were to pay tuition.

The Jefferson plan provided for the appointment by the aldermen of a superintendent of schools. He was to be a man of "learning, integrity and fidelity to the commonwealth." Each superintendent was to have charge of ten schools, and his duties were to be much like those of the modern superintendent of schools. He was to hire teachers, examine the pupils, visit the schools, and have general control of them. The schools were to be financed in the same manner as other county activities.

Jefferson's plan also made provisions for the establishment of secondary schools. High school districts were to be made up of several elementary school districts. The high schools were to be built on plots of 100 acres; the buildings and their maintenance were to be paid for out of public funds. Boys were to be selected from the elementary schools on the basis of their promise, and they would then get free education at the secondary school level. Outstanding graduates of the high schools were to be sent at public expense to the College of William and Mary.

Jefferson was not a professional educator. However, he set up the ideals and a pattern for public education. His own state had no middle class—the large landowners had already provided for their own children and had no interest in the education of the people who worked on their plantations. Hence the Jefferson plan did not have a chance in Virginia; it remained for other states to lead the way.

It is interesting to speculate on what might have happened if Jefferson's plan had been adopted in Virginia. It might have speeded up the establishment of free public education by at least a century.

Benjamin Franklin

Benjamin Franklin (1706–1790) was a man of many talents. He is best known as statesman, scientist, and philosopher, but he was also interested in education.

Although Franklin was born in Boston and received what schooling he had in that city, he did not share the educational philosophies of Horace Mann and John Adams. These men believed that education was a state function; Franklin held that it was an individual function. Adams and Mann would tax property owners to raise money to educate the children of all the people; Franklin believed that the money should be contributed by individuals interested in organizing and maintaining schools. He thought that plans should be made, if necessary, for the education of the poor, but that if public money was to be used, it was for pauper education. A great many people in Pennsylvania held the same opinion as Franklin, and Pennsylvania for years looked upon public education as education for the poor.

Franklin proposed no system of education. He was instrumental, however, in founding an academy in 1749. Included in the chapter on secondary education is the story of the academy founded by Franklin which later became a great university.

Franklin did not attend college. He was self-educated, and he was one of the best-educated men in the early days of our nation. It is little wonder, then, that he looked with disfavor upon those colleges teaching Latin and Greek but no useful information.

Believing that education should be practical, Franklin did not hold with the Latin and Greek of the Latin grammar schools: he maintained that all education should be conducted in English. Furthermore, he felt that the subject matter of the schools should be such as to prepare youth for an occupation. It is understandable that in writing out the plans for his academy, Franklin should put so much stress on English—he was a master of writing simple, understandable English, and his students were to learn to read, both silently and orally, and to write English. The pupils should learn arithmetic, too, and how to keep accounts—Franklin mentioned many times in his writings that keeping accounts was very important.

In his plan for the curriculum for his newly established academy, Franklin suggested the wide use of prizes. He suggested that two "scholars" be paired in spelling: each was to ask the other to spell ten words each day; the one that spelled the most words correctly to receive a prize—"a pretty, neat book of some kind."

Did Franklin have any influence in education? Yes. The type of academy he planned spread very rapidly over the country, crowding out the Latin grammar schools that had been common before his time. But most of the academies never did fulfill Franklin's dream. Even his own academy, falling into the hands of a board of trustees, made up largely of members of the church of England, added Latin and Greek to the curriculum. Eventually his academy took on more and more of the college-preparatory aspects of secondary education, which was not as Franklin planned it. Even with his great prestige, he could not establish and run the kind of school he dreamed of. It was not until a century later, when the public high school came into being, that Franklin's plan for a secondary school taught in English and teaching useful things became accepted.

Franklin's plan for individual self-education also had an enormous influence on the youth of his time. You must remember that in Franklin's time there were no free public schools in Pennsylvania. The rate of illiteracy was very high. If a young man wished to get an education he had to do it largely for himself, particularly if he was too poor to pay tuition. Franklin's example was followed by a great many young men.

Horace Mann

Horace Mann (1796–1859), often referred to as the father of our public schools, was educated as a lawyer and practiced law with great success for 14 years. He was elected to the Massachusetts House of Representatives in

1827 and served as a member of it until he transferred to the Senate in 1833. While a member of the legislature he was instrumental in securing the passage of a law setting up a state board of education. Mann left the legislature and the practice of law at a great financial sacrifice to become the first secretary of the newly created state board of education. He did not return to politics until 1848, when he resigned as secretary of the board of education and took the place in the Congress of the United States vacated by John Quincy Adams.

Why did Horace Mann give up law and politics for education? He said that "the interests of a client are small as compared with the interests of the next generation." He was determined to do something for the schools of Massachusetts, for the need for school reforms there was great at that time. The schools lacked adequate financial support, the terms were very short, there was a scarcity of textbooks, the buildings and equipment were inadequate, and there were few properly prepared teachers. In fact there was no provision for the preparation of teachers in Massachusetts—or in any other state, for that matter. There were no superintendents of schools, and no one to supervise and advise with the teachers. A great many children were growing up without going to school. Horace Mann threw all his energies into this problem.

Through his efforts the first public normal school was established in Lexington, Massachusetts, in 1839. In his address at the dedication of the first building Mann painted a glowing picture of the importance of such schools for the education of teachers. He more than anyone else started the movement that provided America with normal schools, teachers' colleges, and colleges of education for the adequate preparation of those who teach our children.

Horace Mann's greatest contribution to the literature of education lies in the 12 annual reports he made as secretary of the Massachusetts State Board of Education. In them he wrote on the conditions of education in his state and elsewhere, and discussed the aims and purposes of public education. He believed and taught that education should be nonsectarian, universal, and free, and he set up a system of education in Massachusetts to facilitate meeting these goals. Students of education who are interested in his work will find much valuable material in these reports.

In 1853 Horace Mann was instrumental in the founding of Antioch College at Yellow Springs, Ohio. He became its first president and remained there until his death. Thus he influenced college and on a lower level public education as well. Having fought for free public education in Massachusetts with great success, Mann became interested in extending some of his reforms to the college level, and in Antioch set up a college that was nonsectarian and coeducational. Both of these ideas were revolutionary a hundred years ago and occasioned bitter criticism by other college men of the time. His most quoted statement was one he made to his students in a baccalaureate address delivered shortly before he died: "Be ashamed to die until you have won some victory for humanity."

The influence of Horace Mann reached not only to the other states in this country but also to South America. He was well-known in Chile and Argentina by reason of a man named Domingo Faustino Sarmiento, a native of Argentina who had been exiled from his country. During his exile Sarmiento lived in Chile and became a very important citizen of that country. Commissioned by the government to visit the United States and make a report of the school system, he spent considerable time with Horace Mann. Upon his return to Chile he wrote a book reporting his trip. It contained a great deal about Mann's ideas on education and it also included sections of the school laws of Massachusetts. His report, however, had little influence on the educational practices in Chile.

Sarmiento later returned to Argentina, whence he was sent by his government to the United States as Minister. Once again he turned his attention to our system of education. In 1868 he was recalled to Argentina to become President. With an opportunity at last to do something for the schools of his country, he remade the school system largely on the American pattern he had learned so well from Mann. Horace Mann is still remembered and much revered in Argentina.

Henry Barnard

Henry Barnard (1811–1900) followed closely in the footsteps of Horace Mann. He too studied law and was admitted to the bar; he too deserted law to dedicate his life to the cause of public education. Barnard spent two years in Europe making a study of education, devoting most of his attention to the work of Pestalozzi's disciples in Germany and Switzerland. His mind was enriched by valuable observations of social and educational conditions, but he appreciated more than ever the institutions in his own country and was convinced that hopes of permanent prosperity depended upon universal, free public education.

After his return Barnard was elected a member of the Connecticut legislature. He promptly proposed and secured the passage of a bill setting up a state board of education—the same sort of educational program that Mann had established in Massachusetts. Again following Mann, Barnard left the legislature to become the first secretary of the board. He carried on in Connecticut the same intensive program that Mann had carried on in Massachusetts. His salary was low—three dollars a day and traveling expenses— but he held the office from 1839 to 1842 and accomplished great reforms in that time. The members of the legislature, however, did not support Barnard and his program and they abolished the office in 1842.

Going to Rhode Island, Barnard there carried on a campaign for better public education. He talked to the Rhode Island legislature and was instrumental in having it enact a law similar to the one he had proposed in

Connecticut. He became the first commissioner of education for Rhode Island and again did pioneer work for education, vastly improving educational conditions in the state.

Barnard held many other important offices in the educational field. He returned to Connecticut later as president of the normal school and ex-officio secretary of the state board of education. Still later he became president of the University of Wisconsin. His last position was United States Commissioner of Education. The first to hold this office, he served with distinction, setting the pattern for many succeeding commissioners.

Barnard's greatest contribution to the literature of education was the *American Journal of Education,* which he founded in 1855 and edited until 1893. During these years it was the outstanding educational journal and did much to help shape the educational pattern in America. Barnard also edited and published, in 1852, a book on normal schools. It is filled with material of great educational and historical value.

OTHER EARLY LEADERS

While Mann and Barnard were doing pioneer work in Massachusetts, Connecticut, and Rhode Island other great pioneers were making educational history in other states. One of them was Calvin H. Wiley, a native of North Carolina. Like Mann and Barnard he was a college graduate; he also followed the same pattern by becoming a member of the North Carolina legislature, where he worked for the passage of a bill to set up a state educational organization headed by a state school officer. When the bill creating the office of state superintendent of schools became law Wiley too left the legislature to assume that position. He published a state educational journal, organized a state educational association, wrote textbooks, and traveled about the state talking in behalf of better schools.

John D. Pierce, a Congregational minister, came to Michigan in 1831 and remained there for the rest of his long life. He was instrumental in setting up the Michigan state school system and was the first superintendent of public instruction. Caleb Mills was a pioneer educator in Indiana; and Samuel Lewis was the first superintendent of public instruction in Ohio. The list of state school pioneers should also include Robert J. Breckinridge, Kentucky's first state superintendent, and Ninian Edwards, who was the first to hold that office in Illinois. Thaddeus Stevens should also be mentioned, for as a member of the legislature of Pennsylvania he fought, almost alone, to set up a system of free public education in his state.

THE EDUCATION OF WOMEN

The educational patterns brought from Europe by our forefathers did not contemplate formal education for women. The relative position of

"In memory of Emma Hart Willard who wrote at Middlebury in 1818 the Magna Carta for Higher Education of Women in America." (*Wide World*)

Below: Mount Holyoke Female Seminary. Erected in 1837, the building of 94 × 50 feet stood on ten acres of land and was most imposing. (*Mount Holyoke College*)

Oswego Normal School, 1899. Then, as now, teachers need tools. Unlike today, however, these teachers had very few. Yet, they should be remembered with respect for their contribution. (*State University College, Oswego, New York*)

women's education in the seventeenth and early eighteenth centuries was similar to the civil and political rights held by women at the same time. Equal educational opportunity for girls was secured by an evolutionary process which closely parallels the general struggle for a free, nonsectarian, tax-supported public school system.

In colonial days women had almost no civil or political rights. A married woman's property belonged to her husband, even if she owned it before they were married; and she could not "will" property at her death. In all matters women were subject to their husbands. In such a society it was little wonder that no provision was made for the higher education of women and that only the minimum elementary education was provided. In colonial times girls were admitted to the public elementary schools where they were taught the rudiments of learning; however this seldom went beyond reading, writing, and a little arithmetic.

The colonial colleges did not admit women as students. Most of the early grammar schools and academies, following the European system of education, also excluded girls. Girls were destined to become homemakers and mothers, and they learned all the many skills needed to manage a home successfully from their mothers. Young women were constantly discouraged from seeking academic education. Even intelligent and educated men believed that it was a mistake for women's education to go beyond the barest fundamentals.

During the time our great educational pioneers were fighting for free public schools, a group of determined women were fighting a great battle for adequate higher education for their own sex. A brief sketch of the work of three of these women will exemplify some of the prevailing attitudes and problems. Emma Willard, Catharine Beecher, and Mary Lyon did not work for equal property rights or for political rights, but each insisted on a program of education that would make women the educational equal of men in their own sphere.

Emma Willard

Emma Willard (1787–1870) was born in the village of Berlin, Connecticut, the sixteenth of 17 children. She attended the public school until she was 15 and then entered the town academy where she studied for two years. At the age of 17 she began her educational career as a teacher in a district school during the summer term.

When Emma Hart Willard started teaching, little education was available for women, though the New England states provided public education on the elementary level for girls as well as boys. There were many "female seminaries" that provided a scanty education for girls, but they were generally on a low educational level.

Emma Hart had a great dream. She wanted to organize a system of education for women that would offer the same permanence, uniformity, and respectability as educational institutions for men and yet would be adapted to the needs and interests of women.

From 1804 until 1821 Emma Willard (she married Dr. John Willard in 1809) held many educational positions. She taught a country school, and she taught in in the academy at Berlin. The following year she went to Westfield, Massachusetts, to teach in an academy for girls that had been established in 1800. From there she went to Middlebury, Vermont, to teach in another female academy.

In 1814 she opened a boarding school for girls in Middlebury. Although this was a success, she dreamed of a publicly supported institution of higher education for women. So she turned her attention to the state of New York where with the assistance of Governor De Witt Clinton she presented her plan for female education to the state legislature. She was successful in getting an act passed granting a charter for the establishment of an academy for young ladies. She was unsuccessful, however, in securing the financial support she so much desired. Back in Middlebury again, she published her plan for the education of females. It attracted a great deal of attention and was widely read both in this country and in Europe.

After the disappointing experiences with the legislature of New York Emma Willard was delighted when the common council of Troy, New York, decided to raise $4000 to purchase a building for a female academy. The money was raised and the building was purchased. More money was raised by subscription, a board of trustees was appointed, and in the spring of 1821 Emma Willard opened what was to be her most famous school. At first it was called the Troy Female Seminary, the name being changed later to the Emma Willard School.

In many ways the opening of the Troy Female Seminary marked a new milestone in the education of women. The school was popular and prosperous from the beginning. The leading families of the country sent their daughters there to be educated. Emma Willard turned her attention to the education of teachers, and several years before the first normal school was established she had prepared several hundred girls to become teachers. Many graduates of her school went to the southern and western states and did pioneer work in establishing educational institutions for women.

In 1843 Mrs. Willard became closely associated with Horace Mann and Henry Barnard in a great agitation for normal schools. She wrote several books, including a history textbook, and collaborated with W. C. Woodbridge on a geography that was widely used in the schools for many years.

Catharine Beecher

Catharine Beecher (1800–1878) came from a distinguished family. Her father, Lyman Beecher, was the eminent Congregational minister, her brother the famous Henry Ward Beecher, and her sister the even more famous Harriet Beecher Stowe.

Catharine Beecher grew up in a parsonage. Her young life was very busy because there were 13 children and she was the oldest girl; thus she learned at an early age to perform the many tasks that had to be done in a New England home. The training her mother gave her in caring for children and keeping house was of great value in her later life as a teacher. She did not attend school until she was ten, her mother teaching her in the meantime to read, spell, write, and do a little arithmetic, geography, and art. She entered an academy in 1810, but it provided little that her mother had not already taught her. She began teaching in a girls' school in New London, Connecticut, and in 1828 founded the Hartford Female Seminary, which was long one of the important institutions of its kind in America.

Catharine Beecher was a great pioneer spirit. Like Emma Willard, she had an ardent desire to do something about the education of women in this country, but again—like Mrs. Willard—she expressed no interest in political equality for women. She dreamed of a system of higher education that would provide women with the same educational opportunity the men enjoyed. She was not interested in training women for the professions usually occupied by men. She thought that women should be educated for teaching, nursing, and homemaking; and her ideas concerning the place and work of women dominated her educational planning. She was interested in suitable physical education for women, and she developed courses in her schools that taught them how to be graceful and "to sit, to stand and to walk properly." She also developed the first courses ever taught in home economics and wrote several books for her classes and for housewives.

In 1838 Catharine Beecher moved with her family to Cincinnati, Ohio, and here she continued her interest in the education of women, particularly in their preparation for teaching. She organized and conducted the Western Female Institute, and from it she sent a great many young women into the teaching field; many of them went to the South and to the West.

Miss Beecher organized the Woman's Education Association and traveled widely over the country in its behalf. She raised funds and was instrumental in establishing schools for women in Milwaukee and other western cities. She wrote books and gave a great many lectures, and until her death in 1878 she devoted her time and energy to advancing the cause of education for women.

Mary Lyon

Mary Lyon (1797–1849) was another pioneer who devoted her life to the advancement of education for her sex. She did for college education what Emma Willard and Catharine Beecher had done at the less advanced level in establishing seminaries and institutes. She envisaged a college for women that would be comparable to the colleges already established for men. There was no such college at that time and coeducation had not been thought of.

In 1836 Mary Lyon founded Mount Holyoke Seminary (later Mount Holyoke College) and became its first president. This was not accomplished easily at a time when it was unfashionable for a woman to be interested in higher education. Miss Lyon and her friends went from town to town and from door to door explaining her project and soliciting funds for the new seminary. Finally, after the funds were raised and a building was constructed, America's first higher institution for women opened its doors to a group of eager students in the fall of 1837. Girls who were at least 16 years of age and who could pass a written examination in certain fundamentals were accepted as pupils.

Mary Lyon did not create the demand for higher education for women, nor was she the first to voice it. The founding of Mount Holyoke, however, marked the initial appearance of the great institutions which are today devoted to higher education for women. Wesleyan Female College at Macon, Georgia, was chartered and legally authorized to confer diplomas on its graduates in the year of 1837. Vassar, Smith, and Wellesley, which were founded later, owe much to Mount Holyoke and to the work of Mary Lyon in breaking down the wall of prejudice against the education of women. Mount Holyoke also prepared teachers who later became leaders in establishing other colleges for women.

THE ASCENDANCE OF DEMOCRATIC EDUCATION

So far this brief summary has been concerned mostly with the men and women who were instrumental in beginning the movement towards our system of free public education in the various states and in advancing education for women. In the context of their time the contributions of these persons was of greatest significance. By 1870 elementary education was available to almost everyone who wished it. The ideal of free universal education had not yet been applied to secondary schools or to colleges, however. Professor R. Freeman Butts has noted that during the century 1770 to 1870 the idea was to provide some education for all and much education for a few.[14] From 1870 to 1960, according to Professor Butts, the keynote of a century of democratic education was "more education for more people."[15] American education has made much progress towards this objective since 1870.

In 1870 a majority of elementary-age students were enrolled in school, but by 1960 more than 99 percent were in attendance. In 1870 approximately 8 percent of children aged 14 to 17 were actually in secondary school; by 1960 nearly 90 percent were attending. These facts show our current approximation of universal elementary and secondary education.

[14] R. Freeman Butts, "Search for Freedom—The Story of American Education," *NEA Journal*, March, 1960, pp. 37–42.
[15] *Ibid.*, p. 42.

The increase in higher education enrollments have been even more marked. In 1900 approximately 4 percent of all youth aged 18 to 21 were attending posthigh-school institutions; by 1960 almost 40 percent of this population were enrolled in colleges and universities. In 1870 adult education was almost universally limited to our largest metropolitan centers where "Americanization Education" courses were offered to those immigrants preparing for citizenship. By 1960, courses in general, vocational, and avocational education were available to millions of adults.

The movement towards a more democratic education had not been limited to concern for the quantity provided. Important progress has also been made towards improving the quality of American education. Advances in quality, however, are more difficult to effect than are quantitative changes. Different experts have different ideas as to what constitutes quality in any given area, and achieving the consensus level necessary to make progress on a broad scale is a formidable task! The struggle towards quality in education is too complex to discuss in a brief review, but a few of the significant happenings must be noted.

Even before universal elementary education was an accepted idea, necessary reforms were being urged on the existing schools. The colonial objective of literacy for all was shown to be narrow and constricting, and schools were asked to broaden their offerings and to add courses ranging from art and history to physical education and natural sciences.

Secondary education has also undergone much reform since 1870. The most important changes necessitated by the acceptance of the comprehensive secondary school attendance for virtually everyone accentuated the problem of proper course offerings in junior and senior high school. Since 1900 there have been at least three noticeable trends in curricular emphasis in secondary education. From the earliest times a very rigid set of college-preparatory requirements dominated our high schools. In the period loosely bounded by the end of World War I and the beginning of World War II college preparation gave way to life-adjustment and personal development as major emphases in secondary education. Since the close of World War II a new wave of reaction has affected junior and senior high schools. Academic excellence, particularly in the areas of science, mathematics, and foreign languages has become the prime objective of many schools. This later trend can become nothing more than a return to the college-preparatory program of our schools in 1900; it can also, however, lead to a program of secondary education which does a better job of academic preparation while it continues to meet the needs of all students whether or not they are college-bound.

The efforts towards freedom in American education are continuing. Progress will not be easily achieved, nor will it occur universally, but it is encouraging to know that most Americans are aware that improved and improving education is imperative. The ultimate goal is to build an educational enterprise which will free the minds of people and equip them as free citizens and free persons.

RELATED READINGS

Butts, R. Freeman, and Lawrence A. Cremin, *A History of Education in American Culture,* New York, Holt, Rinehart and Winston, 1953.

Cubberley, E. P., *Public Education in the United States,* Boston, Houghton Mifflin, 1934.

Good, Harry S., *A History of American Education,* 2d ed., New York, Macmillan, 1962.

Meyer, Adolphe E., *An Educational History of the American People,* New York, McGraw-Hill, 1957.

Weimer, Hermann, *Concise History of Education,* New York, Philosophical Library, 1962.

Right: Young "Pilgrim's Progress." Turning back the clock to the 1620s, elementary school children from Providence, Rhode Island, compare ideas gathered during a visit to Plimoth Plantation, a recreation of the original Plymouth Colony, and plan their own Pilgrim project. (*Three Pilgrim pictures, Wide World*)

Right: As the Indians of early Washington State brought gifts to honor the big Chief at a Potlatch Feast, so these "Indians" bring symbols of the fruits of their study of the history of Washington. (*Seattle School District*)

No other person has exerted as great an influence on the American classroom as the great scholar and teacher, John Dewey. (*Columbia University*)

Political indoctrination was a major facet of Nazi schools. Contrast this with third-graders who write their own "Code of Conduct" in preparation for the time when they will share in governing their own society. (*Above, Wide World; left, Seattle School District*)

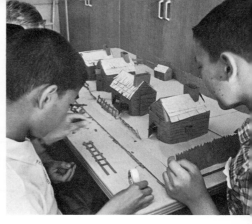

The project continues as the students create models of Pilgrim homes.

Turning the clock radically forward, the students culminate their workshop on Pilgrim life using today's closed circuit TV to communicate their conclusions to three classes of teachers.

Chapter 4 / PHILOSOPHICAL FOUNDATIONS OF AMERICAN EDUCATION

THE TEACHER'S PHILOSOPHY

Any student preparing to be a teacher ought to be developing a clearcut philosophy of education. When the prospective teacher completes his pre-service education he takes his educational philosophy to the public school with him; there, put to the test, it will determine the kind of teacher he will

71

be. In fact, the most important thing about any teacher is the way he thinks about the problems of education and the profession of teaching. Differences in philosophy make some teachers dynamic forces in the lives they touch, and others mere routine advisors in a course of study. Differences in philosophy explain why some teachers are content to work in schools where they make few professional decisions for themselves, usually on the basis of expediency, whereas others must teach in schools where education is vital and purposeful. Differences in philosophy explain different attitudes towards subject matter. Some teachers regard the cultural heritage as something to be divided into inflexible "subjects" to be mastered; others organize subject matter to help children attain worthwhile educational objectives. Differences in philosophy also explain why some teachers have trouble with discipline in the classroom, while others live in happiness and harmony with their pupils.

The teacher's philosophy includes, in addition to the way he looks at life and education, the terms in which he judges values. Every teacher should strive to have a true scale of values. The man who teaches merely for money, or for something to do while studying law, or because he can't get another job, cannot be successful.

In a democracy teaching is one of the most important of all professions, because a democracy determines its future by determining the kind of education it offers and the quality of its teachers. Therefore, no one should attempt to teach who does not recognize the importance of education and does not desire to share in building a greater democracy.

An adequate philosophy of education does not exist in a vacuum, nor is it purposeless. Quite the opposite, a functional philosophy of education provides the answers to at least three basic questions: What is education? What ought it accomplish? How can it accomplish these objectives? Nothing could be more "real" or directive.

In the day-by-day operation of a school or classroom, numerous questions arise. Queries which demand an answer include:

What is the function of subject matter?

How much freedom should students be given?

What is the proper relationship between the English teacher and the athletic program?

Should pupils be homogeneously grouped?

Should any subjects be required of all pupils? Should all pupils' programs contain only required subjects?

What is the proper relationship of the teacher to the parent, the pupil, the community, the school administration?

Should seven percent of the pupils "fail" any course? Should any students "fail" any course?

A philosophy of education will not provide ready-made answers to these or any other sets of specific questions, but a functional philosophy of education *will* supply a rationale without which satisfactory answers cannot be obtained.

EDUCATIONAL PHILOSOPHY IN A NATIONAL CONTEXT

Because a nation's schools play a vital role in shaping the destiny of the country, leaders of government are concerned with the point-of-view guiding their schools and teachers. The White House Conferences of Education which are called periodically by the President of the United States are indicative of the interest in education shown by leaders of our country. Numerous national conferences, committees, and commissions of noneducationally centered organizations have given repeated attention to the proper objectives of education in the United States.

President Harry S Truman appointed a Commission on Higher Education to inquire into the function of higher education in a democracy. Their report, issued in 1946, included an especially clear and concise statement of the place of education in a nation such as ours. Thus, it provides an excellent frame of reference with which to begin a study of differing philosophies of education.

Education is an institution of every civilized society, but the purposes of education are not the same in all societies. An educational system finds its guiding principles and ultimate goals in the aims and philosophy of the society in which it functions. The two predominant types of societies in the world today are the democratic and the authoritarian, and the social role of education is very different in the two systems.

American society is a democracy: that is, its folkways and institutions, its arts and sciences and religions are based on the principle of equal freedom and equal rights for all its members, regardless of race, faith, sex, occupation, or economic status. The law of the land, providing equal justice for the poor as well as the rich, the weak as well as the strong, is one instrument by which a democratic society establishes, maintains, and protects this equality among different persons and groups. The other instrument is education, which, as all the leaders in the making of democracy have pointed out again and again, is necessary to give effect to the equality prescribed by law.

It is a commonplace of the democratic faith that education is indispensable to the maintenance and growth of freedom of thought, faith, enterprise, and association. Thus the social role of education in a democratic society is at once to insure equal liberty and equal opportunity to differing individuals and groups, to enable the citizen to understand, appraise, and redirect the forces, men, and events as these tend to strengthen or to weaken their liberties.[1]

The statement, "an educational system finds its guiding principles and ultimate goals in the aims and philosophy of the social order in which it functions," is true now and has been true through all the history of education. The schools of Athens and Sparta differed because the social and political philosophies of the two cities differed. The early schools established in the New England and the Middle and Southern colonies differed because of the difference in the social philosophy of the settlers.

---

[1] *Higher Education for American Democracy*, The Report of the President's Commission on Higher Education, New York, Harper & Row, vol. I, 1946, p. 5.

Democracy and authoritarianism differ widely in social and political philosophy, so education in countries practicing democracy are different from that in countries with a totalitarian government. A study of education in countries under communism reveals numerous ways which it differs from education in democratic America. In communistic countries children are taught that the state is supreme, in America the emphasis is on the rights of the individual citizen who's government exists to serve him. The Russian child, according to the official rules for children adopted by the Soviet of People's Commissars in 1943, was taught "to obey without question the orders of school director and teachers," and Russian teachers were taught that "a morally educated individual, according to our understanding, is one who in his conduct subordinates his own interests to the service of his Motherland and his people. Such service presupposes wrath and hatred toward the enemies of the Motherland who imperil the battle-won rights of the people. . . ."[2] In Hitler's Germany the children were also taught to "obey without question."

Democracy in government is effective only when there is an educated electorate, and it makes a difference what kind of education the citizens get. If children are educated never to think things out for themselves but to take orders and "give obedience without question," a nation can never develop a citizenry capable of ruling itself. Intelligent obedience is a necessity for the maintenance of order in any society, but the unquestioning acceptance of authority inevitably results in an unhealthy concentration of power.

The American public school system has correctly been characterized as a "laboratory of democracy." Schools are social institutions established, controlled, and supported by society for the purposes of maintaining its own stability and determining the direction of its own progress. Upon the public schools of America rests the responsibility for establishing among the people the practices, ideals, and attitudes which are to shape the course of our democracy during the coming years. Education and democracy are bound in an unending chain of cause and effect—more democracy means more widespread and universal education, and more education of the right kind means more democracy.

It must be remembered that education does not automatically promote the ends of democracy. Some types of education tend to defeat the democratic process. Education is a tool that has been made to work for many masters. Education *in* a democracy must be education *for* democracy.

DIFFERING PHILOSOPHIES OF EDUCATION

Since the beginning of civilization man has had some plan for education, an educational philosophy of some kind. It was noted earlier that the first

[2] George S. Counts and Nucia P. Lodge (trans.), *I Want To Be Like Stalin*, New York, John Day, p. 42.

schools were organized for the purpose of teaching children, particularly boys, how to live in an adult society. The first educational philosophy, then, was probably one of preparation for the future.

Education as Preparation

The first schools created in America were largely dominated by the philosophy of preparation. In New England boys and girls were educated so that they could read the Bible and eventually become adult members of the church. When Harvard College was established in 1636 its function was to prepare ministers for the Congregational Church. The Latin grammar school was established a short time later in Boston to prepare young men for Harvard. The dominance of a preparatory philosophy was universally accepted in colonial days.

The theory of preparation is based on the idea that each unit of a school system is successful to the degree that it prepares for the unit just ahead and that the whole system serves best as it prepares for life. According to this theory—always applied from the top down—the colleges dictate the curriculum of the secondary schools, and the high schools in turn dictate that of the elementary schools. This is true today to a limited extent, for most high school curricula are dictated, in part at least, by college entrance requirements. However, the secondary schools have had much less influence on the education of the elementary school.

In a general way all education is preparation and certain areas must necessarily emphasize deferred goals. Vocational education is offered solely for the purpose of preparing the youth for adult life, thus education as preparation is the logical aim for vocational education. A boy learns to lay bricks in a vocational course so that he can earn a living laying brick; a girl learns shorthand and typing so that she may become a secretary. However, education as preparation is an integral and worthy part of vocational courses, it is an inadequate philosophy for general education.

Education as preparation is a very limiting approach to education. It neglects the fact that children live in the present, that they face present problems. It is difficult to motivate a child to learn something solely because it will be helpful to him when he grows up. Furthermore, such a philosophy fails to take cognizance of what is known about how people learn.

For many years "preparation" was the most important objective of elementary education and the curriculum was slanted to adult problems. Problems have a great educative value and are attacked with great interest if the pupil can see the connection between them and his life. When children are assigned tasks that have no immediate appeal it is often necessary for the teacher to resort to artificial means in order to get the work done. The most common means are threats, punishments, and bribes. The child then does his task to escape an unpleasant experience or to receive a prize.

Many educators have pointed out the weaknesses of the philosophy of preparation as a central value for education. John Dewey, in his *Democracy and Education,* called attention to the fact that "It is not a question whether education should prepare for the future . . . If the environment, in school and out, supplies conditions which utilize adequately the present capacities of the immature, the future which grows out of the present is surely taken care of."[3] He believed that the best possible preparation for living in a democracy as an adult is to live in a democratic society as a youth.

Dr. John L. Childs in his book, *Education and Morals,* also discussed the relative merits of preparation as a philosophy. He wrote, "The moral insistence of the new education that we cease viewing childhood as a mere preparation for a remote future and seek instead a school that would increase the meaning of present experience, was not the product of indifference to adult life; it was rather a product of the insight that the best possible preparation for the future is found in the most significant living in the present."[4]

The psychological evidence available, together with the logic typified by the arguments of Dewey and Childs, lead to the conclusion that preparation alone is an insufficient goal for education in a democracy.

Education as Formal Discipline

The philosophy known as "formal discipline" is another well-known approach to values in education. According to this belief, children go to school not to learn skills and knowledge that might be functional to them at the time they are studied or because they might be of use in adult life, but to get practice that will train their minds. Children are to study and learn, not to develop usable skills, but to develop mental power.

To understand the philosophy of formal discipline it is necessary to know the psychology upon which it is based: "faculty" psychology. Faculty psychology teaches that the mind consists of a number of separate faculties—such as memory, reasoning, and will; and to a formal disciplinist the function of education is to train the faculties by exercise in a manner similar to the way muscles are strengthened by exercise. Since the most difficult subjects provide the hardest exercise, foreign languages, mathematics, and advanced sciences are therefore the most desirable subjects in the curriculum. Additionally, these subjects are functional for vocational as well as for general education. Some faculty psychologists went so far as to suggest that certain faculties are located in specific areas of the cerebral hemispheres and that if a given faculty is a prominent aspect of an individual's personality, the corresponding brain area will enlarge.

Faculty psychology was the accepted theory of learning during most of the latter part of the nineteenth century, and formal discipline was the pervading approach to curriculum-building and instructional practices.

[3] John Dewey, *Democracy and Education,* New York, Macmillan, 1916, p. 65.
[4] John L. Childs, *Education and Morals,* New York, Appleton-Century-Crofts, 1950, p. 148.

Near the end of the nineteenth century and the beginning of the twentieth new research became available which first questioned and then disproved the validity of the theory of faculty psychology. New facts altered significantly the concept of transfer of training which was based on the formal-discipline notions. William James, Charles Eliot, and numbers of other educators and psychologists began to doubt the value of these theories before 1900. Then, around the turn of the century, Thorndike and his coworkers made the first measures of the transfer effect that proved the most damaging. In general they showed that no learning activity has any widespread mental disciplining powers, and that transfer of training is not an intrinsic result of any special subject matter or mental exercise.

An examination of the writings of modern psychologists shows that no accepted student of the field, no matter what school of psychology he adheres to, believes in faculty psychology. There has never been decisive evidence that the mind is divided into segments, each operating separately. Almost all students agree that the mind functions as a whole: when a man reasons, remembers, or wills, it is the whole mind and not a specialized fragment of it that functions.

The major educational application of formal discipline has to do with the "transfer of training." By transfer of training is meant the influence of past training on situations that may be met in the future. As an example, if one spends a large amount of time memorizing, he should, according to the adherents of formal discipline, develop the power to remember and be able to use it in any situation calling for memory. A student might be asked to memorize the multiplication table and learn to spell a dozen new words each day. If he continues memorizing things, he will develop the faculty known as memory and should then be able to transfer this training to any situation involving memory—remembering names, telephone numbers, and addresses with ease. If this theory is true, it should be much easier for the mind trained on spelling words to memorize poetry or to learn the syntax of a new language.

A great many scientific experiments have been conducted to determine the truth concerning transfer, and all of them have resulted in conclusions that there is no such thing as a general transfer. Solving a hundred algebra problems develops the ability to solve similar algebra problems, but it does not help one to understand the world situation or to compute his income tax.

It would seem that in the face of overwhelming evidence, faculty psychology, formal discipline, and the slavish acceptance of transfer of training would cease to be problems in education. However, some practicing educators, particularly on the level of higher education, are unaware of the research or choose to ignore it. So formal discipline still has to be reckoned with particularly in secondary schools and colleges.

Many subjects that are now in high school and college curricula are defended on the basis of their disciplinary value even though most of them were first included because of their functionality. Every subject in the school curriculum was originally placed in the program for some practical purpose. For example, Latin was first studied because it was the language of instruction in secondary schools. The educated person had to know Latin because very little was published in the vernacular, especially in scientific, religious, diplomatic, and professional fields. Latin is not now a living language and most of its practical value no longer exists. Its place in the secondary school curriculum today is usually justified on the basis of its disciplinary value.

The philosophy of formal discipline is untenable to most educators. The many fallacies in its psychological beliefs weaken its position, and its epistemology—the theory of the method and the grounds of knowledge on which it is based—are unacceptable to most scholars. It is in relationship to value, however, where formal discipline fails most noticeably. Formal discipline is a favorite theme of dictators. Training the will and generally "hardening" the mind are as basic to totalitarianism as is a militaristic approach to physical education or blind acceptance of the ideas of a ruling party.

Knowledge as Education

Knowledge has often been confused with education. Indeed, there are those who believe that he who knows the most is the best educated. Almost every college has a required course that has to do with "Western civilization." The several reasons given for including such a course make a good point of comparison of varying approaches to the relationship between education and knowledge. The reason for including such a course varies with the teacher. (1) Some teachers follow the formal-discipline mind-training approach to this course. (2) Some teachers believe that students should take the course in order to know. They reason that every educated person should have a knowledge of the culture of which he is a part, that such knowledge is one mark of a cultured person, and that common knowledge is an important part of education. (3) Some teachers believe that students must know about the past so as to better understand the present and plan more wisely for the future.

What difference does it make what the teacher thinks if the course is the same? A great deal. *Teacher 1* thinks he has done his duty when he makes his students work very hard—his success is measured by how well they work. *Teacher 2* will teach all the facts he can. He will not be concerned how the students learn so long as they can give factual information back to him in an examination. His examinations are frequent, long, and detailed. *Teacher 3* strives to apply to each present-day situation the material which students are studying. He asks, "What can we learn from Hitler that will help us understand the insatiable desire for power and glory of some contemporary leaders?" It seems necessary to conclude that the philosophy of the teacher determines both the content and the method of instruction.

Most educators place main emphasis in education not on knowing for the sake of knowing, but on knowledge which is functional in the guidance of activity. A man may acquire a vast amount of knowledge and still not be educated. It is true that knowledge is a part of education, and that one accomplishes the necessary tasks of life more efficiently if he has a command of certain facts. Most human endeavors require knowledge, but the true aim is knowledge for the sake of doing and not for the sake of knowing.

A DEMOCRATIC AIM FOR EDUCATION

A teacher has a significant effect upon the life pattern of his students. He helps them develop habits, skills, and ideals, and helps them learn to think; he is a major determiner of the kind of citizen they become. A democracy prospers only when it maintains an educated electorate, and it makes a vast difference what kind of education the children have.

The development of a working philosophy of democratic education has been a slow, painful process that can be traced at least as far back as Comenius. Comenius was an ardent believer in democracy. The Moravian Brotherhood, of which he was a Bishop, believed in the common ownership of property and practiced democracy in their relationships. The system of education proposed by Comenius was based on a democratic philosophy which included the idea of education for all children, not just for boys, and not just for the children of the upper classes. He advocated a democratic process in teaching methods and planned a school system much like the one in America today. Comenius was a Christian educator who made much use of the teachings of Jesus, particularly in regard to the importance of the individual, the sacredness of childhood, and regard for human personality.

Large numbers of the Brotherhood migrated to America during periods of unrest and settled in Pennsylvania, Georgia, North Carolina, and Ohio. In fact, the first settlers in Ohio were Moravian missionaries who there built the first house, the first school, and the first churches.

We noted in Chapter 3 that there were other important educators who followed Comenius. Perhaps the ones who added most to the democratic concept of education were Locke, Rousseau, Pestalozzi, Froebel, Franklin, Jefferson, and Horace Mann.

One modern educator who stressed the democratic philosophy of education was John Dewey. His effect on American education has been very great, and his ideas have also influenced education in many other countries. *Democracy and Education,* one of his most significant books, presents a thorough discussion of his democratic philosophy.

DEMOCRATIC PHILOSOPHY AND THE ENVIRONMENT

The process of educating a child is a social process because education in a democratic society is a social function. Knowledge may be gained in solitude, particularly if the learning is memorizing, but education is more than learning—education is living.

Dewey said, "We never educate directly, but indirectly by means of the environment." How does one learn to speak correct English? Only by reading a grammar book? No, it must include association with people who speak correct English.

The greatest teacher is the life around a child, his environment. In fact, the best teaching is done by means of a controlled environment. It is difficult, for instance, to teach art appreciation by talking or reading about objects of art; a love of beauty is best taught by surrounding the child with artistic things. Music too is best taught by giving the children a chance to listen to music, to make music, to compose music.

The major component of the child's social environment is, of course, other people, and the teacher and the children comprise the social environment of each child in school. The richness of this environment depends upon the contribution of each of the members. If the members of the group are of the same national origin, have the same religion, and come from the same economic stratum of society, the environment is very much restricted. If, conversely, the school group is composed of persons of varying national backgrounds, divergent religious beliefs, and if their fathers work at widely differing occupations, the environment becomes rich. The environmental aspects of the teacher's preparation are also significant. A teacher whose own childhood was spent on the Atlantic coast is able to give his students on the Great Plains a vicarious experience with the ocean that is far more meaningful than only reading can impart.

Too often teachers and parents attempt to "hammer in" things they wish children to learn. The process usually followed is one of repetition accompanied by bribes and punishments. At times the teachers and the parents appear to have succeeded, but this is not education. Anything that does not become a part of the child's life experience does not become real to him. The hammering-in process is training, not education. With the same methods a seal can be trained to blow a horn and a horse to paw out numbers.

A child can be trained too, but this process should not be confused with education, and it is easy for the casual observer to mistake physical control for educative control. Physical control can be obtained by using extrinsic factors; educative control comes only when there is understanding and co-operation. The old saying "You can lead a horse to water, but you can't make him drink" has its counterpart in "You can make a child sit still, but you cannot make him think." Physical control is necessary, but physical control without educative control never leads to experiences that are educative.

DEMOCRATIC EDUCATION AND GROWTH

John Dewey has said, "In directing the activities of the young, society determines its own future in determining that of the young."[5] The type of

---

[5] Dewey, *op. cit.*, p. 49.

society youth will someday develop will "turn upon the direction of children's activities as were given at an earlier period. This cumulative movement of action toward a later result is what is meant by growth."

When a child changes from what he was yesterday into what he is today, a process of growth is taking place. As long as growth continues in the right direction, education is taking place. It is the function of parents and teachers to see that growth is continuous and properly directed. If growth is a constant process during school life, it will continue after the child leaves school. Growth that begins in school and continues throughout life is the goal of modern education.

The concept of growth makes education a process that takes place both in and out of school and a process that continues after formal education is ended. One of the conditions that makes education in the right direction difficult is that growth may take place under unfavorable conditions outside of school. For example, a child may learn language that is inaccurate and incorrect and contains many expressions that are grammatically unacceptable. All of these things he brings to school with him. If he continues to grow in the same direction he will, as an adult, use poor English. It is the function of the school to guide growth in the right direction. If the school influence can overcome the other influence, the result will be satisfactory.

What was said above concerning language is true of all habits a child forms. The school strives to have him form good habits even though forces outside school may favor growth in another direction. When the school and the home unite in the proper growth pattern, it is easier to start the child growing in the way he should and for such growth to continue throughout life.

According to Dewey, "The primary condition of growth is immaturity." This may seem to be a mere truism—saying that "a being can develop only in some point where he is undeveloped." However, there is more to it than this. Immaturity in itself suggests the possibility of maturity, or the ability to grow. The child, although helpless at first, has more possibilities of growth than any other animal; in other words, he has more growing to do. The guidance of growth in the right direction is the main function of the school; it bridges the gap between the immaturity of the child and the needs of the adult world. How well it does this, depends upon how well it provides the conditions for proper growth.

DEMOCRATIC EDUCATION AND THINKING

Proper education in a democracy should enable the citizens to understand, appraise, and redirect forces, men, and events, as these tend to strengthen or to weaken our liberties. Suffrage is a prime example. When citizens vote, they not only elect those who are to govern them but also pass judgment on a number of laws and admendments to city charters and state constitutions.

The voting citizen is given a long and complicated ballot which requires him to make intelligent decisions on a number of important questions. It is not uncommon to have a dozen propositions to vote on. The voter should be able to read, of course, but it is of far greater significance that he understand, think, and pass judgment. Thus education in a democracy must be concerned with teaching prospective citizens to understand and think and pass judgments. If they cannot do these things, they cannot vote wisely. Therefore they will not be good citizens.

One purpose of education in a democracy is to teach boys and girls to think their way through problem situations. As Dewey noted, ". . . information served from thoughtful action is a dead, mind-crushing load." It does not matter how much material a child may memorize: unless he understands it, there is no education. Thinking is the only method of education that is intelligent, and it is a part of *all* intelligent action. The correct approach does not envision certain subjects as those wherein children learn to think; learners should always be helped to think about the problems at hand.

School teachers in a totalitarian society cannot allow for free thought processes. No dictator can tolerate citizens who can think, therefore the emphasis on education under a dictatorship is indoctrination and thoughtful reflection is viewed as a dangerous deviation.

Thinking is closely related to experience; in fact, no experience is educative unless it involves thinking. Hence a democratic philosophy of education does not favor school practices that involve "unthinking obedience" and the memorizing of "acceptable" solutions to problems. It is important that children have experiences that involve thinking, and thinking is impossible without certain materials that are related to earlier experiences, actions, or plans.

Thinking also involves a problem. The thought process is not initiated unless there is something to think about, a problem to solve. Democratic education attempts to have students solve problems that are of importance to society and to the learner. Dewey believed that the method of thinking and of good problem-solving follows the same general pattern. He suggested that they concern five steps: (1) the occurrence of a genuine situation or experience meaningful to the learner, (2) the development of a problem within this experience which stimulates the learner, (3) the gathering of data pertinent to the problem, (4) the formation of a solution to the problem which satisfies the learner, and (5) the testing of the new generalizations by application to other experiences.

Although there is no consensus among philosophers or psychologists concerning whether the "Dewey problem-solving method" applies in all experiences involving thinking, the five-step method remains one of the clearest analysis of the process.

Important as thinking is, it is inaccurate to believe that all teaching should lead directly to thinking. Certain things children do at school have, and should have, other objectives. One of the major purposes of playing volleyball is to exercise the muscles of the body. Students playing records do so primarily for the joy of listening, and drawing may be done for the pleasure of expression. Taking part in a play may have appreciation as its main objective, and playing games still another purpose.

Does this mean that there is no thinking involved with these activities? No. There may be thinking involved in every one of them. It is difficult to imagine any school activity that may not involve thinking as a concomitant to the objectives noted above if the experience is organized to encourage thought-provoking response. It is also true, however, that some school exercises are more readily connected with thinking than others.

DEMOCRATIC EDUCATION AND CURRICULUM

All school education is deliberate, or planned, education. The curriculum presents an environment to the pupils which has been carefully selected and organized. According to Childs, "The function of the school is to provide a selected environment and schedule of activities for the nurture of the young in those appreciations, outlooks, and behaviors considered most important and essential to the life of the group."[6] If our most important heritage is our democratic way of life, and few would argue conversely, the primary task of American schools is to organize the materials and activities so as to enhance the preparation of acceptable citizens of a democracy.

If there is general agreement that the democratic aim is the primary goal of education in America, there is no consensus concerning the best methods of achieving the desired end. Some educators argue that the process of selection and organization of curricular materials and activities is too significant, too complicated and demanding a task for any but adult members of society. They maintain that it is the teachers and administrative staff who must largely determine what is to be taught. Other educators believe that the schools should follow pupil interest instead of adult prescription in selecting the materials to be taught. It seems logical to assume that neither of these courses of action need to be followed slavishly, that both are valuable when used properly. Even though the school is organized to develop certain preconceived attitudes, outlooks, skills, and behaviors, it still can work with and not contrary to child interest. The idea that a school must be aimless and chaotic to be "progressive" is far from true. A school may teach children to think, may lead them to have worthwhile experiences in a democratic environment, may involve the learner in planning the curriculum, and still follow a preconceived pattern of objectives.

DEMOCRATIC EDUCATION AND EXPERIENCE

A child learns through experience. Experience results when something happens which the learner understands and reacts to. Each new experience is

[6] Childs, *op. cit.*, p. 4.

added to old experiences. "The reconstruction or reorganization of experience which adds to the meaning of experience, and which increases ability to direct the course of subsequent experience" is education, according to John Dewey.

It is impossible for a child to learn without experience because it is impossible to communicate anything directly to another who does not share a common experience. Reading affords a good example. At one time it was thought that reading was a matter of putting words together, therefore much attention was given to the development of vocabulary, and numerous vocabulary studies were made. Vocabulary alone is not the problem, however, because a learner may know all the words and not be able to read a certain passage. To read, he must share an experience with the writer. The following sentence is composed of words found in the vocabulary of an average fifth-grade child: "An airplane flies so that the angle of attack of the wing is between the angle of zero lift and the stalling angle." There is not a single difficult word in that sentence. However, when it was read to a group of graduate students only those who had prior experience with airplanes understood its meaning: that is, they could "read" the words but they could *not* "read" the sentence. Even if a student should pronounce all the words properly a hundred times and understand the meaning of each word, he would still learn nothing from the sentence because he lacks the experience, and experience is the key to all learning. Mere verbalism results when we attempt to teach apart from experience.

THE PHILOSOPHY OF THE SCHOOL SYSTEM

It is important for each teacher to have a sound philosophy of education. It is equally important that a school system conceive a statement of democratic ideals to which all teachers and administrators can adhere. Questions of educational policy, great and small, depend upon philosophy. Shall we establish a nursery school? Shall we build a technical high school? What kind of elementary school building shall we plan? What kind of student grouping should we use? What type of report should the teachers make? These and hundreds of questions must be answered by the school system. The answers will depend largely upon which philosophy of education is followed.

The philosophy of school administration should be democratic. It is difficult to develop citizens for a democracy if the school system does not practice democracy in its program, and it is equally difficult for democracy to be a part of the educational program unless it is also a part of the administrative organization. It was noted earlier that the schools in a totalitarian state are set up to serve the state and to produce citizens who fit into the pattern. Hitler's schools were designed to produce young Nazis, and they were disturbingly successful. Not only their educational pattern but their administrative organization was organized on a fascistic basis. If we are to develop democratic citizens, our pattern of education and our administration as well must be democratic.

A teacher is always interested in the salary schedule, the tenure regulations concerning teachers, and the fringe benefits of a school system in which he is considering a position. The philosophy of the school system is of even greater significance to the candidate. In many communities the professional staff has a written statement of their educational philosophy; it is wise for the prospective teacher to obtain and study such a document if it exists. Another good way to discover the functioning value system of a school is to talk with the teachers who are already working in the school. The professionally orientated teacher never signs a contract until he has determined the philosophical bases on which the school operates.

METHODS vs MATERIALS

Which is more important in education, subject matter or method? Such a question has received more attention than it merits, especially in the recent past, and is closely related to the question of teaching children or teaching subjects. Method was not important in our early schools; subject matter was supreme. There was no question about whether a teacher taught arithmetic or children—she taught arithmetic, particularly when the philosophy of preparation or knowledge dominated education.

Conversely, method was all-important to the extreme progressivist of the 1930s. Some educators improperly interpreted the writings of Dewey and others and operated under the false premise that progressive educational philosophy was interested in the means of learning to the exclusion of attention to the ends. Although few schools followed such practices, including many who talked about it at greatest length, some teachers were totally uninterested in what children studied or learned so long as they approached the subject at hand willingly.

When education is properly thought of as meaningful experience, the teacher is primarily interested in the growth and development of children. In the best schools both subject matter and method are of great importance, but neither is valued at the expense of the other. The intelligent teacher uses subject matter in a functional way so that children achieve worthwhile educational objectives.

IS EDUCATION A SCIENCE?

Another controversy which has been given attention involves the philosophy of education seen as a contrast to the science of education. Some proponents of science maintain that education is not a philosophy but a science, while some philosophers argue that education is not and cannot become precise enough to be a science. The fact is that education must have both a philosophy and a science. It must have a basic philosophy to determine its goals, its emphases, and its methods. It must have a science to help solve problems that demand research and the use of the scientific method.

Both philosophy and science have an intrinsically valuable function to perform for the profession of education. Science experiments and discovers new facts, philosophy determines the meaning and value of facts. It is philosophy that enables the educator to construct goals in education and help answer questions regarding subject matter and teaching methods. Science produces new facts concerning child growth and development. It leads the way to the development of tests and the use of statistical procedures in education. Science has accelerated progress in schoolhouse construction by dealing successfully with matters of safety, fenestration, and heating and ventilation. The philosophy of education helps a school system decide whether to build a technical school or a comprehensive high school, but science helps them decide what kind of material to use in its construction. It is a teacher's philosophy that helps decide on such matters as examinations, marks and grades, but it is the science of education that shows him how to construct tests and how to compute grades.

RELATED READINGS

Childs, John L., *Education and Morals*, New York, Appleton-Century-Crofts, 1950.

Dewey, John, *Experience and Education*, New York, Macmillan, 1938.

Hook, Sidney, *Education for Modern Man*, New York, Dial Press, 1946.

Hutchins, Robert M., *The Conflict in Education in a Democratic Society*, New York, Harper & Row, 1953.

Maritain, Jacques, *Education at the Crossroads*, New Haven, Yale University Press, 1943.

Phenix, Phillip, Ed., *Philosophies of Education*, New York, Wiley, 1961.

Whitehead, A. N., *The Aims of Education*, New York, Macmillan, 1929.

It requires hand-eye coordination and form discrimination to avoid the round peg-square hole pitfall, and this two-year old is proving that her maturation level is equal to the task. (*Hochman from Monkmeyer*)

The most valid and reliable tests of student ability are administered on an individual basis. This student is being tested and she thinks of it as a new and exciting game.

Below: This student's manual dexterity is being checked by a performance test. Data gathered in such a manner form the basis for vocational guidance and counseling. (*Photos above and below, Hays from Monkmeyer*)

The ability to see likenesses and differences in size, shape, and structure is a prerequisite to successful reading which most reading readiness tests, such as this one, attempt to analyze. (*New Mexico State University*)

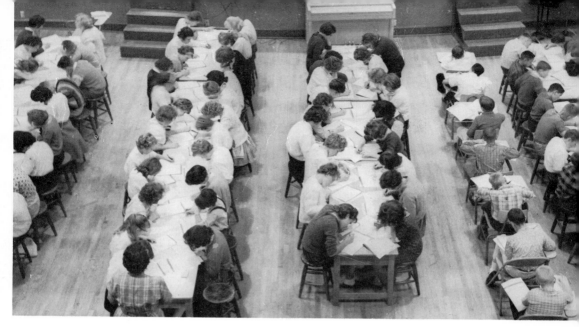

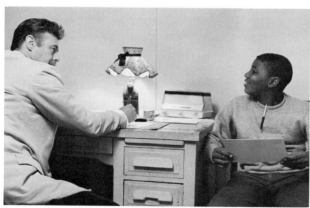

To help teachers and counselors aid student progress through continuing grade levels, most school systems administer achievement tests to all pupils several times during their school careers. The results of this test will help insure easy articulation of the elementary-junior high transition for these pupils. (Seattle School District)

Left: "You know, Mr. Johnson, this test score makes me even happier that you and I chose the program for me that we did." (Suzanne Szasz)

Chapter 5 / PSYCHOLOGICAL FOUNDATIONS OF AMERICAN EDUCATION

DIRECTING LEARNING

A teacher's major role is that of director of learning. Parents expect children to learn the useful and valuable things that will equip them to become educated, functioning citizens in their communities and in their nation. Because of the primacy of the learning-director role, a teacher is judged largely

89

in terms of his success in this area. Children come to school to learn, and if the pupils learn the things they should learn and develop the habits they should develop, the teacher is successful.

Achieving success as a director of learning depends upon the ability of the teacher to utilize the knowledge of at least two aspects of psychology: (1) what is known about human growth and development, and (2) the research concerning how, when, and why people learn. These topics comprise a major portion of the psychology courses in most teacher-preparation programs; and because psychology is to the educator what biology is to the physician, psychology can be termed the basic science of education.

CHILD GROWTH AND DEVELOPMENT

Chapter 4 dealt with some aspects of the philosophical relationships between growth and education. Growth is a concept that also has many psychological connotations. Education begins at birth and when the educative experiences are fruitful a person's educational growth continues as long as he lives, although his physical growth stops at maturity. Good education, therefore, is education that promotes and provides for continuous improvements in a person's behavior. Growth that ceases with the ending of school is, at least partially, wasted effort. Education and growth are processes, not fixed ends to be attained.

The Original Nature of the Child

Much has been written concerning what a child brings into the world with him in the way of knowledge and learning. Some of it has been mere speculation based on folk-lore and over-simplified answers to perplexing questions. There have also been, however, some scientific reports based upon study, experimentation, and observation of infancy and early childhood.

A great many activities involve the child soon after birth, the majority of them associated with the maintenance of life. Many of these movements are unorganized and random and are soon replaced by more specialized and deliberate activities. At one time psychologists believed that there was an instinctive or "inborn" basis for the behavior of infants and for the later developing patterns of the behavior of the growing child they considered that these actions and developing patterns were largely due to certain well-developed tendencies present at birth. More recently, however, psychologists have been less dogmatic about the child's original nature. In general, however, they believe that early learning is a much more important factor than the earlier psychologists thought.

A study of education shows that the history of scientific psychology has been marked by a steady decrease in interest in the number of instincts and "inborn traits" attributed to humans. This is not to say that psychologists are now in complete agreement on the subject of original nature. There is much disagreement resulting not only from the lack of complete scientific knowledge but from the influx of varying philosophical and theological ideas. Some psychologists and educators continue to believe that much of a person's behavior is predetermined at birth. On the other hand, there are some who feel that all, or almost all, behavior is learned. The following statement is often quoted as an extreme example of the latter viewpoint:

Give me a dozen healthy infants, well formed, and my own specified world to bring them up in and I'll guarantee to take any one of them at random and train him to become any type of specialist I might select—doctor, lawyer, artist, merchant-chief, and, yes, even beggarman and thief, regardless of his talents, penchants, tendencies, vocations and race of his ancestors.[1]

The teacher's concept of original nature has an important effect on his thinking about teaching, education, and children. If he feels that most behavior and growth patterns are inborn, he may take a "so-what-can-I-do-about-it" attitude. If, however, he is convinced that learning plays the more important role in behavior, he will assign more extensive responsibilities to education and teaching will become a more important function.

The Teacher's Concern with Growth

A teacher's immediate interest is in what is happening to his pupils at the present time. He must focus his attention on how best to provide them with conditions that will maximally promote growth, hence education. However, the wise teacher knows that the history of each child is useful and necessary to him. What is happening to a child is more meaningful when it can be compared to what has happened to him. Furthermore, a knowledge of a child's growth history will help the teacher in planning more valuable educative experiences for him.

To understand the growth of the child, it is necessary to study him longitudinally. That is, he must be followed through many years of physical and mental development. Children grow at different rates, respond to different types of environments, mature at different ages. The teacher must be conscious of the growth pattern of every child he teaches.

When a teacher receives a new pupil, he wants to discover everything he can about him. He needs to know the child's present status physically, mentally, and educationally. He must know much of his past history to understand his present status. Much about his present status can be determined by means of certain tests and measurements. It is not difficult to determine how tall a child is, how much he weighs, how old he is, how many words he can spell, or how well his vocabulary is developed. Important as this information is, it is not as important as information concerning his present status in its relation to his past history. It is well to know his score on a certain test, but it is more important to know the relationship of that score to his score on a

---

[1] J. B. Watson, *Behaviorism,* New York, Norton, 1930, p. 104.

similar test a year before. Present status is vital, but rate of growth is more so. It is important to know the mental age[2] of the child, but it is more valuable to know how much his mental age has changed since the last time he was examined. Furthermore, it is necessary to know the relationship of his mental age to his chronological age. We know that he is getting older, chronologically, all the time. But is his mental age increasing just as fast? A child with a mental age of 6 and a chronological age of 4 will need very different treatment in the classroom than a child with the same mental age but a chronological age of 9. They will learn at different rates. They are growing at different rates. The teacher must also know what special aptitudes his pupils have, how rapid their rates of growth are, and what the length and character of their past education have been. Knowing these things, the teacher is in a better position to judge whether a child's present achievement measures up to his possibilities.

The pupil should grow in his mastery of knowledge, in his development of skills, and his understanding and appreciation of art, music, literature, and in the society in which he lives. As an individual he should grow in emotional balance, poise, self-reliance, health, and develop a sense of social responsibility. These skills and understandings do not appear suddenly. They increase gradually, and each affects the others. It should be remembered that growing is not just "adding to." Growth involves assimilation and reorganization. A boy is not a little man.

We have identified education with growth and development. Teaching is concerned with education, and therefore it has much to do with growth. Teaching at its best is concerned with stimulating and guiding growth.

SOME SPECIAL ASPECTS OF GROWTH

Growth and Environment

Education is concerned with environment. In fact, the school is second only to the home as an environmental force in the lives of children, and growth is the result of the interaction of the child and his environment. A child's heredity is fixed at the moment of conception and no environmental force can alter this fact. Therefore it is fruitless to argue the relative importance of a child's heredity and his environment. People do grow and learn, and the environment is the variable factor over which intelligent control can be exerted. It is the teacher's task to see that when a child interacts with his environment, worthwhile growth in the right direction takes place.

---

[2] A child's "mental age" is determined by comparing his ability to acquire knowledge with the performance of an average child at the various levels of chronological development. If a child has a mental age of 7 it means that he has the mental development of an average 7-year-old child. In other words, he can detect meanings and solve problems as well as an average 7-year-old child. Binet, a French psychologist, first established the concept of mental age.

Regardless of his heritage, the behavior of a child and the pattern of his growth are conditioned by his environment. It is therefore of greatest importance that the school give him the best possible environment. Environment is not here used in its narrow sense of physical objects about a child, but includes all things with which a child has contact. The school is able to present to the child an environment that is regulated, specialized, and controlled by the things which society deems best for growth and development. Obviously the school cannot directly control the environment of the children during the time when they are not in school, and it is interesting to note that much juvenile delinquency takes place after 4:00 P.M.

Heredity does govern many physical characteristics, such as color of hair, eyes, and skin, general size, and so on, but the assumption that mentality is fixed—a supposition once universally accepted—is now open to question. A number of recent studies have dealt with the relative constancy of the IQ (intelligence quotient) which is arrived at by dividing the mental age by the chronological age. Although the findings are still too limited to merit acceptance of a new generalization, the IQ of the subjects in the recent experiments has been altered a significant amount. It seems logical to assume that human ability, as we now are able to measure it, is not totally determined by heredity nor is it rigidly constant. Many psychologists now believe that the IQ can be raised by proper environment and skillful teaching. The intelligent course of action for the teacher is based on the fact that the function of teaching is to help children develop their capabilities to the fullest, regardless of the limit or nature of those capabilities. Perhaps good teaching will help the child achieve a higher level of intelligence, or perhaps it can only help the child exploit the talents with which he was born. For the classroom teacher the problem is largely academic, and the end results are the same. The good teacher helps the individual to become a better individual.

Too often the faults of children are blamed on heredity or on some inborn tendency when actually they are the results of poor environment or unwise education. When teachers realize the importance of providing the right mental and physical environment for children, they will better appreciate their own importance and responsibility. Teaching becomes an exciting adventure when the teacher realizes that heredity did not settle all the problems of education for him.

Continuousness of Growth

Growth, both physical and educational, is continuous. Changes are occurring all the time. They do not emerge suddenly, but are related to previous changes. The fact of growth-continuity was noted earlier, but it is important enough to warrant further discussion because parents and teachers too often ignore its implications. Although the seventh grade pupil may be in a junior high school building, following a departmentalized program in a secondary school for the first time and given some election in curriculum, he is not much different from the person he was three months earlier in a self-contained elementary schoolroom. Human growth is characterized by continuity, not by radical short-term change.

Psychologists have studied continuity of growth carefully, and a great deal is known about it. It is known, for example, that in acquiring a new factor, skill, or ability, the human organism undergoes both preparational and manifest phases. The fact that the underlying growth of all the first set of teeth and of most of the permanent set is present at birth can be verified by X ray. Because only the manifest stages of the development of human factors, skills, and abilities are readily apparent, teachers are prone to attach undue significance to the amount of change which "shows," ignore the preparational phase, and hold a faulty conception of the fact of continuity of growth.

It must also be noted that although there is continuousness of human growth, the various systems and functions have different developmental rates and phases, and the child does not grow equally in all aspects. Pikunas and Albrecht have noted:

> All systems and organs of the human body have individual cyclic and asynchronous rates of structural and functional development. The brain, for example, grows at a very rapid rate during the prenatal and early postnatal stages and reaches its approximately full weight and structural differentiation several years before puberty changes commence. . . . On the other hand, during the early years of life there is only limited increment of the genital organs and system . . . the thymus gland begins to decrease its function and structurally shrinks in the advanced years of childhood, while the sexual glands deteriorate functionally in the forties in women, and about two decades later in men. The other endocrine glands maintain their functional capacity as long as life is continued.[3]

GROWTH AND MATURATION

Maturation is a term used to describe the general process of growth and development that takes place year by year. It refers to the process through which an individual progresses from infancy to full development. Maturation should not be confused with the growth that takes place as the result of learning. It refers to growth that occurs quite separately from learning. The changes that take place in a child because of maturation are mental as well as physical.

All children pass through various stages of physical and mental development associated with the growth of the body and the maturing of its functions. Some of these changes are associated with the development of the

[3] Justin Pikunas and Eugene Albrecht, *Psychology of Human Development,* New York, McGraw-Hill, 1961, pp. 24–25.

nervous system, and many of them are intimately related to the functioning of the endocrines, or ductless glands. The important thing to remember is that the maturational changes take place naturally. That is, they are relatively unaffected by learning and other environmental situations.

Many experiments have been carried on by psychologists in the field of maturation. One of the more famous ones was the experiment conducted by Arnold Gesell and Helen Thompson.[4] They selected a pair of identical twins who were 46 months old. One of the twins was given training in climbing stairs and stacking cubes each day for six weeks. At the end of this period, the other twin was given a two-week training period in the same task. After the two-week training period, it was found that the two twins were equal in their ability to climb stairs and stack cubes. In other words, the two weeks of training at a later stage of maturation was just as effective as the six weeks of training at an earlier period. Such experiments as this one have shown that learning is dependent upon maturation. There is an optimum time at which certain things can be learned most easily. Some things taught with difficulty to young children can be taught with ease to older ones.

The good teacher will keep himself continually informed as to the maturational status of his pupils. If he has this knowledge, educational experiences can be timed more effectively.

INTERESTS

Maturation and learning are closely connected with interests, for as a child grows and develops, his interests widen and change.

Where do interests come from? There was a time when psychologists believed that the answer had to do with the original nature of the child and his "instincts." Early psychology books contained long lists of instincts that led to interests and to a certain extent determined the child's behavior. Many of these instincts were considered present at birth, but others were recognized as developing later as a part of maturation. For example, interest in the opposite sex was thought to be instinctive even though it did not develop until adolescence. Present-day psychologists do not consider instincts as basic motives for acts; they generally recognize the futility of trying to distinguish the drives that are "innate" from those that are "acquired" through experience. However, it is true that many acquired drives or interests may be based upon fundamental organic cravings. We can safely say that a child is not born with interests—he acquires them through experiences which he gets through contact with his environment. Therefore, to answer the question we must turn to an examination of the influence of the environment.

Different types of environment bring forth different interests. For ex-

[4] Arnold Gesell and Helen Thompson, "Learning and Growth in Identical Infant Twins: An Experimental Study by the Method of Co-twin Control," *Genetic Psychology Monographs*, vol. 6, no. 1, 1929, p. 124.

ample, a child who grows up in the home of a college teacher may develop a great interest in books because he was brought up in an environment of books. Some children who live far from a place to swim have no interest in swimming. The youth of England are not interested in baseball. During World War II the armed forces discovered that many farm boys were greatly interested in and very skillful with machinery; these boys had had modern mechanized farm environments. Thus, children develop interests largely on the basis of their environments.

As a child grows through maturation and learning, his interests widen. First they are concerned with home and family. Then they broaden to take in playmates. Later the school extends them. As a child's environment widens through experience, his expanding interests make possible a richer education. New experiences bring new interests; the new interests in turn lead to new experiences. Children's interests change as they grow older. A child of 7 is interested in one type of book or television program; these may have no appeal to him as an adolescent. When he becomes a man he puts away childish things for more mature ones. Interests are products of both learning and maturation.

A child's general behavior pattern changes with his changing interests. Maturation, interests, behavior, environment, and education are all tied up together. If a child of 12 behaves like a child of 6, the teacher should look for an explanation. In fact, when any child has interests that are not normal for his age, ability, and environment, the teacher must begin to look for the reason.

"John is going to our local college, then to law school, and then he is coming in with me to practice law," says the indulgent father. John may want to go to an agricultural college to study horticulture so that later he can manage a citrus grove, but concerned with parental harmony and security he may follow his father's interests instead of his own. However, his education will be an uninteresting experience. Too often parents plan their children's lives. The boy or girl who can develop a normal interest in a normal environment, select his own college, and choose a vocation in the field where his interests lie will get a better education. Too often education that runs counter to interests leads to frustration and regret. Too many college students work against their own interests and end up as badly adjusted individuals. Any college professor who takes the time to talk with students will unearth many who are interested in one field and yet are working in another.

The wise teacher studies interests, capitalizing on these driving forces in his teaching. He helps develop new interests by excursions and other exposures to new environments. Parents should also study their children's interests. They should realize that interests change and develop, not by parental demand, but only as the result of new environments, additional learning, and the normal maturation of the individual.

EMOTIONS

Emotions are closely connected with interests, in fact, any real interest is more or less charged with emotion. A child is interested in the things he likes, and he always seeks satisfaction. Both liking and satisfaction are emotions. It is difficult to think of any behavior pattern that is not in some way concerned with emotion.

What are emotions and where do they come from? It is not easy to define "emotion." However, we know that it is a mental state that has to do with joy, anger, dread, amusement, disgust, fear, and a great many other states in which a person is moved or excited, or has other strong feelings. Emotions are ever present; they pervade all thought and action.

Psychologists once looked upon emotions as mental states that accompany certain instincts. Thus "combat," which was thought to be an instinctive action, was accompanied by anger or rage, which is an emotion. Both the combat and the anger were considered to be inborn, that is, instinctive. The psychologists made long lists of instincts and their accompanying emotions. The parental instinct was accompanied by tender emotions such as love; assertion and display were accompanied by elation and a feeling of superiority. Now, however, the evidence points to other explanations of the origin of emotions—explanations that are less instinct-oriented. Here again we find that the teacher and the parent are not faced with something that is inborn and "uneducable."

The emotional behavior of children is important to the teacher for at least two reasons. He needs to understand it because it affects health and learning —and he is interested in improving both.

EMOTIONS AND HEALTH

Much research has been done in the field of emotions and health. The earliest and perhaps the best-known research has been concerned with the relationship of emotions to digestion. It has been demonstrated that strong emotions influence the flow of the digestive juices—such emotions as rage, anxiety, or fear often bring on indigestion. Emotions also affect the circulatory system—the heart beats more rapidly and the blood pressure is increased in some cases. There is also a close relationship between the emotions and the functioning of the glands of internal secretion.

Later when you study psychology you will learn more about the nature of the emotions and their relationship to health. Here, however, we may generalize by saying that such emotions as joy, happiness, contentment have a positive educational value, whereas such emotions as sorrow, fear, worry, anxiety, rage are detrimental. Hence school work that is accomplished pleasurably with satisfaction is conducive to normal growth and development.

But school work that is attended by unhappiness and frustration is detrimental to general health.

EMOTIONS AND LEARNING

"Whatever serves rather directly a deep emotional need is apt to make for strong and sound motivation in learning, for in all probability all reasoning processes have emotional moorings."[5] This conclusion, stated by a group of experimental psychologists at Sarah Lawrence College, points up the importance of emotions in the learning process.

If a child works with joy, understanding, interest, and willingness and views his work with satisfaction, real learning takes place. If, however, the student is driven to an uninteresting task which he approaches with fear, dread, disinterestedness, anger, and compulsion, the results are likely to be without value. The wise teacher knows the value of emotions and the proper use of them. The teacher who punishes pupils for making errors in their work and the teacher who gives a prize to pupils who make no errors in their work are both using emotions—and both of them are using emotions incorrectly. Emotions should be used to foster intrinsic interest in the subject at hand, and not extrinsically as punishment or reward.

The type of learning known as appreciation is especially related to emotion. The appreciation of the best in music, art, architecture, dress, books, and plays has a strong emotional aspect. The curriculum may deal with facts and concrete examples, but the significant end result sought is an *emotional* experience.

Emotions differ with the various stages in the growth of the individual. Maturation and learning make the emotional responses of a high school pupil vastly different from those of a child in kindergarten, so the teacher must know a great deal about the emotional reactions at various ages and allow the student to live in accordance with the emotional pattern of his age. A teacher who says, "Now, be a little man!" to a weeping 6-year-old with a bloody finger does not know his psychology: a 6-year-old should not be asked to show the emotional behavior of an adult. Treating high school students as infants is equally erroneous.

PERSONALITY

In this discussion of human growth and development the emphasis has been on physical, mental, and emotional factors. The topics might have been organized under a single, general heading—"personality," because the total growth of a child can be summed up as the development of personality.

[5] Lois Borclay Murphy, Eugene Leonard, and Madeleine Grant, *Psychology for Individual Education*, New York, Columbia University Press, 1942, p. 17.

What is personality? Here, as in many areas of psychology, there are differing viewpoints, especially if a specific answer is demanded. There seems to be consensus, however, that personality can be defined generally as the characteristic pattern of the individual's behavior, his attitudes, his motives, and his perceptions. No two persons have exactly the same personality because each has a different heredity compound and a different environment.

The teacher is vitally interested in the personalities of his pupils. In a sense it can be said that the teacher's most important responsibility is to help pupils develop adequate personalities and find a satisfying view of themselves in their relationships with others. Everything that happens in school contributes to the development of the personalities of the children involved. How is Johnny's total behavior affected by the fact that he always gets the lowest grades? How will Mike's superior skill in sports affect his personality? What happens to Mary when the teacher makes her stand in the corner for whispering? What kinds of attitudes and motives might be learned by the college student who reported the following incident?

"When I was in Mr. A's history class, I offered a suggestion about something—the American Revolution, I think. He said that it was very good, and asked where I got it. When I said it was my own opinion, he became quite indignant and said that high school students were not allowed to have opinions of their own."[6]

The questions noted above are not merely academic. Good teaching cannot take place if the teacher is not aware of the importance of personal relationships in his classroom. The good teacher attempts to become aware of the personality of each pupil. He may not know as much about each of them as he would if there was only one child to teach: the problem is not a simple one but is multiplied by the number of persons in the class. However, it is the teacher's task to find out as much as he can. The following anecdote is a good illustration of a teacher who was ineffective because he did not know the characteristics and basic orientation of one of his pupils:

. . . A bright, nervous, high-strung third-grade child refused point-blank to read aloud a simple story about animals that talked because she regarded it as silly. The order was repeated, the stubbornness increased, and the exasperated young teacher told the child she could not leave school until she had read the story aloud. At five o'clock the deadlock was broken by the principal, who required merely that the girl read a passage from any book, whereupon the youngster proudly pulled from her desk a copy of *David Copperfield* and read a passage with gusto. . . . The work was far below the level of her interests and ability; the episode was the climax of an accumulated exasperation at work which she considered beneath her. And she craved the satisfaction of showing what difficult material she could and ordinarily did read.[7]

---

[6] Ross Stanger, *Psychology of Personality*, New York, McGraw-Hill, 1954, p. 392.
[7] S. L. Pressey and F. P. Robinson, *Psychology and the New Education*, New York, Harper & Row, 1944, p. 188.

A child's personality development is strongly affected by how people whom he considers important feel about him and react toward him. Adults are important people to the young child, and the teacher is one of the most important adults in a child's world. It is imperative that the teacher know each pupil's unique personality, in so far as possible, and behave toward him in light of that knowledge.

Mental Growth and Personality

Personality is closely related to intelligence. General intelligence largely determines whether a person is slow, infantile, brilliant, or unintelligent in his thinking and actions. It also has a positive influence on the child's relationship to his environment, and hence on his growth.

To learn to understand children and to help them live within their responsibilities and limitations is of greatest importance in the development of personality. Some teachers and parents consistently attempt to have children do things that are beyond their capabilities. The child is assigned a task and is scolded, punished, and disgraced if he does not do it. He is publicly denounced to his parents by a report card that he must take home from school, and at the end of the year he must face failure of promotion and have to look forward to doing the whole miserable thing over again next year.

Some teachers and parents, on the other hand, consistently ask children to do things that are beneath their capabilities. The child is assigned tasks he is able to complete with half-hearted effort. He develops poor work habits, loses the keen intellectual curiosity characteristic of superior intelligence, and finally is so bored with school work that his general achievement becomes only mediocre and his grades merely passable.

Improper treatment over an extended period of time profoundly affects personality. The student who is consistently led to failure and the student who is consistently left unchallenged will both cease to grow intellectually; the former because eventually he becomes totally discouraged and convinced that he cannot be successful, the latter because he reverts to the lowest level of his capacity. Neither tends to become the kind of citizen needed in a democracy. A free society will not prosper as it should without the best contribution from each of its citizens, and the basic function of the school is to help each student develop his potential to the fullest. Again, therefore, it is imperative that a teacher learn about the capabilities, backgrounds, interests, and motives of his students, for only as he is cognizant of these factors can he help the students plan a school life that is both rewarding and interesting.

Emotions and Personality

Emotions are very important in the development of personality; they often determine its dominant characteristic. We describe an individual as being hateful, loving, bashful, friendly, quarrelsome, or moody. In each case we are using an emotional state to describe personality. It is difficult to generalize regarding the relationship of emotional experiences to personality. The frequently recurring emotional experiences of children are part of growth and hence of education. Our remote ancestors gave much freer expression to their emotions than we do: they could scream with pain and roar with laughter. But our civilized society frowns upon such extreme emotional exhibitions. Modern civilization says "thou shalt not" to most emotional outbreaks. "Don't" is too often said to children, particularly in the average home. The modern teacher is not a "don't do that" person, he plans and works in a "do" atmosphere, which means that he helps the children to develop the right kinds of emotional outlets.

The main thing for the teacher to remember concerning emotions is that personality is best built when children have emotionally satisfying experiences. They should grow in their ability to do, understand, and enjoy.

THE LEARNING PROCESS

In addition to using what is known about human growth and development, the teacher, as a director of learning, must have a valid psychology of learning to guide his actions. Learning and teaching form the obverse sides of one process. Although it is true that much learning takes place outside the school, the school is set up as the place where children learn in the most efficient manner possible. The buildings and equipment are planned to facilitate learning and the teachers are hired as experts in the learning process. Skill in facilitating learning is as necessary to the teacher as skill in courtroom practice is to the trial lawyer. Therefore, it is imperative that the prospective teacher know and be able to utilize the implications of such things as motivation, readiness, effect, method, and psychological testing.

Motives in Learning

Motives are necessary for learning. They release energy for the task at hand, lead a person to remain inactive or to react, either inwardly or overtly, and thus tend to direct behavior. There is no such thing as unmotivated learning. The motive may be weak or strong, poorly or well-directed, external to or within the process, but it is always present. In the classroom, then, it is not a question of whether the teacher will motivate his pupils to learn, the only question is "*what ways* will the teacher use to motivate pupil behavior?"

Two widely divergent approaches to the motivation of human behavior are available to the teacher, and any specific motivational procedures he uses can be classified under one of them. In conjunction with learning there is internal motivation and external motivation: motivation is internal if it lies within the act itself and satisfying experiences result naturally, it is

On those rare occasions when person-to-person relationships lead to temporary unhappiness, the skillful teacher not only repairs the bent ego, but uses the experience as a positive device for learning. (*Carl Purcell, National Education Association*)

"Hi, Tommy! Come see what we're doing!" In the nursery school enthusiasm reigns, and acceptance is natural and easy. Tommy's having a wonderful time, thank you. (*Standard Oil Company, N.J.*)

Left: These teachers—a fifth and a sixth grade instructor—coordinate the results of a two-year testing program and perceive a clearer picture of the results of their efforts.

Below: Handicapped?, yes; incapacitated?, never! Seven of the fine musicians in this school's orchestra are blind. (*Three photos left and below, Seattle School District*)

Proper diagnosis and expert treatment by this school system's speech therapist help to alleviate a student's stuttering problem.

external if it is applied from without and the satisfaction is gained from something not indigenous to the act. The student who learns to play trombone so that he can play a trombone and participate in the school band is following an internal motive; the student who practices trombone because his father punishes him for not practicing, or because his father pays him for practicing, or because his father does both, is following an external motive. External motivation is based on the premise that people are basically "seekers of reward" and "avoiders of pain," whereas internal motivation is based on the idea that people are basically "goal-seekers." The student who studies a Shakespearian play for the joy of understanding and performing it is motivated by intrinsic forces, the student who studies his required Shakespeare so that he can receive a passing grade and avoid being declared ineligible for basketball is driven by an extrinsic force.

The teacher who relies on extrinsic motivation presupposes that children will resist learning, that they must be forced to do worthwhile things. The director of learning who uses intrinsic motivation proceeds on the assumption that children love learning. What does research say about motivation? Is there any evidence to guide the teacher?

A great deal is known about motivation today. For example it is known that any psychology of learning which assumes children do not like to learn is fallacious. Children do like to learn, in fact they are full of questions indicative of their desires to learn. Children want to know: "What is that?" "How does it work?" "Why do we do this?" They are not happy with unanswered questions; they have an insatiable curiosity about everything around them. Children take their curiosity and great desire to learn to school with them, and usually retain it until they reach a point in their school program where the learning experiences cease to have meaning and purpose for them.

Most psychologists agree that human behavior is purposeful and "goal-centered." People do not go through life seeking rewards and avoiding pain; human behavior is characterized by the process of taking and maintaining

When the nursery school furniture needed renovation, this class took the opportunity to combine an interesting project with an intrinsically valuable service to their community. (*Standard Oil Company, N.J.*)

definite direction toward achieving goals—some of them immediate, some deferred, and some scarcely or never attainable. Drastic action on the part of another person can temporarily swerve the individual from direct progress toward a goal, but the goal will not be forgotten. When the tasks in the schoolroom are similar or at least complementary to the goals which the pupil has, the motivation to proceed is intrinsic to the task and the teacher need give no thought to "*making* the students work and learn." The boy who sees no purpose, no desirable goal in the science class will be a reluctant scholar at best. Yet the same boy will toil willingly to adjust the carburetor on his jalopy or to classify the minerals in his rock collection. When the curriculum is purposeless to the student it becomes necessary for the school to invent artificial devices to motivate behavior. Such devices as marks, privileges, prizes, threats, loss of privileges, punishments, and failure are commonly used. Such extrinsic motivators are poor substitutes for intrinsic purpose.

Another important consideration related to motivation is the permanence of learning. Many of the facts and information that children learn are forgotten; they do not become a permanent possession unless they are constantly used. Thus the facts that are learned under coercion are soon forgotten because when the external motive for learning is removed there is no reason to use the material learned. However, if the motive for the act lies within the act itself and if the material learned is valuable to the learner, he will continue to use it and it becomes a permanent possession. A child never forgets how to walk or talk because he walks and talks every day, but he soon forgets meaningless dates and facts because he has no use for them.

The formation of attitudes, tastes, predispositions, appreciations, and ideals are also closely related to motivation. A student is constantly forming attitudes about school, his teacher, himself, other pupils, and ways of doing things. No one questions the fact that a child forms attitudes in school, but the kind formed is another question. The answer to the question is found mainly in the approach to motivation used by teachers and school officials. If the student is bribed or threatened he forms one kind of attitude; if he works with joy and enthusiasm and has worthwhile experiences he forms another kind. Adult attitudes differ quite as much. The man who always asks "what is there in it for me?" is the product of one kind of home and school education. The individual who asks "is it good for the community?" is the product of another education. Attitudes formed in school tend to be permanent.

READINESS TO LEARN

Earlier in this chapter there was a discussion of maturation—growth which takes place separately from learning. Readiness to learn, one basic principal of learning, is closely related to maturation.

A good example of the importance of readiness to learn is to be found in the area of beginning reading. It has been discovered by experiment that a child must have a mental age of 6 to begin successfully to read; some research seems to show that 6½ years of mental age is preferable. Attempting to teach a child to read before he has reached this level of mental development is usually futile. Under the stress of a great desire to succeed, the immature child will probably become able to "parrot" sounds and even recognize some words on sight, but the concepts which the words symbolize will have little real meaning for him and the rate of forgetting will be exceedingly high. More than mental age is also involved in readiness to read. A child must have developed to a point where he can see likenesses and differences, remember word forms, and do some abstract thinking. Readiness to read is also related to the pupil's physical, emotional, and social development. But, even so, he may not be ready to read. He may be interested in the material in books but not in learning to read so long as he can get some adult to read to him. There are many cases on record of bright children who did not learn to read because they did not need to, but when parents and other adults stopped reading to them they learned the skill quickly.

What is true of beginning reading is also true of beginning to read scientific materials at a later date; it is also true of arithmetic, spelling, and other subjects. There is little value in attempting to teach a child before he is ready to learn.

The principle of readiness can also be violated in the opposite way. Readiness with no possible outlet is frustrating and a waste of time and talent. The child who is ready to read should be helped to read, and the student who is ready for algebra should not be asked to again review addition, subtraction, multiplication, and division. Optimum learning results when readiness and opportunity coincide.

IDENTIFICATION OF INDIVIDUAL DIFFERENCES

It is not difficult to conclude that individual differences exist among children. Some differences, particularly physical ones, are apparent. No two persons, not even "identical" twins, are precisely alike in all physical characteristics. In the areas of emotional, social, and intellectual development, deviation from one individual to another is even more marked, although it may not be as immediately discernible.

All kinds of individual differences are significant to the classroom teacher, and he must strive constantly to identify and assess the characteristics which his students possess and exhibit. In some cases the teacher is limited to personal observation and subjective judgment as he attempts to understand his pupils. In other areas of individual difference, however, the teacher has a professional tool known as the "standardized test" to help him as he measures his students. Two aspects of individual difference where the standardized test has been most often used are general ability and school progress; measurement procedures in these areas yield relatively accurate results.

The measurement movement in education began early in the twentieth century. In 1907, C. W. Stone developed the first standardized test in arithmetic. E. L. Thorndike followed with a writing scale in 1908, and soon scales or tests had been devised for many of the measurable products of education. These early tests were crude and did not do a very good job of measuring the attributes they were intended to measure. However, they were better than the guesswork method which teachers had formerly used. Today, teachers have a wide range of valid and reliable tests of progress in school subjects—usually called "achievement tests"—available for their use.

Tests of ability—intelligence tests—also came into use shortly after 1900. These two types of tests—achievement and ability—should not be confused. Intelligence tests have as their purpose the measuring of a person's ability to perform under optimum circumstances. They should not measure what has been learned. Achievement tests, on the other hand, are specifically designed to discover what the individual has learned, what he already knows how to do.

Before continuing a discussion of these tests it is also important to note that neither of them, especially intelligence tests, are precise enough to warrant unquestioned acceptance of results. The educator must interpret test results in the light of the other things which he knows about the persons who were tested. Standardized test results can be grossly misused, they can also be of great assistance if they are correctly used.

INTELLIGENCE TESTS

The first usable intelligence test was devised by Binet, a French psychologist, in 1905. His tests were revised to meet the needs of American children by Professor L. M. Terman, of Stanford University, and his associates. The Stanford Revision of the Binet test is still in common use. However, it should always be given and interpreted by one specially prepared to do such work, for the results of unskilled testers are likely to be very unreliable. Many other individual tests have been developed. Before a teacher can become qualified to administer any of the individual intelligence tests he must have special preparation.

The result of an intelligence test is usually expressed in terms of mental age (MA) or intelligence quotient (IQ). The former expresses mental development in terms of the average for a child of a particular age; the latter refers to the ratio between the mental age and the chronological age. Mental age tells how far a child has developed mentally; IQ, how bright he is.

GROUP INTELLIGENCE TESTS

Individual diagnosis by a competent psychologist or a teacher specially prepared in intelligence testing is expensive. In most school systems it is possible to study only the individual cases that need particular consideration. All the others must be taken care of by a less expensive method. In order to overcome the cost of diagnosis with individual tests, group tests have been devised.

The first group intelligence tests were developed just prior to World War I. The war itself gave great impetus to the movement and the psychological division of the United States Army devised and gave thousands of intelligence tests with very satisfactory results to groups of soldiers. After the war a great many group intelligence tests were published and were widely used in the schools. Group tests were also used on a large scale and with satisfactory results by the armed forces during World War II. At the present time there are a large number of these tests on the market: these range from tests for kindergarten children to tests for adults.

It is impossible, in a book such as this, to discuss in detail the making and the use of group intelligence tests. It is also inadvisable to reproduce any of the testing material. However, all teachers must become familiar with all phases of testing.

USE OF INTELLIGENCE TESTS

Intelligence tests help the teacher to better understand each individual child. When properly given and interpreted, they make the guidance of each child easier and more scientific. Results of such tests, however, must be used with care. All too often a teacher will attempt to classify a child by the results of one or two tests. Those who know the most about intelligence tests use them with the greatest discretion. Although intelligence tests are tools of guidance, they tell only part of the story concerning a child. They must never be considered as telling the whole story about any child and his potentialities.

The use of intelligence tests also enables the school authorities to locate children who are in need of special education. These children are less or more intelligent than the average child.

Terman spent many years making a study of gifted children. He defined as gifted those who had an IQ of 140 or more. He followed a large group of these gifted children through their schooling and into their adult lives. His conclusions are very valuable for anyone interested in gifted children.

Children of IQ 140 or higher are, in general, appreciably superior to unselected children in physique, health, and social adjustment; markedly superior in moral attitudes as measured by either character tests or by trait ratings; and vastly superior in their mastery of school subjects as shown by a three-hour battery of achievement tests. In fact, the typical child of the group has mastered the school subjects to a point about two grades beyond the one in which he was enrolled, some of them three or four grades beyond. Moreover, his ability as evidenced by achievement in the different school subjects is so general as to refute completely the traditional belief that gifted children are usually one-sided.[8]

[8] Lewis M. Terman, "The Discovery and Encouragement of Exceptional Talent," *The American Psychologist*, vol. 9, June, 1954, p. 223.

Many of the problems of teaching involve the intelligence of school children. The materials that are taught and the methods of teaching are conditioned by the intelligence of the children. Information concerning the intelligence of each child helps the teacher to know how to teach and what to teach that particular child. The intelligence test is the tool. Properly used, it can aid a teacher in doing a good job as a director of learning or as a counselor.

STANDARDIZED ACHIEVEMENT TESTS

Achievement tests are the second major type of standardized instruments most familiar to teachers. These tests measure the results of learning. Standardized tests are available in reading, spelling, arithmetic, and other subjects usually taught. They have been constructed with great care by experts and measure what they are supposed to measure with some degree of accuracy. Achievement tests are commonly used to compare how the members of a class score in relation to national averages and in comparison with their own scores on a similar test given previously. Thus they are designed to measure progress or achievement in basic school subjects.

It is important to remember, however, that many of the valuable outcomes of teaching cannot be measured by any paper-and-pencil test. A language usage test will probably indicate how much grammar a student has mastered, but using good English in daily communication is a more important objective of language-arts teaching and can be measured only by listening to pupils as they talk and by checking written work in all parts of the school program. Other goals of education most sought include such attributes as honesty, persistence in work, and initiative. Obviously these things do not lend themselves to standardized testing.

The general principle to follow concerning the use of standardized achievement tests is that they constitute only one aspect of a testing program and should be used when there is a definite problem to be solved which cannot be solved better by some other means. In the past some educators have given standardized tests merely to satisfy their curiosity, or in order to compare—if favorable—their city's averages with some other city's results. Such uses are questionable. However, if a teacher wishes to have detailed information about each student as a guide in teaching, standardized tests are of great value.

At one time it was thought that comparing one city or school or teacher with its counterpart constituted the greatest value to be derived from testing. Now it is known that such comparisons are highly suspect. Merely knowing that the fourth grades in school A score an average of 10 points higher in arithmetic than the same grades in school B is no basis for comparison of the arithmetic program or of the teachers or of the students in the two schools. So many variables must be taken into account that such a comparison is invalid. Perhaps school A spends 20 percent more time on arithmetic than school B; perhaps its children entered the fourth grade far ahead in arithmetic background; or perhaps the test more closely followed the placement of various arithmetic learnings in school A. It well might be that school B has the better, more functional fourth grade arithmetic teaching of the two schools. Much more information is needed before any kind of comparison can be made accurately.

While the value to education derived from the proper use of standardized intelligence and achievement tests is widely recognized, it is also important to recognize the danger of tests becoming the ends of education rather than a means to achieving a larger aim. It is easy for the public and for some teachers to begin to think of education as the ability to get a certain score on a certain set of educational tests. Such a philosophy ignores much of what is important in education. Even though skill in fundamental subjects is one of the important products of education, it is not the total product. Education must not be interpreted in terms of a manufacturing process in which so many units of reading, geography, and arithmetic are put into a machine and a finished product—an educated individual—is turned out. No matter how well selected and proportioned the mixture of raw materials is, or how well it is adapted to the capacities of the learner, unless worthy ideals, appreciations, and character development have been a part of the process the ends will not be worthwhile.

Teachers can measure a child's growth in height and weight, and have instruments to measure mastery of spelling and arithmetic, but until it is also possible to measure his growth in the other important things of life, education cannot be measured. Perhaps a different set of tests is needed, but it must be remembered that the amount of reproducible knowledge which the standardized test reveals, although of real value, should not be confused with the total aim of education.

GUIDANCE

In addition to being the scientific basis for a teacher's actions as a director of learning, psychology also provides the foundation for the important professional functions of guidance and counseling. In the actual day-to-day operation of a classroom it is difficult, if not impossible, to separate these two roles of a teacher. As a teacher directs the learning of his pupils he must also guide and direct their interests. It is important that children learn to read and write and learn about the world in which they live. It is also important that they develop as individuals. "Growing up" cannot be learned from books but must be done by the child himself under the close supervision of his teacher. The problems of the individual pupil are a responsibility of the teacher. Even when a teacher's attention is directed primarily toward their achieving mastery of subject matter he must not ignore them as individuals in his classroom. As a teacher plans learning experiences, makes lesson schedules, and chooses testing devices, he must be cognizant of the drives and interests of his pupils. When the science teacher discovers that his students need further instruction about the solar system and decides to have the pupils see an instructional film instead of reading another textbook on the subject because he has discovered that this particular class learns best from a varying approach, it would be impossible to say whether that decision is made as a director of learning or as a guidance worker.

Guidance is also concerned with helping students make intelligent educational and vocational plans. Toward this end much information about the student's ability, interests, and personality must be gathered. On the basis of this information, an effort is made to help him become a well-adjusted, successful student and to make intelligent plans for the future. In most school systems the process of data-gathering begins prior to actual school attendance, by means of home visits or a carefully planned teacher-potential student-parent meeting often called a "spring roundup." Much information concerning the home background, health record, and general maturity level is needed early by the child's first teacher—whether preschool, kindergarten, or first-grade teacher—and the record which is begun at this early date follows the child throughout his school career.

Adequate records are basic to all guidance work. Although there are many different types of records, most of them contain information relating to health, intelligence, school progress, family, and activities of the child. Almost all school systems have adopted or developed a set of accumulative records and a method of gathering, recording, and using the material in the students' folders.

If all children were alike and came from similar homes and had the same kinds of problems, extensive records would not be necessary. But no two children are alike. They may have the same IQ, the same chronological age, and live on the same street and still be very different. Consequently each child must be dealt with as an individual. Teaching may be done in groups, but learning is done one by one.

Guidance is imperative at all levels of school. The elementary school child must be helped to make the best possible start of his formal education; the junior high school pupil is confronted by dozens of new problems in his new school as he begins his secondary education with larger groups of classmates who are also in a novel situation; the senior high school student is also in a new situation and faces the additional problem of making a vocational choice. The need for guidance seems obvious. At one time, however, schools ignored everything about the pupil except his progress in the subjects for which he was enrolled. Not only did this limited approach ignore the fact of student individuality, it was not conducive to the very thing it emphasized. Therefore today's schools and teachers are interested in the whole child and in all his problems.

In general there are two methods of handling the function of guidance and counseling in schools. Many city school systems have guidance departments with directors in charge and guidance officers who work with each individual school in the system. The guidance department also employs psychologists, physicians, remedial teachers, and other experts who deal with cases that need special attention. However, these specialists do little individual work with normal pupils and even in a large school system with its complex organization it is the classroom teacher who must carry on the guidance work with about 98 percent of the children. The classroom teacher uses the guidance specialist as a resource person and consultant in connection with his own efforts, he sends to the expert for special testing and counseling those children whom he does not understand or cannot help. In the rural and small urban school there is seldom any special administrative organization to handle guidance. In such schools, which are in a vast majority, all the guidance work is done by the classroom teacher, with the assistance of the principal for cases he does not understand. Almost all beginning teachers enter the profession in small schools where they encounter a great deal of guidance work to do with little help.

Because today's teacher is a combination director of learning and guidance counselor, each teacher must be willing and prepared to accept his part of guidance work. The teacher does not set aside a part of each day for guidance; it is an integral part of everything he does. The boy who is excited about fighting forest fires after seeing a forestry movie wants to know right then and there how one gets to be a forest ranger and can he do it? Questions of that type constantly arise and are answered as a part of classwork by intelligent teachers.

Because guidance deals with the happiness and adjustment of individuals it is a difficult and demanding task. It is at once the most frustrating and the most rewarding part of teaching. Unless a person enjoys others and wants to work with and for them, he should not consider teaching as a life's work.

RELATED READINGS

Frandsen, Arden N., *How Children Learn,* New York, McGraw-Hill, 1957.

Hill, Winfred W., *Learning: A Survey of Psychological Interpretations,* San Francisco, Chandler Publishing Company, 1963.

Jenkins, Gladys S., Helen Shacter, and William W. Bauer, *These Are Your Children,* Chicago, Scott, Foresman, 1953.

Jersild, Arthur T., *The Psychology of Adolescence,* New York, Macmillan, 1957.

Seidman, Jerome, Ed., *Educating for Mental Health,* New York, Crowell, 1963.

Trow, William Clark, *Teacher and Technology,* New York, Appleton-Century-Crofts, 1963.

Handsome, well-lighted rooms, equipped with TV receivers, functional, movable furniture, and mobile wall partitions are an expensive investment, and, like any good investment, bring a rich return. (Board of Education, Columbus, Ohio)

Below: When the school board meets to discuss next year's salary schedules, their deliberations cause a great deal of interest. (Minneapolis Morning Tribune)

The modern American textbook has reached a level of beauty, excellence, and functionalism unequalled anywhere in the world. (John F. Cuneo Company, Melrose Park, Illinois)

The dental and medical clinics found in many progressive school systems are examples of the vital auxiliary services which a complete educational program requires. (U.S. Public Health Service)

Right: School is out for the day and these boys and girls who have had the advantages of the rich, full program in a consolidated school will soon be delivered to their own front gates. (Strickler from Monkmeyer)

The members of the Citizens Advisory Committee in this community meet early each Wednesday morning and have coffee with a side order of statistics. (*Two top photos, Seattle School District*)

Concrete (and brick, steel, and wire) evidence that the citizens of this community support bond issues.

Getting up steam. Early morning commuters, waiting to board their trains, were pleasantly surprised to find PTA members offering doughnuts and steaming coffee along with a letter-writing packet and a request that they use it to write a letter to their state legislator urging him to support adequate state aid to public schools. (*National Congress of Parents and Teachers*)

Chapter 6 / LEGAL AND FINANCIAL FOUNDATIONS OF AMERICAN EDUCATION

INTRODUCTION

In 1960 approximately forty-five million Americans—one out of every four persons—went to school and almost two million teachers and administrators were required to help educate them. The number of people involved in education had risen rapidly, a rise far greater than the rise in population:

between 1870 and 1960, while our population was increasing four and one-half times (from about 40 to 180 million), our public high school population was increasing approximately 80 times. No change in this trend is forecast: the United States Bureau of the Census estimates that our population will reach 222.3 millions by 1975, and schools are certain to have a greater proportional increase. High school enrollments of approximately 15 million students in 1963 represent a 50 percent increase over 1955, while colleges and universities are facing at least a doubling of their enrollments in the next decade.

During the school year 1961–1962 expenditures for public elementary and secondary schools (excluding capital outlay and interest) totaled more than $12.9 billion, or $414.00 per pupil in average daily attendance. Higher education institutions spent an additional $5.6 billion, making a total of approximately $18.5 billion, or less than 3.6 percent of the gross national product during the same year. Since 1930 the correlation between educational expenditures and the gross national product has remained relatively constant, at about 3.5 percent. The large increase in the total dollars spent on education reflects the rise in the national product. However, the increase has not been sufficient to keep pace with the rise of enrollments noted earlier and the result is a proportionately smaller expenditure of the national wealth per pupil. In view of these facts, it cannot be said that Americans overspend on education. It is to be noted that in 1967 schools and colleges in the United States will require at least double the level of support received in 1957 to enable them to offer the same amount and quality of education to an expanded enrollment.

All educated citizens in our country should be aware of the problems our schools are facing; a student of education specifically must know much more because it is his responsibility to provide leadership in the areas of public education. Just as people look to the medical profession for guidance in health matters, so they should expect leadership in educational matters from members of the education profession. Good leaders know the background of present-day problems as well as the current situation. No area of education offers greater challenge to the educator than that of gaining and maintaining proper support of public education.

The problems facing educators today are not novel. Since colonial days the nation has constantly sought better and more efficient ways of supporting education. Some of the battles for free public schools waged over the years have been described in Chapter 2. It is a significant fact that some of the more important ones dealt with problems of financing a desirable amount and quality of education. A problem of this type is never solved. The problem itself keeps changing so that new solutions must constantly be sought.

Many of the battles public education has had to face are closely related to laws and interpretations of laws. As a function of government, education has legal bases which must be understood before today's problems of enrollment and finances can be properly attacked. The legal foundations of education in the United States are extremely complex because schools are established, maintained, and controlled by local, state, and federal statutes and decisions.

The Constitution of the United States, the basic law of the country, did not include education as one of the functions of the federal government: education was one of the areas of government left to the states. State governments, in turn, have given local boards of education most of the direct responsibility for organizing and operating local schools. In recent years, however, the traditional lines of responsibility and authority have been somewhat obliterated: state governments have provided an increasing proportion of the support for education as compared to local sources and the federal government has become more and more involved in education through grants of money to state and local school systems and teachers. In the main, though, education in the United States remains basically a state function; in actual practice it is administered at the local level with the federal government providing supplemental aid for special programs and areas of great need.

THE STATE IN PUBLIC EDUCATION

This nation does not have a national system of education, nor does it have hundreds of thousands of systems (one per community). The United States has 50 systems of education because education is a state function with plenary authority for education vested in state governments. Perhaps no statement about American education is more significant or has more implications.

The system of state control of education has evolved because in a democracy education controlled from the national capitol is not desirable. Final responsibility for education is not given to local communities or school districts because these units are too small to legislate successfully on general problems, especially in the areas of support and control, areas which significantly affect the educational program. Furthermore, all subdivisions of the state—such as counties, townships, and school districts—are creations of the state. Therefore each of the 50 states has provided for education in its constitution and thus made education a function of state government.

School boards in several states have gone to court in an attempt to prove that schools belong to the local community or district, but in every state where this question has been tested at the supreme court level the decision has strengthened the position of the state. The Supreme Court of North Carolina, for example, stated, "The schools are, in essence, local branches of the state government." Without state sanction no taxes may be levied, no teachers hired, no books may be bought or school buildings constructed, and all teachers employed by school districts are legally state employees.

Most students agree that the state-centered organization of education that has developed in the United States has enhanced democratic control of education. The citizens who are the voters in the school districts of the state also elect the members of the legislature and the other state officers. If a majority of the citizens desire a change in their educational program, they express their wishes through the election of a legislature which then passes the laws that control the local school districts.

In an undemocratic society there is a hierarchy of educational authority, usually centered in a federal department of education under an appointed director. The educational program is established by the central office and passed on down to the counties and school districts. The local schools are administered by governmental appointees who receive their authority from above. In a democracy, conversely, the authority comes up from the people. The amount of state control and the amount of discretion given to the local school districts varies widely in the different states, but each state has some type of state educational organization. Usually the state department of education is headed by a state board of education and a chief state school officer.

State Boards of Education

There are many patterns of organization for state boards of education. In some states a single board acts as the policy-making body for the state, in other states a number of boards share the responsibility and often overlap in their functions. Regardless of the specific pattern of organization, however, every state has provided for a state-level policy-making function for education. This is clearly in line with the state-centered system of education this country has followed.

New York established the first state board of education in 1784. It was originated as the "Board of Regents of the University for the State of New York." However, no such university was provided for and this board has concerned itself largely with secondary and higher education on a state-wide basis. Massachusetts, under the leadership of Horace Mann, followed in 1837 with what proved to be the first board concerned with all levels of education. Connecticut was next, its state board being established under the leadership of Henry Barnard in 1839.

There are several different methods of selecting the members of a state board of education. One method is to designate certain state officials as ex-officio members of the board, another method is appointment by the governor, and a third is election by the people. Most students of educational administration agree that the designation of certain state officers as ex-officio members is the least satisfactory of the methods, yet this system accounts for some of the members in about half of the states and all members in at least two states.

In most states all or some members of the state board of education are appointed by the governor. In seven states they are elected by the people; in Colorado one member is elected from each of the four Congressional districts and a fifth member from the state at large; in Texas one member is elected from each Congressional district; in Nebraska one member is elected from each of the nine judicial districts. In Wyoming the members are appointed by the chief state school officer, in New York they are elected by the state legislature, and in Washington they are elected by school board members.

There has been much discussion among educators as to whether a state board should be appointed or elected. The objection to the election of a board by popular vote is the fact that educators are too often elected. This is the case in Michigan, where the board is elected and is usually made up of professional educators. At present most authorities favor appointment because it assures a lay board. A lay board does not attempt to assume executive functions; it legislates and appoints the state's chief school officer, usually the state commissioner of education. Its members have an impartial concern for the educational welfare of the entire state rather than for some one institution. Although Colorado's board is elected, the law provides for lay members. Perhaps the best type of state board is one composed of a small group of laymen appointed by the governor, as in Massachusetts, Kansas, and California. However, its term of office should be long enough so that no governor can appoint all or even a majority of the members in a single term.

The number of members of a state board of education varies from 3 in Mississippi to 21 in Texas. The size of the Texas board is increased whenever the number of Congressional districts is increased. The experts agree that a board made up of an odd number—either five, seven or nine—is to be preferred. A small board often assumes administrative functions, and a very large board breaks up into committees instead of functioning as a whole.

The functions of a state board of education vary widely in the several states. In most states the board determines the general educational policy. In some states it has supervisory responsibility over elementary and secondary education; in others it controls the institutions of higher education. In Michigan it functions mainly as a board of trustees for the teachers colleges—in almost half the states it is responsible for these colleges. In most states it is responsible for vocational education. In some states very little authority is given to the board, aside from the appointment of the chief school officer. A state board of education should be a legislative body, it should appoint the chief school officer and carry on its administrative functions through him and with his assistance. The members of the board should, of course, have no authority as individuals but should function only through the board acting as a whole.

The Chief State School Officer

Beginning with New York in 1812, all 50 states have made provisions for a chief state school officer. He is usually designated as the superintendent of public instruction if elected, and as the commissioner of education if appointed. His powers and duties differ considerably in the various states. Where there is no state board of education he is the head of the state school system. The term of office ranges from one to six years, with most states providing at least four years.

The authority vested in the chief state school officer may come from a constitutional provision or from legislative action. In states where he is a constitutional officer the duties of the office and sometimes even the salary are written into the constitution.

There are several different methods of selecting the chief executive of a state school system. In 26 states he is elected by popular vote, but the present tendency is away from popular election. In 17 states the chief state school officer is appointed by the governor.

A city superintendent of schools or the president of a state college or university is not elected by popular vote. Such offices are filled by appointment by a lay board after consideration of a great many possible candidates. Authorities in this field believe that the state's chief school officer should also be appointed to office—by the state board of education, in this case. This is the method of selection now used in 17 states, and it has worked well.

The state commissioner of education should be the leading educator in the state, yet less than half the states require any educational or professional qualifications for this officer. He should be efficient, a real leader in educational thought. When such a commissioner is supported by a wisely chosen board, he is able to assume his rightful place as the chief state school officer. The most important educational policies should be formulated by him and submitted to his board for approval or rejection.

State Control of Education

In addition to having the legal responsibility of providing schools for all children, each state also has the duty of exercising control over these schools. As is true with other vital matters, the state legislature has such control.

It is the state legislature, not the Congress, that makes the laws concerning the levying of taxes, the certification of teachers, the construction of school buildings, and the general control of education. In Delaware the state has almost complete control of education, in Nebraska the state has a minimum of control. Between these two extremes are found all degrees of control.

How does this difference in state control manifest itself? In a great many ways, particularly in relation to course of study, certification, finances, school building construction, and textbooks. One state prescribes a definite course of study and all the schools are expected to follow it. Another state allows each school district to work out its own educational program. In some states the textbooks are selected and bought by the state and all the schools, particularly those on the elementary level, must use them. Other states allow each school district to select and buy its own textbooks. There are many differences in certification procedure, some states granting many types of teaching certificates, others only a few. In some states the state alone can grant certificates, in others the colleges may grant them. Some states have very rigid regulations concerning the construction of school buildings, regulations which are enforced by a state architect or building department, while other states make no special attempt to control the type of schoolhouse construction.

State Support of Education

The major portion of most local school budgets is met by taxes levied and collected within the local school district. This does not mean, however, that the authority for such taxation also rests at the local level. The state government has always formulated the basic laws under which school moneys are raised and expended. Even in the prenational period the colonial governments enacted legislation permitting school taxes to be levied by local and county units. The main support for education is still the local school tax which for the school year 1961–1962 provided 56.3 percent of the revenue for public schools.

The schools of the colonial and early national periods were supported in a most haphazard manner. Money was often raised by a combination of sources—such as tax on real and personal property, through gifts and donations, and rates and tuition—to meet whatever portion of the budget other sources failed to provide. Many teachers were "paid" in part with farm produce, the pledging of personal services by citizens, and board and room in first one home then another. Obviously progress has been made since those earlier days, but the struggle to achieve and maintain sufficient support for schools on a continuing basis remains one of the most crucial problems of education. Almost every new session of the legislature in each state finds the financing of schools for the coming biennium one of its most persistent and difficult issues.

Many states have accumulated permanent state school funds from federal land grants and from other sources yielding interest that can be distributed to local school districts each year. However, these funds are relatively small and an appropriation of additional money from the general fund of state revenue is needed to support local schools. State money thus provided to local school districts is distributed in a great many different ways. The oldest method, which is very unsatisfactory, is to distribute the money on the basis of the school census, which usually includes all the children in the district from 6 to 21 years of age. The school therefore gets an apportionment of money for children not in school as well as for those attending private school. The inequality of such a method is obvious. A method of apportionment on the basis of the actual number of children in school is to be preferred over using the school census as a base, and if the apportionment takes cognizance of the number of days taught it is still more just. Most students of educational administration agree that the best method is to pay local districts (1) on the basis of the number of teachers employed in the schools, and (2) on consideration of the financial need of the district. Such a plan would make it possible for all districts to maintain at least a minimum program of education. This is not true in cases where the state takes little part in the financing of public schools. In such states there is no equalization of educational opportunity because some districts have the resources to support excellent schools whereas others find it impossible to maintain even a minimum program. Such inequality runs counter to the basic premise of a democratic society: that every person has the right to equal opportunity.

During and since World War II much attention has been devoted to the state's part in the total program of financing education. It has become increasingly evident that the local school district is too small a unit to finance the total educational program. Most of the money raised locally comes from an ad valorem tax on property which must be shared with the other segments of local government. Some state governments also levy a tax on property with the result that too great a burden is placed on this one source of revenue. States have many other sources of revenue not available to local taxing units—the principal ones are sales and income taxes. It is largely from these sources that the state raises money and distributes it for the use of local school districts. The proportion of the total cost of education paid by the states varies from 4.0 percent in one state to 79.6 percent in another. Each year a larger percentage of the total cost of education is being paid from state sources, and with increased participation of the state in the financing of education has come increased state control over education.

COMPULSORY EDUCATION AND COMPULSORY ATTENDANCE

It was a big step from the unorganized methods of teaching of our early days as a nation to acceptance by all the states of the idea that education is the function and the duty of the state. In the beginning education was financed by such sources as gifts, lotteries, and tuition, and the struggle to establish the present program of education took time. First it was necessary to get people to agree that all children were to be provided for and that the cost was to be paid out of the public treasury. Property owners in the early days objected to paying for the education of their neighbors' children, but the principle was finally established by law and court decisions. Today it is a generally conceded fact that ignorance is the greatest enemy of a democracy and children are educated so that they will be better able to discharge the duties of citizenship. It is felt that the program benefits not only the child but also the community and the nation at large.

Compulsory education and compulsory attendance were provided for by law first in Massachusetts (compulsory education interpreted to mean that every community is compelled to provide schools; compulsory attendance signifying that all children are compelled to attend school). The Colony of Massachusetts led the way in 1642 when it passed a law giving the selectmen of each town the power to provide schools for the children. The purpose was to "see that the children can read and understand the principles of religion and the capital laws of the country." This law was something new and it had great significance in the instituting of free public education in America. In 1647 Massachusetts added to the law of 1642, requiring that each community of 50 or more families must employ a teacher and that each community of 100 families or more must provide for the establishment of a grammar school.

Again it was Massachusetts that led the way by passing the first compulsory school attendance law in 1852. Following this example, every state has passed such a law, the last state to fall in line being Mississippi, in 1918. These laws provide that children of certain ages must attend school, an idea that was bitterly fought at first. Children were needed at home, on the farms, or in the shops; furthermore, it was not democratic to compel a parent to sent his children to school. These and other arguments sound childish now, but in 1852 they were very real.

In a book such as this it is impossible to cover the whole subject of compulsory attendance. It is important to note, however, that the principle has been established as part of every state's program of education even though the ages of attendance and the means of enforcement vary greatly among the states.

LOCAL CONTROL OF PUBLIC EDUCATION

Although the state is the legal unit for the control of public education in the United States, the actual administration of the schools is delegated to smaller subdivisions, usually the county, the township, or the local school district. Each local unit elects a board of education, and this board employs the superintendent and teachers. The local board adopts the budget, levies the taxes, approves plans and lets contracts for school buildings, adopts textbooks, establishes transportation routes, and in general legislates on all administrative problems of the schools. Of course the board of education acts through the superintendent of schools and its actions must always come within the legal pattern established by the state legislature.

The administration of education largely through local school districts is a development within our American democracy that has no parallel in Europe, although most of our educational pattern originated there. This plan keeps the schools close to the people and enables any community to have the kind of schools it desires.

The type and size of the local school units vary in the different states. In Delaware the state assumes a large part of the administration of education. In most of the southern states and in Utah and New Mexico the county is the most important unit. In the other states the township or the local school district is the prevailing unit. There are about 125,000 school districts in the United States. In some states there are more school board members than teachers. However the present trend is toward fewer districts and larger administrative units. Each year a great many school districts are consolidated; the larger units thus created make for better administration and supervision.

Small, incomplete units are still quite common, although most educators are agreed that the administrative unit should be sufficiently large to provide a total educational program of elementary, secondary, and adult education fiscally sound and educationally efficient and defensible. The consolidated or unified district should be large enough to provide efficient administration and to provide desirable special services, but it should not be so large that the patrons lose identification with the schools.

Opposition to consolidation and unification comes largely from two sources. First there are those with vested interests in a community or area who feel that they will suffer financial loss in any reorganization of school districts. There are also those who believe that their own immediate area should have complete control over their own little school. It is not unusual to find groups of small, independent districts maintaining nearly identical and inefficient programs within a small geographic area, each district proudly retaining separate identity while the children struggle along with substandard education. All of this is corrected by consolidation.

COUNTY AND "TRADE CENTER" UNITS

The county as a subdivision in the administration of education can be of great importance. The county is much more satisfactory as a tax unit than is the smaller local district. In states where the local district is the chief unit for school taxes the tax load is very uneven. It is not uncommon to find two adjoining districts, one paying a large school tax and the other a small tax to maintain comparable school systems. This is particularly true in states in which the railroads are taxed by the local school districts through which they run. The county can provide a better distribution of the tax load, for when it is the unit the tax rate and educational advantages can be the same for all districts.

The county plays an important part in education in two different types of school administration. In many states—Utah, for example—each county is organized as a single school district, and all taxation, distribution of funds, and supervision and administration of the local schools is on a county-wide basis. But in other states we find many school districts in one county. Here, the county still plays a part in school administration: there is a county superintendent of schools, usually elected to the office who must deal with all county-wide problems such as the school census, the distribution of funds, the registering of certificates, and matters involving more than one district. He must have a corps of assistants if he is to do a satisfactory job, including sufficient clerical help to be free from the details of statistical reports; and he should also have assistant supervisors to help him supervise the schools of the county.

From the standpoint of supervision, the county unit is more desirable than the small school district, especially when the districts are largely one-teacher rural units. However there is a better large administrative unit than the county. Many states have found it preferable to form larger units by consolidating a group of school districts around a trade center as the nucleus. This is particularly desirable when one part of a county is remote from the county seat but near a large trade center in the next county. In general, if there is to be consolidation of schools as well as school districts, all the families affected should be able to send their children to school in the community where they trade, spend leisure time, and attend church. This type of organization also makes it easier to map out school bus routes. Most authorities on school administration favor the trade center rather than the county as the administrative unit. In fact, there has been no recent adoption of the county unit system, but there are many cases of large-scale consolidation around a trade center.

A comprehensive program of education can be offered only where the local districts are large enough so that there are enough children to justify employment of the necessary teachers and provision for complete services at a reasonable cost. How large a unit is required? The answers vary. The best suggestions have been made by the National Commission on School District Reorganization of the National Education Association. According to its report:

At least 1,200 pupils between the age of six and eighteen were necessary for a complete school program at reasonable cost. This however is to be regarded as a minimum. If possible 10,000 pupils of these ages would be better to guarantee a complete program. With the smaller group it would not be possible to have such personnel as a psychologist, nurse-teacher, special educators for atypical children, librarian, and the necessary health and research staff. However, the smaller unit is just as satisfactory if it can join with other like districts in employing and using specialists in the various fields.[1]

Of course the above recommendations are far from being achieved. In Nebraska there are 3100 school districts, over 90 percent of which have schools employing fewer than ten teachers. Most of these districts have only one school and one teacher and provide no special services.

THE LOCAL SCHOOL DISTRICT

The local school system controlled by the people of the community is America's greatest contribution to the field of education. In the larger systems we find the highest salaries, the best buildings, the most adequate furnishings and supplies, and in general the best superintendents, principals, and teachers. The adoption of larger units of administration in the rural areas would contribute much to their educational program.

Every local school district in this country derives from the state its right to levy taxes, employ teachers, construct buildings, and carry on an educational program. The local school district is governed by a body usually called the "school board" or "board of education." The amount of authority exercised by the local school board varies widely in the different states. In some states it is given almost complete independence. In other states almost every act of the board is determined in some detail by state laws or the rules of the state department of education.

The Board of Education

The local board of education, as it functions in the United States, represents a uniquely American approach to the control of education. It has been said that the local board of education is the most American and the most democratic governmental body in the world, and few would deny the validity of the claim. In countries that do not have democratic control of education the line of authority descends from the top. The superintendent of the local schools is appointed from and by the national government; he represents federal authority. Thus the control comes from the top down, and those most directly affected—the local citizens—have the least power over the local schools. In the United States the functional authority for the local school system is vested in the local board of education, a group selected by a vote of the local citizens or, in a few cases, appointed by elected officers of the city government. In either case the board members owe their position, and thus their allegiance, to their fellow townsmen. The chief administrative officer

[1] *School District Organization: Report of Commission on School District Reorganization,* American Association of School Administrators, Washington, D.C., 1958, p. 321.

of the school, the superintendent, is appointed by the board of education and owes allegiance not to a national government but to the board of local people who appointed him. In this way the control of education in America ascends from the people most intimately involved—the local citizens.

It would be extremely difficult to overemphasize the place of the school board in American education. Although the state holds supreme authority in education, every state legislature has delegated almost all the control of education to local school boards. It is significant that this state authority is not delegated to superintendents of schools, or to teachers or other professionals, but rather to lay members of the community. Public schools are important to democracy and should be under the control of the most able people in the community. Serving effectively on a school board is one of the finest contributions that a public-minded citizen can make. It involves great responsibility, it takes much time, and it calls for the highest type of leadership.

Organization and Operation of Local Boards of Education

Boards of education vary from state to state and from community to community within each state in size, method of selection, internal organization, specific authority, and other attributes. In the 25 largest cities in the United States the number of members ranges from 5 to 15. Some rural school districts have as few as 3 members while other small communities have as many members as cities of 500,000 population and more. Most authorities in this field argue for relatively small boards of education and agree that regardless of the size of the school district, an uneven number, preferably 5 or 7, is the optimum size for best operation.

There are two general methods of securing members for a board of education: election by the qualified voters of the district, or appointment by some official or group. In eight of our largest cities the members of the board of education are appointed, in most cases by the mayor of the city. This is true in New York, Baltimore, Chicago, and some other cities, particularly in the eastern part of the country. In Philadelphia and Pittsburgh the members are appointed by judges of the court of common pleas. In some other cities, particularly in Alabama, Georgia, and other southern states, the members are appointed by the city council. A board that is the creation of the city government is often tempted to mix into city politics, and such a situation certainly is not conducive to furthering the best interests of the schools. In most communities, including 17 of our largest 25 cities, the members of the board are elected directly by the people. Students of educational administration are in almost universal agreement that board of education positions should be elective.

When the members are elected, the following conditions are essential, for obvious reasons: (1) the members should be elected from the community at large and not as representatives of districts or wards; (2) they should be

Future Farmers of America, an organization which is an integral part of the vocational Agriculture Program in the school, grade and cull chickens. (*U.S. Office of Education*)

Left: Vocational education in the form of an automobile mechanic's shop gives many boys the opportunity to develop a saleable skill—and tune their hot-rod as though it were a violin. (*Detroit Public Schools*)

elected on a nonpartisan ticket; (3) the election should not be held on the day when political city-leaders are chosen; (4) elections should not be held more often than once in two years; and (5) the terms of office should expire at different times to prevent a majority of the board from being elected at any one time. Democracy is better served when the schools are under the control of a lay board whose members are elected by the people for that specific purpose.

Most school board members serve without pay, and no recognized authority believes that they should be paid. When there is payment to board members it is always small, usually an honorarium for attendance at the official meetings. Because the best members are women and men who look upon membership on a board of education as an opportunity to serve their community, the payment factor has no significance for the members, and should be abandoned in the few places where it is used.

Not all school boards are vested with the same authority. The greatest difference is found in the relationship between the board of education and the city government in matters of finance. There are two types of fiscal control of local school districts of such significance that a district is often classified by the type it represents, either dependent or independent. In fiscally independent school districts the board of education is authorized by state law to levy taxes or to have some other agency levy taxes specifically "earmarked" for school support, subject to any legal limitations which might

The budget for multi-sensory teaching aids translated into a richer learning situation. (*Lincoln Public Schools, Lincoln, Nebraska*)

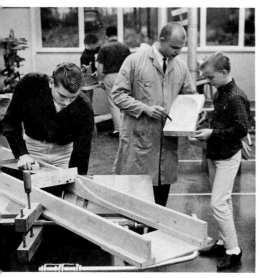

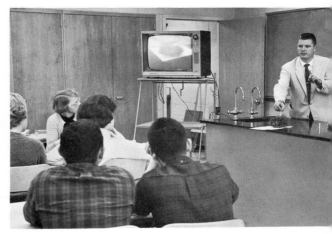

Because their teacher is able to put the sea urchin "on camera," twenty-five students can simultaneously examine its structure. (*Three photos below, Seattle School District*)

A well-equipped industrial arts workshop contains a great variety of supplies and equipment, including many expensive items.

Right: When the biology classroom has a salt water aquarium, the sea can be brought to the land-locked scientist.

exist. In these districts the board also is empowered to spend the funds received from these taxes without consulting any outside agency. Other boards of education, in fiscally dependent school districts, must submit their annual budget to the mayor who includes it in the total budget for the city. The necessary taxes are then levied by the city as a part of its overall finance program.

It is not surprising to discover that a fiscally independent school district is to be desired rather than a dependent one. When school funds become a part of the general operating budget of city government they are often jeopardized by the patronage systems, inter- and intrapolitical party struggles, and the power of vested interests that are more characteristic of the operation of city governments than of school districts. Schools that are independent in financial matters are able to plan and direct a better educational program.

It is not the function of the board of education to administer a school system. The board legislates and passes on policies recommended to it by its chief administrative officer, the superintendent of schools. The most important single task for a board of education is to select a superintendent of schools as the educational and executive head of the school system. It is the superintendent who should administer the schools; it is the function of the board of education to consider and determine matters of policy. For example, the board should legislate on such matters as the construction of new buildings, the opening of new schools or departments, or the policy of salary payment, but not on such matters as what teacher, janitor, or clerk should be assigned to a certain school. The board approves the teaching standards for the school system, but the superintendent and his staff interview and select the teachers who are then appointed by the board upon the superintendent's recommendation.

A few school boards have established a type of control, usually called a "dual system of administration," employing a superintendent of schools to administer all educational matters and a business manager to handle all financial matters by direct authority from the board. This plan has not been satisfactory, and most school systems have the unit type of control wherein the superintendent is in charge of all administrative functions and the business manager is one of the several assistants responsible to the superintendent. Because it is virtually impossible to separate educational decisions from the financial commitments they almost always require, the unit system is obviously more desirable.

THE SUPERINTENDENT OF SCHOOLS

As chief executive officer of a school system, the superintendent must be a man with ability to inspire the confidence of his coworkers. He should have the necessary technical education for his position (and this requirement is being interpreted more and more in terms of a Ph.D. or an Ed.D. from a recognized college of education); he must know modern education, school finance, school buildings; and he should be adept in the skills of democratic leadership and good administrative technique.

There was a time when the superintendent of schools literally "ran the schools" himself. Only 25 years ago it was not uncommon to find the superintendent making the budget, computing the tax levy, keeping the books. He also employed and assigned the teachers, bought the supplies, hired the janitor, kept the fire insurance in force, and represented the schools before the community. The superintendent also was a teacher; he taught several classes, and coached the athletics, and worked with the dramatics and school paper. He was also the counseling staff, and in addition he handled the discipline problems with which the other teachers proved inept.

Today's superintendent seldom has to do all these things. Although the final responsibility, for the school system accomplishing these and the many other tasks of the modern school, still rests with the superintendent, the actual details are cooperatively planned and are carried out by assistant superintendents, supervisors, a business manager, and many others.

There are two basic concepts concerning the proper role of the superintendent in a school system. One was adopted from the military and the other from the concept of democracy. The older idea, still found in some school systems, holds that the superintendent has the same relationship to his school personnel that a general has to his army. His assistant superintendents are the colonels who receive orders from the general, and the school principals are the lieutenants who carry out the orders from above. The supervisors are the sergeants, and the classroom teachers the privates. Such a superintendent envisions administration in terms of "line-and-staff," in true military fashion. At one time when there were fixed curriculums, single textbooks, and uneducated teachers, this militarization was common practice.

Today's superintendent looks upon administration as a basic function of expediting the teaching-learning process in the classroom. He further realizes that a school cannot successfully teach democratic principles if its own operation is totalitarian in nature. The focus of the school is on the classroom, not on the superintendent's office, and the curriculums of the school system—its only reason for existence—are living, growing things. In the modern conception the classroom teacher becomes the key professional worker and plays the major role in shaping the total educational program and putting it into practice. No superintendent today has cause to administer by orders and directives. The community's educational program is planned as a cooperative process involving teachers, principals, and superintendent, and often members of the community and pupils in the schools. A good superintendent leads; he does not command.

THE PRINCIPAL

Each school in a city school system is under an administrative officer, usually called a "principal," appointed by the superintendent to handle the problems of that school and its immediate community. He is responsible for the organization and administration of his school under the general supervision of the superintendent's office. The care of the school, the supervision of instruction, the direction of the janitorial staff, the keeping of records, the solving of problems involving pupils and the community are among his most important tasks. It is impossible to have a good school system unless the principals of the schools are well-fitted for their work.

Teachers and principals work together in providing the best possible educational program for the students in their schools. The principal, as the superintendent's representative, is the actual head of the school, but in any efficient system there has to be complete cooperation and wide participation by all concerned.

THE SCHOOL PLANT

Each local school district must provide the necessary school plant for carrying out the educational program, and since the school plant is conditioned by the program of education, the first step in setting up a satisfactory physical plant is the adoption of a building program and a philosophy of education. Every decision concerning what to build depends on how the schools are to be organized and what is to be taught. The building program will differ for a school system having a junior high school program from one having an eight-grade elementary school and a four-year high school. Therefore the adoption of a plan of organization is fundamental to a building program.

The type of teaching and organization in an elementary school determines how an elementary school building will be planned. In a later chapter we shall examine the various types of elementary school organization; here it should be noted that the building for an elementary school organized on the "platoon plan" must be planned very differently from one for a school having the usual grade organization. Even when there is to be a room for each grade, the details depend upon many educational factors. Some elementary schools provide special rooms for art, music, physical education, industrial arts, science, and home economics. These schools provide special teachers in these fields. However in many elementary schools now being built the home rooms have benches and other equipment necessary for teaching the various special subjects. This means that the rooms must be larger. The planning of a senior high school building is also influenced by the type of educational organization. Does the high school program call for study halls? If so, they must be provided in the building.

In addition to the educational philosophy and the resulting program of organization, many other factors must be taken into consideration. First it is necessary to determine the building needs of the district by making a study of the existing plant and the population trends of the community. It is futile to begin a construction program without considering what the needs are likely to be 10 or even 20 years ahead. These needs can be determined with some accuracy by technical methods that have been developed by student or school administration.

THE FEDERAL GOVERNMENT IN EDUCATION

As previously noted, the United States does not have a national system of education; rather, this country has 50 systems of education. Those who framed the national constitution did not include education as one of the functions of the federal government, in fact at no time was a national system of education seriously considered by the writers of the basic law of the United States. Thus by virtue of the famous "elastic clause" of the constitution, education was one of the functions left to the states. The perversion of schools and teachers that has occurred in countries with highly centralized systems of education is striking evidence of the wisdom of a decentralized approach.

When Adolph Hitler seized control in Germany in the early 1930s the first thing he changed was the public-school system. The task was made easier because Germany already had a highly centralized school system that had existed under both the Kaiser and the republic. It was organized and ready for Hitler to manipulate, and in a very short time the Nazi school system emerged. The books that had been used were burned unless they fit Hitler's philosophy. Curriculums were changed to fit the Nazi doctrine and the teachers who did not asquiesce were dismissed. Military training became a required part of every boy's schooling, and girls were trained to take their part in a Nazi world. Propaganda took the place of education, history became indoctrination. No longer was the search for truth encouraged because truth was not important when boys and girls were to be fitted for life in a controlled world. By the time fighting commenced in World War II, less than ten years after Hitler's ascendancy, the schools and youth organizations of Germany had created a generation of fanatics who believed in him and were ready to die for him.

Even before Hitler came to power in Germany the schools of Italy had been seized. When Mussolini became dictator of Italy the teachers, the books, the curriculums, and the youth programs of the country's schools were all reconstructed in the Fascist pattern. Stories of the ancient glory of Rome and the greatness of Mussolini filled the school books, and children were taught to emulate their leader and subordinate their lives to the will of the state. It took much time and effort after the war to redirect the Italian schools towards democracy.

Japan has also had a highly centralized system of public schools. The children were taught that the emperor was the divine descendant of a sun goddess, and education in Japan was a mixture of religion, emperor worship, and moral training. It produced adults who believed that the greatest aim for man was to die for his country and his emperor.

Nor are all examples of highly centralized, totalitarian-orientated school systems historical. Kings, kaisers, czars, directors, ruling parties, and classes have used and still use a national system of public schools to further their own ends. In fact, usually one of the first acts of a dictatorial government is to slant education in their favor, and any such government that can maintain power sufficiently long to educate a generation of children yields great power.

With a decentralized system of education the specific thinking of the current national administration cannot be forced upon the schools. The schools in America were the same under the Eisenhower administration as they were under Truman, Roosevelt, or Herbert Hoover because the election of a Republican or Democratic national administrator does not endanger the position of a single school administrator or teacher. A new administration cannot change a single textbook or alter the curriculum of a single school subject. In a democracy the pattern of education is not laid down by a national official or group, it grows up from the people. That is why education remains a state and local function instead of a national function in this country.

It cannot be concluded, however, that the federal government plays a minor role with regard to education in the United States. The federal government is becoming involved in education at an ever-increasing rate, and the precedents, both in written statutes and by legal tradition, can be traced to the time prior to the ratification of the national constitution.

First Federal Land Grants for Education

The first support of public education by the federal government was in the form of a land grant, made in connection with the organization of the Northwest Territory. In 1785, as part of an ordinance organizing the Northwest Territory, Congress decreed that the sixteenth section of each township organized in that territory should be set aside for "the maintenance of public schools within said township."

In 1787 Congress reaffirmed its action of 1785 when it passed an "Ordinance for the Government of the Territory of the United States northwest of the Ohio River." This ordinance contained the famous declaration: "Religion, morality, and knowledge being necessary to good government and the happiness of mankind, schools and the means of education shall be forever encouraged." This was the first educational pronouncement of our Congress. Daniel Webster recognized the importance of the Ordinance of 1787 when he said, "I doubt whether one single law of any lawgiver, ancient or modern, has produced effects of more distinct, marked, and lasting character than the ordinance of 1787."

The first state from the Northwest Territory to be admitted to the Union was Ohio. The enabling act for its admission in 1802 contained a provision that the sixteenth section of each township should be given to the inhabitants thereof for public schools. This land grant for public education was continued for the other states carved from the Northwest Territory and later for the states farther west when they were admitted to the Union.

The ordinance organizing the Northwest Territory provided that the sixteenth section of each township should be set aside for the schools of that township. This plan did not prove to be a wise one because in some townships the land was valueless, in others it was very valuable. Consequently, all the land grants made later by Congress were made directly to the states. Thus it was possible for all the schools in a state to share equally in all the land. With the admission of Oregon and Minnesota, Congress increased its grant for public education to two sections in each township, and still later to four sections as in the case of Utah, Arizona, and New Mexico. In 1907, when Oklahoma was combined with Indian territory and admitted as a state, Congress made an additional grant of $5,000,000 to the state school fund in lieu of the usual grant of school land from the Indian territory. Only three states admitted after 1800 failed to receive school lands. These were Maine, West Virginia, and Texas. Maine and West Virginia were formed from existing states, and Texas had made its own land grants as an independent nation before joining the Union.

The granting of land for public education was not due entirely to an interest in education on the part of the members of Congress. Some of the states had already set the precedent. Furthermore, the federal government owned vast areas of unsettled land and Congress was much interested in selling this land and in having the West opened up and developed. The federal government still owns millions of acres of land in the western states. In fact, it owns 98.8 percent of the state of Alaska, 84.5 percent of the state of Nevada, and 45.5 percent of the land in California.

The story of what happened to the "school land" in the various states is interesting. Much of it was offered for sale at once and was disposed of at a very low price; the money received usually became part of the state's permanent school fund, the interest on it being used for the schools. Many states still own much of the land that was given to them. Usually this land is leased and the rentals are added to the school fund. In many western states the land is leased for grazing, in some states coal and iron mines are operated on school lands, in others the land contains much valuable timber.

Some states have made their school lands endow education magnificently, but others have lost or wasted this endowment.

In addition to the land grants to the states, Congress has provided for certain other grants that have been used largely for education. Thus in 1837, when the national debt was paid and there was a cash surplus of $28,000,000 in the federal Treasury, Congress decided that these surplus funds should be returned to the states. Most of the states used the money in the support of public education. At various other times funds have been provided through the gift of salt, forest, and swamp lands to the states. These lands were then sold or leased by the state to provide funds for education.

The latest provision made by Congress for deriving funds for education from the land was the act passed in 1920, commonly known as the Mineral Leasing Act. Under it, the states receive from the federal government a portion of the royalties paid for the production of nonmetallic minerals on public lands. Included on the list are such things as coal, phosphates, oil, oil shale, and sodium.

Each state decides, within certain limitations, what use is to be made of the funds received under this act. Utah adds the income to the permanent state school fund; California devotes all these funds to junior colleges.

Federal Legislation for Education

At the beginning of the War between the States there was a shortage of trained military men, and also of men trained in agriculture and mechanics. The government needed officers to command the army, farmers to produce more food, and engineers to devise and build the machinery of war. So Congress turned to the schools for help and, in the Morrill Act, furnished the money to establish colleges of agricultural and mechanic arts.

The Morrill Act, which was passed by Congress and signed by President Abraham Lincoln in 1862, set aside certain lands to be used by the states in establishing these colleges. It provided for a grant of 30,000 acres of land for each Senator and Representative in Congress. This grant conveyed to the states over nine million acres. The amount received by the individual states for the sale of these lands varied from $50,000 to $750,000.

Some states, such as Colorado, Kansas, Iowa, and Michigan, established new and separate colleges of agriculture and mechanics arts. Others, among them Nebraska, Minnesota, and California, made the college a part of the state university. Before the end of the century every state in the Union had such a college, established either in connection with an existing college or as a new institution. These colleges seem to have fulfilled the desire of Congress, for they have become large, strong, and very important in the educational pattern of America.

In 1887 Congress passed the Hatch Act. It provided for an appropriation of $15,000 annually to each state and territory having an agricultural college, for the purpose of establishing an experiment station "to promote scientific investigation respecting the principles and applications of agricultural science." Such stations were set up in all the colleges that had been established under the Morrill Act. Later legislation vastly increased the money appropriated for these experiment stations, and also financed extension services to be provided by the land-grant colleges.

The federal government continued the practice of spending money for education in the Smith-Hughes Act, passed in 1917. This act provided that the government should appropriate annually for the various states large sums of money for education in industrial arts, home economics, and agriculture, contingent upon each state matching dollar for dollar all the money it received for this purpose. It also set up the Federal Board for Vocational Education to administer the act. Vocational education spread rapidly through the United States after 1917. The fact that 1917 was a war year is important, for the same considerations that caused Congress to pass the Morrill Act in 1862 led to the passage of the Smith-Hughes Act.

Since 1917 many other provisions have been made to help finance certain kinds of education. During the Depression in the 1930s the National Youth Administration and the Civilian Conservation Corps were set up and financed by the federal government to provide education for certain groups of young people. The George-Deen Act brought financial aid to distributive occupations education. Additional funds for vocational education were appropriated by the George-Reed Act of 1929, the George-Ellzey Act of 1934, the George-Deen Act of 1936, and the George-Barden Act of 1946. Present operating provisions for vocational education are contained in the Smith-Hughes Act and the George-Barden Act. The George-Barden Act authorizes maximum amounts which may be appropriated and allocated to the states and territories for each field of vocational education, including (1) $10,000,-000 for vocational agriculture, to be allotted on the basis of farm population, (2) $8,000,000 for home economics, to be allotted on the basis of rural population, (3) $8,000,000 for trade and industrial education allotted on the basis of nonfarm population, and (4) $2,500,000 for vocational education in distributive occupations, to be allotted on the basis of total population. No state or territory shall receive less than $40,000 per year for the first three fields, nor less than $15,000 for distributive occupations. States and territories must match, dollar for dollar, federal funds for vocational education, although of recent years state and local funds for vocational education have been four or five times as great as federal funds.

Financial Assistance to Federally Affected Areas

Many local school districts incur financial trouble because of the activities of the federal government. For example, the location of a large airfield in a community might bring several hundred additional children to the public schools, but land used by the Air Force would not be subject to tax. In fact, such an airbase might take much valuable property off the assessment rolls and thus reduce the taxes in the district. Situations of this kind arose during World War II in great numbers. For this reason the federal government provided funds to construct schoolhouses and pay the operation costs of the schools in these federally affected districts.

Assistance for school districts in federally affected areas was provided for in several laws. Two laws provided for the construction of schoolhouses, and another law made contributions toward the school-operating expenses (in lieu of taxes) in districts that had lost assessed valuation because of property taken over by the federal government. During the calendar year, 1961, for example, some 4,000 school districts received more than $275,000,000 for these programs.

THE NDEA

One of the most extensive programs of federal aid to education was initiated recently when Congress passed the National Defense Education Act of 1958 and in 1961 extended it to continue through June, 1964. These acts are further evidence of the fact that when local and state governments are unable and/or unwilling to provide funds for specific programs which are demanded by the people, the federal government has taken the initiative in effecting the ideas involved. Such was the rationale of the Morrill Act with regard to agricultural education in 1862, the school lunch program, and almost all of the "land-grants" discussed earlier.

In the case of the NDEA, the relationship of education to national survival provided the impetus. Recurring unfavorable comparison of American to European graduates in the areas of mathematics, science, and foreign languages led Congress to grant large sums of money for improvement in these areas and for identification and counseling of superior students who would most probably profit by added emphasis in these areas. The amount of money spent under the various provisions of this law during the fiscal year 1961 are indicative of the specific nature of the act, and are evidence that the Congress felt strongly about the need for improvement in these areas.

The United States Office of Education has estimated that during 1961 approximately $31,370,000 in NDEA funds were spent by the states to acquire equipment needed to strengthen the teaching of mathematics, science, and modern foreign languages. Federal money contributed for state supervisory services for mathematics, science, and languages totaled $2,348,000, and grants to states for strengthening statistical services totaled $1,437,000. Expenditures of $15,000,000 were made to strengthen guidance, counseling, and testing programs, and $6,400,000 was allocated to 93 colleges and universities to conduct institutes designed to prepare 3,129 high school counselors.

Also under NDEA in 1961, 198,000 students in 1,410 institutions attended college with the help of money borrowed in the loan program. A total of $73,845,000 was allocated for this purpose.

Under the program of language development, 75 language institutes were conducted at a cost of $6,400,000; $1,750,000 was awarded to 47 language and area study centers; $2,800,000 was given for 765 language fellowships; 46 new language research and study projects were initiated. Further statistics would be extraneous. The major idea is significant, however: as in the past, the federal government is being called upon to provide funds for the support of the educational process at the state and local level.

Proposed General Federal Aid

In 1949 a bill providing for an appropriation of $300 million for education was passed by the United States Senate but was never reported to the floor of the House of Representatives. This was the first of several attempts to get general federal aid to education. The bill had the backing of those who believed in public education but was opposed by believers in private and parochial schools, and by others including those who fear, or say they fear, federal control. Proponents of federal aid say that it is necessary to give help to the poor states that need assistance in providing an adequate level of education. It seems evident that some equalization of educational opportunity is necessary. The states vary greatly in wealth and per capita income. There is a constant flow of people from rural to urban centers, and people move from state to state. Nearly half the residents of California were born in other states. Ignorance and lack of education know no state boundaries. If we are to have a high level of education in our democracy, the poorer states must have federal aid to enable them to maintain a satisfactory educational program. The question concerning federal control of education was answered by the proposed bills, which made the appropriations to the states and allowed each state to supervise the expenditure of these funds. Evidently federal funds can be provided without federal control of education.

It is not the purpose of this section to make a complete survey of all the educational activities financed by the federal government. We have, however, attempted to present evidence showing that its policy has included aid to education even though we do not have a national system of education. Aid to education was begun before the Constitution was ratified by the states; not only has the policy continued but each decade has shown increased federal aid.

THE UNITED STATES OFFICE OF EDUCATION

There was no office, department, or bureau of education in our national government until after the War between the States, although there had been much agitation for one for many years. The act establishing a Department of

Education was passed in 1867 and was approved by President Andrew Johnson on March 2. It provided for a Department of Education but made no provision for the inclusion of the department head in the President's Cabinet. It created the department "for the purpose of collecting such statistics and facts as shall show the condition and progress of education in the several states and territories, and of diffusing such information respecting the organization and management of schools and school systems and methods of teaching as shall aid the people of the United States in the establishment and maintenance of efficient school systems, and otherwise promote the cause of education throughout the country."

Henry Barnard became the first United States Commissioner of Education and held the office until 1870. He did much to set the pattern that was followed by his successors. It should be noted that the law gave very general powers to the department, with no specific duties aside from collecting statistics and giving advice to the various states. However, this Department of Education was not to last long. In 1869 the name was changed to the "Office of Education" and the next year to the "Bureau of Education." That year also, the bureau was placed in the Department of the Interior, where it remained until 1939, when it was transferred to the Federal Security Agency. The old name "Office of Education" was re-adopted in 1929.

During its 14 years under the Federal Security Agency the Office of Education showed considerable growth, acquiring additional special functions. Since 1933 it has administered the federal program of vocational education provided for in the Smith-Hughes and related acts. During World War II it carried on an extensive training program for war workers and managed emergency schools in war-swollen areas.

Although there has been much interest among educators in the creation of a Department of Education with a Cabinet officer in charge, it was not until 1953 that the word "education" appeared in the title of a Cabinet-level department of the federal government. On April 11, 1953, the U.S. Department of Health, Education, and Welfare was created under the secretaryship of Oveta Culp Hobby. The significance of this development cannot be appraised fully at this time, but we may quote the words of the 1953 Annual Report of the U.S. Department of Health, Education, and Welfare: "At the minimum, however, a voice for education at the cabinet level has been achieved, and the problems—and opportunities—of American education are assured of sympathetic consideration in the highest councils of the Executive Branch."

The Office of Education engages in two different types of activities, the first being the collection and publication of statistics and the diffusing of information regarding our school systems. Information is made available through various publications, conferences, and workshops, and by means of direct answer to some half-million inquiries annually. The second aspect of the work of the Office of Education has to do with the handling of large sums of money for various specialized activities. In 1961 the United States office of education handled and/or allocated $518,000,000.

EDUCATION IS EXPENSIVE

The casual observer is sometimes startled by the great increase in the expenditures for education in recent years, but when these amounts are reduced to a percentage of the national income they become small by comparison. In fact the percentage of the national income spent on education now is no greater than it was during the economic depression of the thirties, and without adequate financing the schools cannot operate as they must in a democratic society.

Schools spend more dollars today than previously for many reasons, including the increased costs of expanded services, the longer school year, and the effect of inflation on the money that the school has to spend. Schools, under the pressure of constantly increasing demands by the public, have added to their budgets such items as health services, audio-visual materials, closed-circuit television, and numerous other costly services which were unknown a few years ago. Better, more complete school buildings are now being constructed and this additional cost must be added to the general rise in building costs.

A few decades ago, the school year was commonly six or seven months long. The 9-month, 180 teaching days, school year prevalent in more recent times is now considered a minimum calendar year. An increasingly greater number of school systems operate for 10 and 11 months per year, and this costs money.

Responsible for the greatest share of increased costs for education is the improved salaries for teachers and administrators (salaries of professional personnel usually constitute about 70 percent of the total school budget). A share of the increase in salary is due to inflation, but the major cause of increased salaries is the fact that teachers today are significantly better prepared and have invested a great deal more in their preparation than teachers of earlier years. Fifty years ago the typical elementary school teacher was certified after completing less than a high school education and passing a county examination. During the same period few secondary school teachers had completed a four-year college program. The bachelors degree is considered minimum preparation for the beginning teacher today, and teachers who continue in the profession most often have completed a year or more of graduate study.

All of these factors, and many more, have added to the financial strain on school districts. Today's education is expensive but in terms of the need for education today it cannot be called "unnecessarily costly."

All of the problems of the schools lead us back sooner or later to one basic problem—financing. It is a problem with which we cannot afford to cope half-heartedly. Education has always been essential to achievement of our political and moral objectives.

TABLE 2. PERCENTAGE OF SCHOOL SUPPORT DERIVED FROM
STATE GOVERNMENT SOURCES

State	Percent	State	Percent
Delaware	79.6	Minnesota	37.9
South Carolina	71.8	Maryland	36.5
North Carolina	71.1	Virginia	36.1
Hawaii	70.8	Idaho	32.6
New Mexico	70.6	Indiana	31.4
Alabama	69.1	Maine	29.6
Louisiana	68.2	Missouri	29.4
Georgia	64.1	Oregon	29.4
Washington	61.6	Ohio	29.1
West Virginia	57.0	North Dakota	28.3
Kentucky	55.3	Massachusetts	26.9
Tennessee	55.2	Connecticut	26.6
Nevada	55.1	Montana	25.3
Florida	55.0	Rhode Island	24.9
Mississippi	54.4	New Jersey	23.8
Pennsylvania	51.1	Kansas	22.7
Arkansas	50.0	Colorado	22.1
Texas	50.0	Vermont	22.0
Alaska	47.5	Wisconsin	21.3
Wyoming	45.2	Illinois	20.4
Michigan	43.6	Iowa	11.6
Utah	43.4	South Dakota	8.2
Oklahoma	42.8	New Hampshire	5.7
New York	42.4	Nebraska	4.0
Arizona	40.9		
California	40.4		
		Average for 50 states	40.1

SOURCE: NEA Research Bulletin, vol. 39, no. 1, Research Division, National Education Association, Washington, D.C., February, 1961, p. 14.

It is not enough to meet the problem grudgingly or with a little more money. The nation's need for good education is immediate; and good education is expensive. . . . At stake is nothing less than our national greatness and our aspirations for the dignity of the individual.[2]

SOURCES OF INCOME FOR EDUCATION

Sources of income for public education include local and county property taxes, state support, and federal support. For the country as a whole, local

[2] Rockefeller Brothers Fund, Special Studies Report 5, "The Pursuit of Excellence," New York, Doubleday, 1958, p. 33.

property taxes account for 56.3 percent of the support for public education, state support provides 40.1 percent, and federal support about 3.6 percent, although there is wide variation from state to state and within states. Personal income per pupil enrolled in public elementary and secondary schools varies significantly also, from a state average of $4,397 in Mississippi to $15,984 in Delaware. Extreme variations from district to district within a state exist, with some districts having less than $100 assessed valuation per child while others have more than half a million dollars behind each child.

State support is increasing in relationship to local support, largely in an attempt to equalize educational opportunity for the children of the various districts within a state. Much of the state support comes from general fund appropriations, although there are many earmarked revenues which are used for education only. The percentage of school support derived from state government sources averages 40.1 for the 50 states with variations from 79.6 percent in Delaware to 4.0 percent in Nebraska. Table 2 shows the state by state percentages.

Even greater variation is seen in the total expenditures for education. There has been a general upward trend in the amount of money spent on education even in relationship to increased numbers of students, as Table 3 shows.

TABLE 3. CURRENT SCHOOL EXPENDITURES PER PUPIL IN AVERAGE DAILY ATTENDANCES BY STATES RANKED IN ORDER OF HIGHEST EXPENDITURE IN 1961–1962

State	1961–1962[a]	1959–1960[b]	1953–1954[c]
1. New York	$615.00	$585.00	$356.00
2. New Jersey	526.00	512.00	338.00
3. Illinois	502.00	457.00	293.00
4. Connecticut	497.36	420.00	265.00
5. Oregon	477.00	448.00	328.00
6. Delaware	475.00	460.00	315.00
6. Wyoming	475.00	454.00	317.00
8. California	471.98	494.00	323.00
9. Massachusetts	450.00	413.00	285.00
9. Rhode Island	450.00	417.00	240.00
9. Washington	450.00	430.00	287.00
9. Wisconsin	450.00	421.00	285.00
13. Arizona	445.00	390.00	292.00
13. Montana	445.00	427.00	316.00
15. Maryland	443.00	415.00	233.00
15. Ohio	443.00	388.00	215.00
17. Alaska	442.52	585.00	n.a.[d]
18. Minnesota	442.00	415.00	312.00
19. Michigan	440.13	424.00	264.00
20. Nevada	440.00	435.00	260.00
21. Pennsylvania	436.67	421.00	241.00
22. Colorado	426.00	406.00	292.00
United States (Average)	414.00	390.00	247.00

State	1961–1962[a]	1959–1960[b]	1953–1954[c]
23. Kansas	410.00	384.00	255.00
24. Iowa	405.00	400.00	295.00
25. Louisiana	398.17	370.00	230.00
26. Indiana	390.00	372.00	252.00
26. North Dakota	390.00	345.00	250.00
28. Missouri	386.17	355.00	232.00
29. New Hampshire	386.00	363.00	266.00
30. Texas	381.00	330.00	223.00
31. South Dakota	380.00	350.00	273.00
32. New Mexico	361.00	365.00	250.00
33. Vermont	356.00	339.00	250.00
34. Nebraska	355.00	320.00	245.00
35. Hawaii	350.00	378.00	
36. Utah	347.00	340.00	210.00
37. Florida	341.00	310.00	214.00
38. Oklahoma	335.00	320.00	235.00
39. Maine	330.00	326.00	195.00
40. Idaho	309.00	285.00	215.00
41. Virginia	302.00	275.00	185.00
42. North Carolina	290.00	240.00	173.00
43. West Virginia	280.00	275.00	175.00
44. Georgia	275.00	236.00	177.00
45. Arkansas	261.00	242.00	115.00
46. Kentucky	256.04	275.00	160.00
47. Alabama	250.00	217.00	112.00
48. South Carolina	232.00	223.00	168.00
49. Tennessee	231.00	228.00	145.00
50. Mississippi	220.00	225.00	103.00

Sources:
[a] "Rankings of the States: 1962," Research Division, National Education Association, Washington, D.C., February, 1963, p. 16.
[b] NEA Research Bulletin, vol. 39, no. 1, Research Division, National Education Association, Washington, D.C., February, 1961, p. 22.
[c] "Financing Public Education in the Decade Ahead," National Citizens Commission for the Public Schools, New York, 1954, p. 55.
[d] Not available.

THE LOCAL SCHOOL BUDGET

On the local district level, proper financial planning requires knowing the various amounts and sources of income and the expenditures that will have to be made. Such information is contained in the annual school budget. A budget is an organized means of forecasting expenditures and revenues—a financial plan for the fiscal year prepared in the light of the educational needs of the community.

The first step in the budget-making process is the assessment of need. Basic and detailed information is secured from school principals, heads of division, department heads, teachers, custodians, and other employees. The actual techniques of obtaining and evaluating the needs varies considerably from district to district, but whatever the specific techniques used it is not possible to provide the best possible educational program within the limits of financial ability without careful consideration of needs.

When the educational needs have been listed and assessed the actual development of the budget can proceed, taking into account such things as the expenditures for preceding years, changes in costs of various items and services, growth patterns, contemplated additional services, and possible reductions and deletions. Items must be well-justified for inclusion, and decisions must be made on the basis of contribution to the educational program.

In the usual school budget the expenditures are distributed so that about 5 percent of the budget goes for administration and 70 percent for instruction and maintenance of the physical plant and equipment, transportation, the payment of interest and insurance, and other expenditures. Local conditions will cause much variation in actual budgeting procedures and decisions. The average expenditures are not suitable criteria for judging any specific situation, but a great majority of local budgets closely approximate the percentages given above.

RELATED READINGS

Austin, D. B., Will French, and J. D. Hull, *American High School Administration*, 3d ed., New York, Holt, Rinehart and Winston, 1962.

Chamberlin, Leo M., and Leslie W. Kindred, *The Teacher and School Organization*, 3d ed., Englewood Cliffs, N.J., Prentice-Hall, 1948.

Educational Administration in a Changing Community, Thirty-seventh Yearbook of the American Association of School Administrators, Washington, D.C., 1959.

Knezevich, S. J., *Administration of Public Education*, New York, Harper & Row, 1962.

Morphet, Edgar L., Roe L. Johns, and Theodore Reller, *Educational Administration: Concepts, Practices, and Issues*, Englewood Cliffs, N.J., Prentice-Hall, 1959.

Puffer, K. H., *How Good Schools Are Run*, Freeport, Maine, The Bond Wheelwright Company, 1962.

PART II

The Organization of American Education

INTRODUCTION

The first section of the book centered around some of the more important ideas and events that formed the foundations of American education. The threads identified in these growth areas will continue to be apparent as the discussion is continued.

The second section is concerned with the various units of the modern American school system: the kindergarten and nursery school, the elementary school, the secondary school, and higher education. Many volumes have been written about each of these schools: what is done here can only be a brief overview of the backgrounds, the functions, some of the major issues, and the significant trends in each one.

In the interest of clarifying the discussion, each of the units will be discussed separately, but it must be remembered that no school operates in a vacuum. The strength of any secondary school, for example, is closely related to the strength of the elementary schools from which the pupils come, and to the nature of the colleges some of its graduates will attend. Each of the parts is an entity, and each bears certain characteristics and has special contributions to make. To be effective, however, the parts coordinate into a larger whole. This total view will become recognizable as something is learned about all the parts.

The growth of American education to its position of eminence in the world today is inherent in the story of America's primary, elementary, and secondary schools, as well as its colleges and universities. Even the very abbreviated discussion that one volume allows should make the student proud of his educational heritage and determined to help continue its growth.

CRITICAL ISSUES
IN AMERICAN EDUCATION

Each of the statements below is representative of an opinion commonly held concerning American education today. Most of them indicate a definite position on issues that are closely related to the topics discussed in Part II of the text.

It is suggested that you follow the same procedure and use the same scale with these statements that you applied to the Critical Issues list preceding Chapter 1.

What's Your Opinion?

1. Systems of uniform examinations given by boards of education in some states should be eliminated from the American public schools.
2. The movement to substitute "activities" for "subjects" in the school curriculum has operated against the best interests of American education.
3. Each state should be free to order its own education without being obliged to heed the decisions of the U.S. Office of Education.
4. We should cease to put emphasis upon education in childhood for the deferred values of later life.
5. College entrance requirements are too academic in character for the good of secondary schools.
6. High school students are too immature to participate with their teachers in planning their own learning activities.
7. The main purpose of secondary education is to train the faculties of the mind: viz. geometry increases the power to reason; foreign language, the memory.
8. Educational experts rather than classroom teachers should make the curriculum.
9. High school children should be given a genuine part in selecting the activities of their school curriculum.
10. By the curriculum is meant all the experiences which children have under the sponsorship and direction of the school, rather than all the subjects which comprise the program of studies of the school.
11. A child's achievement in school should be expressed in meaningful statements about his growth in understanding, appreciation, and attitudes rather than in numbers and letters.
12. Coercion is necessary in schools because a good curriculum calls for the learning of many things, the value of which the young person cannot appreciate.
13. More opportunities should be found for youth to secure work experience.
14. Schools should provide each pupil with more guidance relating to educational, vocational, avocational, and social problems.
15. Schools should present a realistic account of social and economic conditions in their communities even though the picture may not be desirable.

16. The secondary school should be made the responsible agent of the state for safeguarding the well-being of youth until they are absorbed in adult life.
17. The conflict between the elementary school, with its emphasis on child growth and development, and the secondary school, with its emphasis on subject matter, can best be resolved by "up-grading" the elementary school subjects.
18. Only those students who can profit from a rich academic program should be admitted to college.
19. The senior high school should cease giving credit for activity-type courses such as physical education and driver training.
20. Homogenous grouping, especially on the basis of ability is an undemocratic procedure and has no place in the American school system.

The First Infant School in Green Street, 1827. Though archaic in approach, the rudiments of today's activity-centered nursery school were obviously part of the program. (*The New-York Historical Society*)

Below: Mrs. Carl Schurz opened the first kindergarten in America in a pleasant room at her husband's parents' home. There were originally six pupils. (*Watertown Historical Society, Watertown, Wisconsin*)

Illustration in a manual on Froebel's methods. Activity and participation were two main principles of Froebel's kindergarten.

Below: Virginia Day Nursery, 1906. (*Museum of the City of New York*)

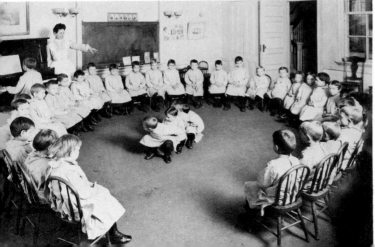

Kindergarten pupils in 1893 were involved in working with Froebel's "Gifts." In these objects he saw the whole material universe epitomized and symbolized. (*New York Public Library, Prints Division*)

Below: Dr. Maria Montessori. Her approach to the kindergarten stressed individual attention in a highly structured atmosphere.

When it's story time in today's nursery schools, the atmosphere is relaxed and the order and attention are natural. (Standard Oil Company, N.J.)

Below left: Someone drives, someone rides, someone pushes—and everyone enjoys the wagon. Below right: Bud discovers gold, Mark scales an Alp, John prepares his space craft to re-enter the earth's atmosphere—and some people equate play with time-wasting! (Both lower photos, Children's Bureau, Department of Health, Education, and Welfare)

Chapter 7 / THE NURSERY SCHOOL AND KINDERGARTEN

PRE-ELEMENTARY EDUCATION

Comenius was a forerunner of modern kindergarten and nursery school educators. In the seventeenth century this Moravian bishop proposed a system of education for young children that would allow them to first enter public school at the age of 6 or 7. Comenius, however, was interested in the type of educative experiences that the children had had prior to entrance into formal schooling. In what he called "The School of the Mother's Knee," he published a detailed plan for mothers to use as they taught their children.

In discussing the age of school entrance and the kind of education that should precede it Comenius wrote:

> In truth, it is no great delay to wait until the end of the sixth year or the beginning of the seventh, provided always that care be taken as has been advised, that there be no failure at home during those first years of this age.[1]

Comenius provided that the mother, at home, should give the child from birth to age 6 or 7 a careful education in "piety, good morals, reverence, obedience, and due respect to superiors; in wisdom, and promptness in action, and distinct pronunciation."[2]

Importance of Pre-Elementary Education

That the proposal of Comenius was well-accepted is attested to by the fact that from his day to the present the most common age at which children begin school has been about 6 or 7. In state after state it has been decreed that a child must pass his sixth birthday sometime in the fall of the year he is in the first grade. The pattern of no organized or formal education for the first six years of a child's life has become common, although there is evidence to show that formal education might well begin earlier.

Educators believe that the most important years in the education of an individual are those at the beginning of life. The habits, attitudes, and ideals acquired during these early years continue to give direction to behavior in adult life, and psychologists often trace the cause of maladjustments in adults back to incidents which occurred in infancy or early childhood. These facts, among others, make the movement to extend the school program to children of pre-elementary age sound, both educationally and psychologically, yet the United States has been slow in providing education for young children. It is true that there are public school kindergartens and some publicly supported nursery schools, but for the majority of children formal education begins near the age of 6 when they enter the first grade.

Why has there been reticence to provide education for young children? Basically it is because the average person does not envision the necessity of early education clearly enough to favor the additional cost of providing this education, and there is no question that the extension of the public school system for one, two, or three years would be expensive.

Historical Background of Pre-Elementary Education

As noted above, Comenius was one of the first to advocate the education of young children. This education, although designed for children, was orientated to adult values, and it stressed piety, obedience, respect, and promptness. His insistence on the primacy of these values marks him not as a modern educator but places him, rather, in the context of the seventeenth

---

[1] John Amos Comenius, *School of Infancy*, Boston, Heath, 1896, p. 81.
[2] *Ibid.*

century. He did, however, call attention to the fact that children should be educated, and this was sufficiently unique for his time.

Another important early contribution to childhood education was made by Rousseau. Rousseau was one of the first to direct attention to studies for the preschool child. He insisted that education for children should be natural and childlike, and said: "Nature desires that children should be children before they are men." This approach is strikingly counter to the obedience and piety desired by Comenius!

It was Pestalozzi, however, who first put the education of young children on a functional basis. In effect he combined the best ideas of Comenius and Rousseau and organized and successfully operated a school for little children. From Comenius and Pestalozzi came the idea that young children should be provided with an education; from Rousseau's philosophy came the belief that the education should be suited to the children. Pestalozzi founded his educational philosophy not on rules and obedience, but on understanding and love. The effects of his pioneer work were far-reaching. It was from Pestalozzi that Froebel got his inspiration, and it was in the Pestalozzian school that Froebel learned the methods which characterized the kindergarten he was to create later.

THE NURSERY SCHOOL

The nursery school forms the first bridge for the child from the home into the outside world. It is evident, therefore, that the nursery school plays a significant and delicate role in the growth and development patterns of the children who attend. The child who has a successful and rewarding experience in nursery school is aided in adjusting not only to future school situations but also to his total extra-home environment. Thus the nursery school years are of special importance in the total educational pattern.

Historical Background of the Nursery School

The first modern nursery schools were established in England during World War I as a service to mothers who were needed for work in defense industries. The first nursery schools in America were founded a few years later. In 1920 the United States Office of Education reported three nursery schools, and by 1930 the number identified by the Office of Education has increased to 262. These figures are probably somewhat less than the actual number of nursery schools in existence at the time because of the difficulty in contacting all possible schools and because of a tendency for many nursery schools to be run on a part-time basis unrelated to any public or private school system. Whatever the precise number of nursery schools in existence in 1920 and 1930, it is possible to conclude that this decade marked the beginning of nursery school education in America. Since those earlier years, there has been much research in the field of child psychology and in the

education of young children that has aided the development of the movement and made significant changes in the scope of the task which a nursery
school undertakes.

The federal government has sponsored nursery schools at two different
periods: during the 1930s when the program was considered as a part of the
social legislation under the Works Progress Administration, and during
World War II when the program was part of the legislation mobilizing the
nation for war. In the 1930s federal monies were provided to establish nursery schools in order to give employment to teachers, custodians, lunch-room
workers and others, and to provide care for the children of families working
for the WPA. During World War II nursery schools were established and
partially supported under provisions of the Lanham Act especially to care for
children whose mothers were working in war plants or related industries.
However, these latter schools were not mere day nurseries providing organized baby-sitting services; much attention was paid to their educational
plans and objectives.

Some nursery schools were operated during World War II by business
organizations engaged in war work, the most notable being the ones set up
by the Kaiser Corporation for the children of shipyard workers. These
schools did much to popularize the idea of organized nursery school education.

The forward push provided by the war-inspired nursery schools has had
significant influence on education since the war. Many of the schools that
were established on an emergency basis during the war have been consolidated with local school systems and are now operated on a continuing basis.
In general, large city school systems have been more interested in maintaining nursery schools than have the smaller communities.

In some cities nursery schools have been developed as laboratory projects
in connection with high school courses in homemaking, while others have
been maintained by churches and other philanthropic organizations. There
are also private nursery schools which are run for profit, and experimental
schools run by universities as a part of teacher-education programs.

The cooperative nursery school has gained favor as a recent trend in early
childhood education. These schools are run by parents under the supervision
of one or more certificated nursery school teachers. In a typical cooperative
nursery the mother of each child spends a proportionate share of time working at the school, thus making it possible for her children to have the experience of nursery school life in localities where private or experimental
nursery schools are overcrowded, inaccessible, or prohibitively expensive.

Age of Nursery School Children

The nursery school is designed for children of prekindergarten age. There
are children of varying ages in the different nursery schools in the United

States, but the typical age range is from 2 through 4. Many nursery schools take children for one year only, when they are 4; others accept younger children and keep them longer. Nursery schools worthy of the name should not be confused with the day nurseries established only to care for children of working mothers during the hours of employment. Day nurseries are not necessarily educational institutions. The nursery school, conversely, is an educational institution, interested in providing for young children the best possible conditions for growth and development. The children in a nursery school may come from homes where the mother has outside employment, but the emphasis is upon what happens to the child, not on service to the mother.

The Educational Program in the Nursery School

The nursery school teacher does not obviously teach. A casual visitor to a nursery school might conclude that the primary function of the teacher is to watch over the children as they play, work, and live together. However, the nursery school teacher is constantly on the alert for learning situations that may arise out of the work and play of the children. She starts where the children are and takes advantage of every opportunity to show relationships, point out a lesson, or guide children's interpersonal relationships into constructive channels. She knows the importance of always being ready to provide a variety of materials, and she helps create conditions that promote growth. Most of the learning situations in a nursery school are spontaneous and their fulfillment depends upon the receptivity of the teacher. Thus she must have a special ability to take cues from the children and mold them into meaningful learning situations.

In her book, *Living and Learning in the Nursery School,* Marguerita Rudolph says of the nursery school teacher as she builds educational experiences: "Her leadership must be sensitive and subtle; and she must have skill in understanding human emotions as well as in guiding intellectual growth and safeguarding physical welfare. . . . The success and the limitations of a nursery school teacher are determined and influenced by her inner powers for growth and learning, as well as by her experience and her training."[3] The nursery school teacher is constantly learning and continuously building an educational program for her pupils.

Relationships Between the Nursery School Teacher and the Children

The personal relationships between the teacher and the child in a nursery school situation can be the most rewarding in the teaching field. Although very young children grow to feel a security in their teacher similar to the security they know at home, the nursery school teacher knows her primary function is to help each child grow in independence. To accomplish this aim,

[3] Marguerita Rudolph, *Living and Learning in the Nursery School,* New York, Harper & Row, 1954, p. 146.

the wise teacher assumes a variety of roles, greatly augmenting the role of "mother away from home." Here is one of the differences between the day nursery and the nursery school under the guidance of a trained teacher.

The nursery school teacher is an arbitrator. When situations arise involving two children she steps in only when it becomes necessary, careful to show she understands both sides of the controversy. She is aware of the needs of the child at fault—if indeed one is more responsible for the trouble than the other—as well as those of the child who is not. The wise teacher does not eliminate all frustrating experiences, but she is always aware of what is going on, without the children's knowledge. She is a guardian—watchful of things that could harm them; she is a comforter—always ready to listen to problems, however small; she is sensitive to the degree of independence the children have obtained, and extends motherly assurance to the more immature. By watching and listening to a child when he is expressing himself in some artistic medium, she can learn much about that child, and she is trained to recognize the signs of disturbance that often become apparent in a simple finger painting or in casual conversation during play. When she becomes aware that a particular child is having difficulty, she is prepared to give him special attention and, if it becomes necessary, reports to his parents and facilitates the process of referral to psychological or psychiatric consultation.

While the competent teacher is being all these things to all the children, her responsibility towards the physical and emotional well-being of her pupils have far greater implications than those which effect only the nursery school period. It is in this segment of formal education that the patterns and feelings about school are initiated and developed in each child. If the student is secure, busy, and happy; if his questions are answered and he is given ample opportunity to explore and experiment; if there are sufficient materials so that he discovers the satisfaction of self-expression; if an ample variety of activities stimulate him and encourage growth; and of greatest importance, if he loves his teacher, he will develop a favorable attitude toward school that will prove invaluable to him as he continues his education.

Relations Between the Nursery School Teacher and the Home

The nursery school teacher has the added responsibility of initiating the records that will follow the child through school. Since she has no previous record to consult when special problems arise, she must work closely with the child's parents. Besides learning about the child through observation, she needs much additional information that can be obtained only from the parents. Through this close association with the parents, she develops a greater understanding of the child. If it is evident that there are problems in the home, she can often compensate for them by giving the child special attention.

The nursery school teacher must be skilled in handling the special teaching problems presented by the exceptional child—crippled children, and those who are hard of hearing, who have poor vision, or who are mentally retarded. In cases such as these a close association between the teacher, the parents, and the child's physician is mandatory. Often the teacher, working with the parents and the doctor, can help the handicapped child develop a confidence in himself that will render unnecessary a continuing pattern of segregated education in later life.

THE KINDERGARTEN

In 1840 Friedrich Froebel gave the descriptive name, *Kindergarten,* to his school for young children at Blakenburg, Germany. His pioneer efforts were to have a great effect on education in Europe and America, but not in his own country—Prussia. In fact, although the kindergarten itself was adopted rather generally in England and in other European countries, it had little influence on education at the time. Education in Europe during Froebel's lifetime was a strict, formal, and largely routine affair. Into the midst of this formal educational philosophy Froebel projected a school for 5-year-olds that was based on songs, games, and pupil activities. The contrast between Froebel's kindergarten and all other forms of elementary education was very great and it is no surprise that Froebel's school languished in such an atmosphere.

The kindergarten was not readily accepted until the emergence of a democratic philosophy of education (such as the United States has attempted to achieve). The progressive movement in education had much to do with the spread of the kindergarten because the spirit of informality and happiness stressed in the primary grades of progressive elementary schools complemented the kindergarten philosophy. It was largely the influence of John Dewey on elementary education that made such a situation possible.

The Early Years of the Kindergarten In America

In 1854, at an educational congress in London, Henry Barnard observed a kindergarten based on Froebel's plans. Barnard was deeply impressed by the possibilities of such a school and published the first American account of this type of school. Because of the influence Barnard had in the educational field, his report created considerable interest in the kindergarten and encouraged the efforts of the early kindergarten workers in the United States.

In 1855, the year following the Barnard report on kindergarten education, Mrs. Carl Schurz, a recent emigrant from Germany, established the first kindergarten in the United States at Watertown, Wisconsin. Because Watertown was a German community, the kindergarten was a German language school.

The Watertown kindergarten was conducted by Mrs. Schurz only until

1858, but the desire for pre-elementary education was still evidenced in the United States, especially in German-speaking communities where many people knew of kindergartens by virtue of their old world backgrounds. It is not surprising, therefore, that the second kindergarten in the United States established in Columbus, Ohio, under the direction of Miss Caroline Frankenburg, was also a German-speaking school. Later, kindergartens were established in other German communities, many of them in connection with academies which were conducted in the German language.

It is significant to note that the kindergarten in the United States first appeared in German communities. The kindergarten was something new, fresh from the fatherland. At that time there were many large groups of Germans living in America who carefully preserved their language customs, culture, and educational patterns and when anything new came from Germany they were interested. Furthermore, it should be remembered that large numbers of these Germans had come to America to escape from the militaristically orientated society of Prussia, and thus the very reasons why the kindergarten was banned by Von Bismark made it welcome to the peace-loving German of the new country.

The first English-speaking kindergarten in America was opened in 1860 in Boston, Massachusetts, by Elizabeth Peabody, the famous sister-in-law of Horace Mann. Miss Peabody was conducting a private school when she became acquainted with Mrs. Carl Schurz. She was so intrigued with the idea of the kindergarten that she turned her attention to this phase of education. After spending the years 1867–1868 in Europe studying the kindergarten, she returned to America to devote the remainder of her professional career to this field. She is especially remembered for a series of lectures on the philosophy of Froebel and his plans for the kindergarten.

With the advent and spread of kindergartens in the United States came the necessity of kindergarten teacher-preparation institutions. The first professional training for kindergarten teaching was given at a school established especially for this purpose in Boston in 1868. The first normal school to add kindergarten preparation to its curricula was in Oshkosh, Wisconsin.

Although the kindergarten has its birth and early growth in America as a private, most often German-language school, it was necessary for the kindergarten philosophy to be accepted and implemented through the public schools systems before it could be available to an appreciable number of children. Boston established a public school kindergarten in 1870, but it was discontinued after a few years, then in 1887 the kindergarten again became a part of the Boston public school system. However Boston was not the first public school system to establish kindergartens as a part of the permanent education program. Credit for this must go to St. Louis, Missouri, where kindergartens became a part of the school system in 1873, largely through the influence of Susan Blow working with an outstanding superintendent of schools, William T. Harris. Miss Blow was a German scholar and a leader in the kindergarten field who, more than anyone else, attempted to put into the American kindergarten all the materials and activities used by Froebel in Germany. In this she failed because the kindergarten of Froebel had to be modified before it could become an acceptable part of American educational pattern, but the influence of Susan Blow was strong in the early years of the kindergarten in America. The St. Louis kindergartens of Miss Blow's were highly successful in their time, and Superintendent Harris also became a strong supporter of the kindergartens during his tenure in St. Louis. Later Mr. Harris became United States Commissioner of Education and in that capacity notably influenced the spread of the kindergarten movement in America. From St. Louis and Boston the value of kindergartens as a part of the publicly supported system of education became recognized in many major cities and communities, especially in the north and east sections of the country.

An international exposition also served as a vehicle to spread the kindergarten idea. In 1876 the centennial of the United States was celebrated by an exposition in Philadelphia which included exhibits embodying new ideas in the educational world. One of these exhibits was a demonstration kindergarten. Thousands of the people who saw it returned home determined to make kindergartens available in their communities.

Adapting the Kindergarten to American Education

The kindergarten was something of an educational fad in the 1880s, and many school systems included it because it was the new thing to do. However, if the kindergarten had not developed a new, Americanized philosophy and new methods, it would have died out as have most educational fads. It is significant to note that the kindergarten had to rid itself of much of the philosophy of Froebel, its originator, to become acceptable. Froebel's philosophical rationale was mystical and symbolic, and everything he did for or with children had some hidden meaning. For example, a group of children sitting in a circle or playing with a ball connoted unity to Froebel. Susan Blow tried to attach these meanings to the activities of children as Froebel did, but such ideas could not be accepted in America. Children played with a ball because it was fun; they sat on the floor in a circle because they could see and hear each other better that way and because they preferred to sit in a circle. The pioneer American kindergarten educators made their significant contribution in the context of their day, but the lectures of Elizabeth Peabody sound stilted and unreal today and the plans of Susan Blow at least Germanic.

Present-day kindergartens are an American product. The current schools have preserved the spirit of Froebel without his philosophy or his materials. Among the influences that have changed the appoach to kindergarten education are the methods proposed by Dr. Maria Montessori, an Italian. Professor Montessori, a doctor of medicine and a psychologist, had great success in developing materials and methods to be used with children of low intelligence. Later she attempted to adapt these methods and materials for teachers of normal children and in 1922 published *The Montessori Method,* a text which outlined and explained her thinking. Her book created widespread interest, and many American kindergartens and nursery schools claim to follow her method, although few recognized educational psychologists would agree that a "Montessori method" actually exists. Her work did add a new dimension to the kindergarten: great emphasis on the mental and physical health of the children, and attention on the part of the teacher to preventive health methods.

The Educational Program in the Kindergarten

The temptation in the kindergarten is to teach too much rather than too little. Children at age 5 are active and eager to learn, but the kindergarten is not the place where formal instruction should begin. The kindergarten teacher's objective is not to teach children to read, for example. It is true that some of them will be taught at home, some of them will be able to read to a limited extent, while others will pick up reading during the year. For most children, however, the kindergarten is not a place for planned reading instruction. Neither is it a place where arithmetic is begun. Children do become more or less number conscious at this age, and many of them will know some arithmetic, but the teacher does not deliberately teach lessons in the subject.

What does the kindergarten educational program include? It includes teaching children to work and play together. Kindergarten pupils learn much about living together, eating, playing as a group, and resting. They like to learn to manipulate things, so they use tools, build houses, play games. They must learn to live safely; they care for pets; they learn much about taking care of themselves, if this has not already been taught at home. They develop a readiness for the more formal work of first grade, such as reading readiness. Health education ranks very high in importance in the kindergarten, and many of the educational experiences are built around this area. Music, in the form of singing and rhythm bands, is also important. The child exercises great freedom in various methods of expressing himself in artistic ways. Finger paintings may appear only chaotic to an ordinary adult but to the kindergartner and his teacher they are basic expressions of ideas, moods, and emotions. The kindergarten teacher is conscious of teaching a total child, and is interested in furthering his development physically, mentally, emotionally, and socially. In the process of achieving these important, varied objectives the kindergarten pupil is a busy, happy individual.

One result of a year in kindergarten is the improved readiness for work in the first grade. Many of the things a first-grade teacher must teach to children who have not been in a kindergarten can be eliminated, for children who have had a kindergarten experience have already learned much about living with others and cooperating with their classmates. This is important in a school, and even more important in the child's development.

BUILDINGS AND EQUIPMENT FOR PRE-ELEMENTARY CLASSES

The ordinary elementary schoolroom building is not suited to either nursery school or kindergarten. Rooms must be specially planned and equipped for these school classes.

The preschool environment usually includes both inside and outside facilities, so planned that they can be thought of as a single unit. There are wide doors on the playground side of the room and often a covered area immediately adjacent to both the classroom and the open playground so that the teacher has three types of environment to use. If the site permits, the floor level of both inside and outside classroom areas are the same and are as near to the playground level as possible allowing for the use of certain pieces of equipment in all these areas. Children of this age are encouraged to play out of doors when the weather permits, and the windows on the playground side of the room are usually placed so that the teacher can supervise activities in and out of doors simultaneously. The playground for nursery school and kindergarten use is most often separated from the play space used by the older children. It often has three kinds of surfaces; a paved area used for riding tricycles and wagons and playing with large building blocks, a grassed area where they may tumble and run and play games with balls, and an area surfaced with sand or tanbark where the sandbox is found and where the swings, slides, and other pieces of apparatus are installed.

The pre-elementary room itself is always something special. A nursery school or kindergarten class must have a room large enough so that several different areas can be developed. There will be a place, both inside and out, where animals can be kept because care of pets is a part of the education of children on this level. There is usually a playhouse or housekeeping corner delimited with ordinary boards or made and unmade by the children, using large building blocks. The housekeeping corner is equipped with wooden "sinks" and a "stove," and, sometimes, a cupboard with grown-up clothes to put on while they are playing house. The third important area in a pre-elementary classroom provides a place for playing active games. In this area is found equipment for a rhythm band, and usually a small piano. For the younger children there is equipment for a rest period. All of the rooms have adjoining toilet rooms, with facilities scaled for the use of the children.

This rather detailed description of the pre-elementary classroom is an attempt to provide a glimpse of the varied activities which characterize a nursery school or kindergarten program.

TEACHING IN THE PRE-ELEMENTARY GRADES

Most of the teachers in nursery schools and kindergartens are young women. There are a number of requirements a teacher should meet if she is to qualify as a pre-elementary teacher. The primary criteria are a true love for children and a positive, not negative approach to directing children's activities. She must have also radiant health, not merely enough vitality to go through perfunctory motions but enough to permit her to take an active part in the endless activities of young children; this teaching is hard work. Among the many other qualities that the teacher of young children should have are alertness, patience, poise, approachability, generosity, kindness, happiness, and open-mindedness. In short, a teacher who undertakes work in a nursery school or kindergarten must be of the finest type.

In addition to highest personal attributes, a teacher at this level must have a special education. It should include study of the human body and all the problems involved in healthful living. She must be able to recognize symptoms of children's diseases, be able to give first aid to children who hurt themselves or become ill during the day. She must be well-informed in the field of psychology, with special emphasis on the growth and development of young children and their emotions and their learning processes.

The pre-elementary teacher must have special education in several varied fields. The program involves music, and most school systems require that these teachers carry a tune and play simple melodies on the piano. She should also be familiar with the instruments and materials used in rhythm bands. Art is likewise important, and the teacher must be able to encourage the creative aspect of the children's lives. She must be an expert in developing reading readiness in the kindergarten, mostly through the language and communicative skills programs. In addition, the pre-elementary teacher must be prepared in such fields as physical education and science.

There was a time when it was believed that any pleasant person who loved children could qualify as a kindergarten or nursery school teacher. It is now known that such an idea is false. On the contrary, pre-elementary teaching demands more preparation than almost any other teaching position.

REWARDS OF THE NURSERY SCHOOL
AND KINDERGARTEN TEACHER

The exacting standards and demands of pre-elementary teaching are accompanied by rich rewards. At no other level can a teacher observe such physical and emotional growth in her pupils. The nursery school child may arrive as a baby, crying and clinging to his mother's skirts, shy and inexperienced and insecure, and he will probably complete this phase of his education a confident, secure, happy individual, ready and eager to go on learning.

There are also the smaller but equally valuable rewards that come everyday: experiencing with the child the glow of triumph the first time he conquers fear and goes down the slide by himself; watching the child, who not long before had cried hysterically when his mother left him at school, come running happily in from the car to start his day at school; knowing the satisfaction that comes from enriching the experiences of the children as they take a walk, examine a bug, or express themselves artistically in movement to music. For one who possesses the special feeling for children so necessary in a pre-elementary teacher, the rewards that come from seeing a child grow, develop confidence, experience the wonders of nature, discover relationships, and gain knowledge and relate it to his experiences—all the wonders of learning—are countless.

RELATED READINGS

Forest, Ilse, *School for Children from Two to Eight*, Boston, Ginn, 1935.

Gesell, Arnold, and Frances Ilg, *The Child from Five to Ten*, New York, Harper & Row, 1946.

Heffernan, Helen, Ed., *Guiding the Young Child*, Boston, Heath, 1956.

Leavitt, Jerome, Ed., *Nursery-Kindergarten Education*, New York, McGraw-Hill, 1958.

Portfolio on More and Better Schools for Children under Six, Washington, D.C., Association for Childhood Education International, 1958.

This illustration from a Lancastrian system manual indicates the extreme regimentation of the program: "Fig. 2. The Book Monitor with the right hand hands the book to the pupil; who receives it in his right hand, with the back of the book to the left; and then passes it into the left hand . . ."

Left: A typical one-room elementary school on the 19th century American frontier. (*Photos above and left, The New-York Historical Society*)

Below left: The arts and crafts experiences in 1900 emphasized the ability to re-create a pleasing model. (*Photos below left and below, the Jacob A. Riis Collection, Museum of the City of New York*)

In the late 1800s, organized charities supported out-of-door schools in poor districts believing they would somewhat offset the unhygienic conditions in slum homes.

The eight students in this reading group have similar reading abilities. Flexible intra-class grouping of this kind facilitates the meeting of individual differences without the stigma of X-Y-Z grouping. (*Lincoln Public Schools, Lincoln, Nebraska*)

The library is the heart of the instructional program of the school, and "Johnny" not only can, but does, read and read and read. (*Photos above and right, Audio Visual Section, Los Angeles City School Districts*)

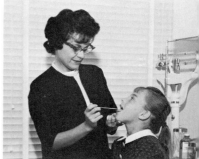

A healthy mind and a healthy body are both requirements for the fullest development of the individual.

Left: An elementary school student council learns about democracy and self-government. (*Seattle School District*)

Chapter 8 / THE ELEMENTARY SCHOOL

HISTORICAL BACKGROUND OF ELEMENTARY EDUCATION

Today it seems incredible that anyone should have questioned the need for elementary education for all young children, yet the fight for free public elementary schools was a long and bitter controversy which began in Europe following the Protestant Reformation and spread to the United States with the first settlers.

Chapter 3 outlined the three general patterns of elementary schools in the

American Colonies—the aristocratic, nonpublic education in the southern colonies; the largely church-controlled, private schools in the middle colonies; and the tax-supported education in New England. As early as 1642 the General Court of Massachusetts Colony passed a law requiring elementary education for children. Another and more extended law passed five years later provided that every community of 50 householders should "forthwith appoint one within their own to teach all such children as shall resort to him to read and write. . . ."

It should be remembered that free public education did not prevail with the adoption of our constitution, but was achieved in slow difficult stages. For centuries only upper-class children in Europe were allowed to learn to read and write; the common people were kept poor and purposely ignorant. The earliest movements to provide free elementary education came with the Protestant Reformation when the newer religious groups wanted all the people to be able to read and interpret the Bible. It was this great religious impetus that led the Puritans in New England to put so much emphasis on education for all children. The 1647 act of the Massachusetts General Assembly is commonly known as "The Old Deluder Satan Act" because instrumental in securing its passage was the argument that the measure would circumvent the Old Deluder because "one of his chief projects was to keep men from a knowledge of the Scriptures." Thus the steps towards free elementary education for everyone were taken first in the colony of Massachusetts. Because education is controlled at the state level, however, each state has a separate history concerning how free elementary schools became universal within its jurisdiction. In Indiana, for example, the fight was led by an educational pioneer, Caleb Mills. In 1847 the legislature of Indiana submitted an act to the voters of that state on the question of taxation for the support of free schools. The vote was taken in 1848 and the free school philosophy was accepted by the relatively narrow margin of 78,000 to 61,000.

To us today, with our emphasis on social legislation and governmental services, the arguments against free elementary education seem narrow and short-sighted, but in an earlier day they convinced many (as is often the case when new social legislation is under consideration). Many of the popular negative arguments were advanced by persons and groups who felt their vested interests were being placed in jeopardy. For example, there was opposition from various religious groups that had already provided elementary schools for the children of their own congregations. Why, they argued, should they be taxed to provide education for other religious groups? The new philosophy also posed a threat to nonparochial private schools. The practice of transferring public funds to private schools was common and these schools did not wish to lose their support, as they most certainly would. A third argument held that free schools—like free shoes, free potatoes, and bread—should be only for paupers. In fact, many of the first free schools were called "pauper schools" and some people believed that free schools would pauperize otherwise good citizens. The major argument, however, held that a man who had no children should not be compelled to pay for the education of another man's children because he would receive no benefit. This was taxation without any return in service, and the contention was commonly accepted as valid until it became apparent that elementary schools were established for the benefit not of parents but of the country as a whole and that everyone profited. As a recent publication of the United States Chamber of Commerce clearly shows, the higher the educational level of a community, the greater its consumption of goods and services and the higher the level of social activity. A nation with an ignorant, illiterate electorate could never have become a functioning democracy, and so the free public elementary school became a part of our educational system.

The pattern of elementary education was much different during the early history of the United States from the pattern today. The imposing and useful buildings now a part of every American community had no counterpart in the early days. Adequate schoolhouses did not exist, and elementary classes were held in vacant carpenter shops, in unoccupied barns, or basements. Sometimes the schools were rotated from place to place to provide education for more children. The school years were much abbreviated, and the teachers were not educated for their work.

The important criterion was to provide some education for all the children at a low cost, thus were advanced such schemes as the "rotating school." The "monotorial schools" were another popular economy-orientated answer to universal elementary education. These were developed in England by Joseph Lancaster and brought to the United States in the 1800s.

The Monitorial Schools

Lancaster, an English Quaker interested in the education of the poor, devised a system whereby a great many children could be taught by one teacher. Each teacher had as his assistants a group of older students called "monitors." The children were gathered into a large room where the teacher in charge would teach a small, unitary portion of the lesson to the monitors who, in turn, would teach it to the children in small groups.

Lancaster was supported by the royal family and other people of wealth and was thus able to organize scores of these "monitorial" schools in England. By virtue of Lancasterian schools, many children who would otherwise have been totally uninstructed received a smattering of education.

The Lancasterian school plans were brought to New York in 1806 by the Free School Society. At that time New York had an inadequate system of church-controlled schools reaching only a small percentage of the children from middle- and upper-class families, the children of the poorer sections of the population seldom received any education at all.

The Free School Society chose the monitorial system of education because it afforded a means of serving large numbers of children on limited funds, equipment, and teachers. A teacher was sent to England to study the Lancasterian system, and a teacher was brought from England to New York. Later Lancaster himself came to the United States and spent the remaining 20 years of his life lecturing and establishing monitorial schools.

The Lancasterian system spread from New York to other parts of the country and in many places was used in secondary as well as elementary schools. It was the official system of education in New York until 1853, when the schools were consolidated with the other parts of the New York Public School system.

The Lancasterian system of education was inexpensive, its annual cost per pupil was often less than $2.00. It catered to a hitherto neglected group of children, brought education for all to the attention of the people, and spread all over the world. However, it was not good education. Few of the results now expected from elementary education were possible. The curriculum had to be fixed, detailed, and narrow because several hundred children taught in one room by one teacher must necessarily study the same things at the same time. Universal literacy was one of the basic aims of the school, but a great many of the pupils never did learn to read and the movement gradually subsided. The large groups taught by one teacher were replaced by schools that employed more teachers, cost more, but did a significantly better job. Joseph Lancaster made an important contribution to education, but not by virtue of his educational method. He is remembered, rather, for his contagious passion to educate the children of all the people.

Apprentice Education

A common form of education in colonial times, and in the early days of our nation, was "apprentice education." It was the practice to "bind out for apprentice education" young boys from families whose parents could not afford to pay for an education. Each boy was apprenticed to some man in a trade who became his master and in all things acted in the place of his father. The period of apprenticeship was usually seven or more years, varying with various occupations. The master bound himself to teach the boy a trade. He was also bound to house, feed, and clothe the boy. And in most cases he was responsible for seeing that the boy received the rudiments of elementary education. Thus thousands of boys were taught to read, write, and do arithmetic while they were learning a trade as an apprentice. This general plan of education was applied to most trades, and to farming, household service, merchandising, and a great many other occupations. In some cases young lawyers, doctors, and schoolmasters were apprenticed to members of the profession.

The rotating and monitorial schools served many children who would otherwise have been denied even the rudiments of formal education; they also had the effect of popularizing elementary education and increasing the demand for free, accessible elementary schools. In terms of today's needs, however, these schools would be considered very inadequate.

Current belief holds that elementary schools should be concerned with the total development of the individual. It must be remembered, however, that there are many other educational agencies: the home, the church, summer camps, youth organizations, and organized commercial amusements. All of these become a part of the total educational pattern of modern youth and the school does not have responsibility for the total development of children. But the elementary school does attempt to provide students with an environment conducive to a broad program of learning. It teaches facts, develops habits and skills and appreciations, and in general prepares the pupils for the society in which they are to live.

ORGANIZATION IN THE MODERN ELEMENTARY SCHOOL

There is no universal practice regarding the number of grades that make up the modern elementary school. In the traditional pattern the child entered in the first grade and continued through grade eight. There are still a large number of eight-grade schools, particularly in rural areas, where one-room schools predominate. The eight-year elementary school is also prevalent in villages having only one elementary school and one secondary school, usually housed in one school building.

The one-room rural school represents the simplest elementary school organization, with one teacher who works directly under the supervision of an elected school board. The teacher has complete charge of the school, teaching all subjects to all pupils, and is responsible for the physical condition of the school. Although the position is one of unusual responsibility, it is most often held by a beginning teacher who receives the lowest pay in the teaching profession. Such schools are gradually disappearing in the process of school district reorganization which brings consolidation of the pupils of several schools into one, more complete, unit. It is not uncommon for a dozen or more one-room rural schools to be gathered into one consolidation.

The consolidated school is organized under a superintendent of schools who is selected by and works under the local school board. If the consolidated system is as small as a typical village school system, the superintendent may also serve as principal of the elementary school. If the consolidation is larger, as is most often the case when one-room rural schools are combined with an existing school system, the new school district may have several elementary schools, each under the direct supervision of a principal. In either case the teachers are concerned only with the children and their education. The problems of supplies, books, finances, physical plant, and general overall administration of the school are the responsibility of the administrative staff.

The common pattern of school organization in city and metropolitan school districts includes an elementary school program of six instead of eight years. In communities of 2500 to 5000 population the six-year elementary school commonly is followed by a six-year junior-senior high school. In metropolitan areas the elementary school most often precedes a three-year junior high school which is followed by a three-year senior high school.

The typical city school system has many elementary schools, each of which has a full-time principal who works under the supervision of the superintendent and, sometimes, an assistant superintendent or a coordinator for elementary education. The teacher's direct contact with administration is through the principal of the school in which he teaches.

Teachers in city school districts are participating increasingly in curriculum development, textbook selection, development of supply lists, and other policy-making functions of school administration. In addition they have the advantage of expert help and supervision. They are usually well-prepared for their job by professional education and experience, and then receive a much higher salary than a rural or small-town teacher.

Intraschool Organization: The Self-Contained Classroom

Except in those districts using the new "ungraded primary" and "ungraded intermediate" school organization (this will be discussed more fully later), elementary school children are organized into groups designated as "grade groups." Thus a teacher speaks of teaching the "third grade," meaning a group of children at that level. In a small school there may be one classroom for each grade, and in a very small school each classroom may contain children of two or more levels; in larger schools there will be several classrooms for groups on the same level. The classrooms can be termed "self-contained" classrooms, a form of intraschool organization favored by most authorities as the best basic unit for elementary education.

The self-contained classroom is so-named because one teacher and one group of children of a certain grade-level work together all day in the room, and because all the educational experiences of the pupils occur within the context of the work of the one room. Thus, each room has a teacher who introduces the pupils to all types of experiences in the various subjects. If the pupils are also to have contact with other, special teachers, the work in these special areas is planned jointly by the homeroom teacher and the special teacher so that it articulates easily with the program in the other subject matter areas. The homeroom teacher studies the background and environment, the needs and interests of his pupils, and plans a flexible program of education in terms of the data he has. This is the oldest form of organization in elementary education, and after trying many other types of organization schools have quite generally returned to the self-contained classroom. The wisdom of having pupils stay with one teacher long enough to feel at home with him and develop a general feeling of security, and the wisdom of having one teacher become well-acquainted with the individual personalities in his group and with their parents, appeals to many educators.

A self-contained classroom should be planned in terms of its many purposes. If the room is to serve as a functional learning laboratory for music, art, physical education, as well as arithmetic, reading, language arts, and geography, it must be conceived and equipped for multiple use. A self-contained classroom must be large, with sufficient space for its cupboards, shelves, and work-tables, and for the more typical table and chairs and chalkboards. It should have display-cases, a sink, an aquarium, and equipment and supplies for art. In short, it should provide an environment that is flexible and well-equipped enough to facilitate learning in a wide variety of areas.

Intraschool Organization: The Platoon

Another form of elementary school organization used by some schools is called the "platoon school," or sometimes the "work-study-play school." The platoon school idea was developed in the early part of this century and achieved widespread acceptance during the 1920s, mostly as an answer to crowded conditions in elementary schools. During the period from 1930 to 1955, however, most of the schools that had adopted a platoon system abandoned the idea and changed to a self-contained organization. Some school systems continued the platoon, usually on a modified basis, because they believed it to be educationally sound, and in very recent years a few school systems have been using a type of organization which is a "modified-platoon" plan.

In the simplest form of the platoon school, the students are divided into two equal groups. Half of them are in homerooms with their homeroom teacher where they study the usual subjects that do not need special equipment while the other half of the children are scattered among the special rooms. At the end of a period these platoons change places. Thus a fourth-grade homeroom teacher may have a fourth-grade group working in arithmetic, reading, and language for approximately one-half the school day, and when the shift is made she will instruct another group of fourth-graders in the same subjects. Thus she has charge of two fourth-grade groups each day. The teachers in the other, special, areas change classes every period. In many platoon schools, these teachers have students from two or more homerooms simultaneously.

The platoon type of school organization enables a school building to accommodate a larger number of children, thus cutting the per capita cost of the educational program. Critics of the platoon form of organization maintain that it is not a plan with an educational philosophy but merely an administrative device. Those who oppose the platoon idea note that it allows little opportunity for coordinating the total educational pattern of the pupils because each period presents a separate educational experience. Another purported shortcoming of the platoon is the fact that the homeroom teacher, with two groups and a schedule which calls for her to be teaching constantly, has little opportunity to study and deal with individual children.

Proponents of the platoon type of organization believe that the great strength of the platoon lies in a superior mastery of subject matter on the part of pupils. They feel that excellence is assured by the fact that (1) each teacher has fewer areas of the curriculum to teach and thus can concentrate her teaching techniques in specific areas of responsibility, and (2) platoon schools tend to seek teacher-candidates with a more highly specialized background of preparation. The rebuttal of those who believe in the self-contained school notes that the gains in subject matter specialization may be at the expense of a broader general education, and that the platoon school gives subject matter a central position instead of being basically concerned with the guidance and welfare of the pupil.

An overwhelming majority of elementary schools are organized on one of these two bases—with the self-contained schools being the more numerous. A prospective elementary teacher should study and, if possible, visit schools of each type. The elementary teacher should be cognizant of the type of school organization he must fit into before signing a contract. He will not be sufficiently prepared to work in a self-contained school unless his own education fits him to direct learning in most, perhaps all, the areas of the elementary curriculum.

Other Types of Intraschool Organization

In actual practice there are few schools that can be considered "pure" examples of either the self-contained or the platoon organization. One commonly-used modification of the self-contained plan provides for one teacher with one group of children all through the year, with certain service areas provided for with special teachers who also work with the students. For example, the library, an important part of elementary education, has a teacher-librarian in charge. The homeroom teacher takes the students to the library at regular intervals where the librarian assists them in selecting books and also teaches them library skills. The program in art, music, and physical education is often operated similarly, or these special teachers may come to the homeroom where their work can be carried out in the same environment. In still other instances, the school system provides for supervisors, coordinators, or "helping teachers" in these special areas, who work directly with the teacher to help her plan the program she follows in art, music, and physical education. In any case the homeroom teacher may be given assistance in the special areas, but it remains her responsibility to organize and coordinate the total educational program for her pupils. For example, a group of fourth-grade students interested in a Thanksgiving Day program would make their basic plans under the guidance of the homeroom teacher, whereupon the librarian helps find suitable books, the music teacher teaches the music, the art teacher helps make the scenery, and the physical education teacher teaches the suitable dances.

Another type of organization in elementary schools is the departmental organization which may be planned much like the daily schedule in a typical secondary school or may be more reminiscent of a platoon school with the children moving out of a homeroom several times a day to receive instruction in special areas. This organization is most prevalent where the elementary school contains eight grades and an attempt is made to enrich the program for the older students.

THE ELEMENTARY SCHOOL CURRICULUM

Although important and interesting, the form of organization of any school is of far less magnitude than is the curriculum. Administration and organization have but one legitimate function—to facilitate the teaching-learning situation in the classroom. And just as American education has seen several, conflicting trends in school organization, consensus regarding the proper approach to curriculum planning has also undergone basic changes over the years.

One significant movement in curriculum construction began about 1920 and lasted for a dozen or more years. In nearly every school system teachers were formed into committees, experts were brought in to help, supervisors and administrators took part. The desired goal was the production of a course of study, in book form, to be put into use by all teachers in all grades. Almost from the beginning the plan failed because it placed emphasis on static, fixed particles of subject matter to be purveyed to all pupils in equal dosages. On the surface it seemed a good idea to have each teacher know at the beginning of the year exactly what he was expected to do for the year, and for supervisors to be in a position to know and help all teachers equally. But the system failed to take into account the differences between schools, rooms, and teachers. For example, School A of a single school system might consist of children from first generation European homes; School B might draw ninety percent of its population from a heterogeneous middle-class society; School C would have students whose homes were bilingual; while School D enrolled children from more expensive homes. Obviously these pupils come from vastly different home environments. Some children attending the schools might not speak English at home, while children in

A good elementary school program meets the needs of all students; the handicapped, the accelerated, those with special talents, and those with special problems. (*Photos left and below, Lincoln Public Schools, Lincoln, Nebraska*)

Below left: The use of a fraction kit is one way in which attractive instructional aids help students give concrete meanings to abstract ideas. (*Seattle School District*)

Like most worthwhile attitudes, safety and responsibility are best "taught" when they can be "caught."

Lunch bags in hand, these third-graders arrive at the school camp. Although a reltively recent innovation, school camps have proven to be such valuable curricular assets that they are being established at a rapid rate. (*Hays from Monkmeyer*)

other schools might have every advantage and assistance from home. Any curriculum built around the experiences of these children would have to vary greatly from school to school, and detailed requirements about the subject matter would have to be modified. Thus the attempt to prescribe a fixed, universally applied course of study for each grade as an educational guide for the teachers was doomed to failure.

When the curriculum was equated with a course of study and when the basic function of supervision was to make certain that each teacher was following the outline and teaching the dictated material at the time it was supposed to be taught, prescribed courses of study led to prescribed daily schedules. These programs were posted outside each classroom and the teachers were required to be "on schedule" constantly. Thus the administrators knew exactly what each teacher was teaching any time during the day. And this was administration at its worst.

Today school systems are writing courses of study, but the current concept of their form and function bears little resemblance to that held in the 1920s. Today it is believed that a course of study should be drawn in large units, not in piecemeal lessons, and that its proper function is to serve as a guide for the teacher, not as a requirement. Each teacher interprets the course of study in terms of the children under his direction. The curriculum is most often conceived in terms of all the experiences which children have under the guidance of a teacher, and the course of study is merely an aid to the teacher as he plans the educational experiences with and for his pupils. What happens to the course of study is of little importance; what happens to children is of supreme importance.

The attention of educators has shifted from producing a neatly packaged course of study to center on the educational experiences of the pupils within the curriculum. There are a number of approaches to curriculum-making in elementary education today, each of which has its proponents. All of them, however, reject the narrow prescription of earlier days.

The Integrated Curriculum

Much is said today about the "integrated curriculum." Its objective is "to develop the understandings and skills necessary to the survival and progress of American Democracy." To this end there is a sequential organization of content appropriate both to the maturity level and needs of children and to the objectives of the curriculum. This implies an organized framework of studies for the elementary school. The integrative core becomes a motivating device around which many of the daily activities are organized. It gives purpose to reading, arithmetic, language arts, and the arts, and serves to integrate the total experiences of a class day. In addition, however, special units of time are devoted to separate subjects. There is much confusion about this concept. If integration takes place, it must take place in the lives of the children as well as in the subject matter. The integrative core attempts to accomplish both.

The Child-Centered Curriculum

Beginning about 1920 and extending through the next two decades, two major developments had great impact on the school curriculum and organization. The first was the "child-centered movement," a reaction against the subject-centered, lock-step curriculum of the past. It was brought into being as a result of the findings of child psychologists and child-study centers. Its proponents made many important contributions to education by emphasizing individual differences, giving attention to the basic needs of all children and to growth and development patterns, feeling a concern for the development of the child's total personality, and emphasizing the importance of "learning by doing." As a result class size became smaller. For example, the annual report of the Chicago schools in 1864 shows that the average class held 81 pupils. Many elementary schools today keep class sizes below 30. Increased attention has been given to pupil motivation and to the relationship of content to the stage of development of the child. The curriculum planning that followed was an attempt to secure appropriate subject content related to the needs and interests of children at different age levels.

The Sociological Approach to the Curriculum

Another major development has been described as the sociological approach to the curriculum. Studies by anthropologists of American class and social structure had a sharp impact on educational thinking. *Middletown, Elmtown's Youth, Who Shall Be Educated,* and other books, clearly indicated the effect of culture and culture patterns on children and youth. In contrast to the child-study movement, this development emphasized the demands of society upon the individual. Coupled with the child-centered movement it led to a concern with democratic living within the school, and to a concern over group processes and human relationships. It suggested that children be given the opportunity to participate in socially desirable enterprises.

Advocates of these points of view have sometimes gone to extremes, but many important changes have come about as a result of their studies. Flexible seating arrangements have largely replaced fixed rows of desks. The furniture is appropriate to a variety of activities: science tables, library corners, art material centers. There is an atmosphere of activity and pupil freedom. The teacher does not stand in front of a group of restless children but works closely with groups in various parts of the room. The freedom is not license, however. Modern education emphasizes guidance and direction to develop pupil standards and self-control. The modern school has great respect for the personality of the individual child, but not at the expense of the group. Many activities are group-centered, and particular attention is given to provide opportunities for pupil involvement in the operation of the school. Student monitors, student councils, nurse's assistants, traffic patrols are fully as important as organized study periods.

Progressive Education

Progressive education in common with most other movements had some over-enthusiastic exponents who went to extremes. Many teachers were not prepared for this type of teaching. Attempts to be "progressive" led to error and confusion, and thus to some unfortunate beliefs about the nature of "progressive education." At one time it was a very respectable expression, but misuse of the philosophy of progressive education has clouded its meaning. It is easiest to tell what it is not. It is not education in which the teacher follows the passing whims of the children, it is not education without a plan and without direction. It is education in which the growth of the child is more important than any area of subject matter. Much of the material in this chapter concerning the modern conception of the curriculum is progressive education at its best. The teacher is a planner, a guide, and a member of the group she is teaching. The sound features of progressive education have become an almost universal part of the modern elementary school.

All elementary schools are progressive in the earliest grades. The nursery school and the kindergarten demonstrate progressive education in its best form, for, as we have seen, the child is the center of all consideration. The school is interested in his health and in how he behaves as a human being. There is constant activity; the children are happy. There is no fixed subject matter to be taught. The three grades that make up the primary school are also usually progressive. But the higher grades tend to become more formal and freedom is curtailed. However, this is not necessary. The really modern school carries the freedom and activity of the lower grades through all the grades above.

INDIVIDUAL DIFFERENCES

Ever since the time of Plato it has been recognized that children have different capabilities for learning. The nature and extent of these differences have been little understood until recently. In 1916 Dr. Lewis M. Terman of Stanford University published his epoch-making book on the measurement of intelligence and the Stanford Revision of the Simon-Binet tests. It then became possible to measure the academic aptitude of children. The tests, however, could be given only to individuals and only by a person trained in the technique. A few years later, group intelligence tests were developed that made it possible to measure all the members of a class at one time.

The true extent of individual differences is somewhat amazing. Typical classrooms of elementary-school children will have one or two individuals in the near-genius or genius class and one or two at the other extreme who are classed as dull-normal or of borderline intelligence, capable of little academic achievement. Between these extremes will be the rest of the class. The differences are largely in academic aptitude. In addition there are tremendous differences in physical condition, in motor development, in social maturity, in family background, in aptitudes for various creative arts, in emotional stability, and in many other attributes.

Differences which children have when they start school are increased with good teaching. For example, the range in reading ability at first grade is about three years. At grade six some individuals may test at a ninth- or tenth-grade level while others are operating at a second-grade reading level. The majority of the class will range from fourth- through seventh-grade reading ability as measured by standardized reading tests. The range in arithmetic is similar. By grade eight the typical arithmetic range extends from third grade through twelfth as measured by standardized achievement tests.

Few parents and not all teachers are aware that these differences are perfectly normal and exist in all classes. The influence of our European background (in Europe, examinations are the basis for promotion in all schools) makes it difficult if not impossible for many people to accept the fact that a child who is below grade-level on the tests can still be making good progress.

It is in this great variety of talents and abilities that the uniqueness of the American culture stands out. Each child is accepted for what he is. He is provided with the maximum opportunity to develop his particular array of talents. Thus the schools make a unique contribution to the development of children whether they become athletes or scholars, scientists or musicians, clerks or business managers.

Ability Grouping

The nature and extent of individual differences have created one of the major organization problems of the American school, and there has been an endless variety of attempts to perfect a form of grouping pupils which will alleviate the problem of providing for these differences. As tests became easier to administer, grouping became an educational vogue. One of the first and simplest plans was known as the "XYZ system." Schools which used this method divided the students into groups on the basis of intelligence-test scores and each group proceeded at its own rate. The learning of academic subjects, particularly in the highest-ability groups, was well-served by this plan, however, most educators doubt whether this constitutes a good type of education. It has been attacked as being undemocratic because it deprives pupils of the opportunity to work and live with all kinds of people and because children and their parents resent the implications of being classified in the second or third caste. XYZ grouping is also opposed as being deceivingly simple. The learning process is not as easily served as the plan implies, and because of parental aspiration and personal motivation, some children are led to strive for higher standards than they can achieve, while others of apparently equal academic aptitude achieve far below their potential.

The greatest fallacy of XYZ grouping is enhanced by the name which is often given it—"homogenous grouping." This term implies that each of the groups are unitary and are composed of pupils of equal or almost equal ability. The fact is that grouping pupils on the basis of any single criterion, including abstract intelligence, may "ungroup" them so far as physical, social, or chronological age is concerned. They present a heterogenous set of abilities to the teacher in all areas except the one in which they were grouped, yet the teacher presupposes a homogenous group and does little to provide for individual differences. Therefore, the very reason for which the grouping was done is ignored.

A great many schools have experimented with XYZ grouping and have discontinued it. A few school systems still use it, some because it provides a convenient way of isolating members of a minority group without having to answer to the charge of racial or socioeconomic discrimination. These are not acceptable bases for educational decisions.

To replace XYZ grouping, many schools have organized classes on the basis of chronological age and physical and social maturity. Each child is placed in an environment conducive to maximum growth in all areas—academic, social, emotional. More recently, schools have experimented with a system which obliterates grade-level designations for the first three years of school. Under this plan the first three grades constitutes an "ungraded primary school," and individual differences are provided for by organizing a variety of subgroups for instruction in the several subjects. Reading instruction, for example, is sometimes divided into as many as 50 ability-level groups. Students move from one subgroup to another with relative ease and are "promoted" out of the primary school whenever they demonstrate readiness to go on, or when it becomes apparent that further time in this unit would fail to promote maximum growth. Most students, to be sure, complete the primary school in the typical three years, but some are ready for promotion in two years, while others can profit by spending four years before going on to "fourth-grade." With the stigma of barely passing (or of failing three separate grades) removed, the psychological barriers to learning are significantly lowered.

Almost all elementary school classrooms use the instructional or subgroups method of meeting individual differences. The number of these groups in any particular subject will depend upon the nature of the differences within the class. The typical number of these groups is from two to four, and membership in each group and in each subject is determined by the pupil's ability in the subject. A few teachers are able to make their teaching completely individual, but more often the class size and the range of abilities make this type of teaching impossible.

Special Education for Exceptional Children

Exceptional children may be classified into three groups: the mentally different, the physically deviant, and the emotionally disturbed. The mentally different group includes the gifted as well as the mentally retarded. The physically deviant includes those with orthopedic, visual, auditory, and speech deviations. While many of these children are educated in small special classes, the majority are still enrolled in the regular classrooms of the public school. Teachers and administrators often fail to identify these exceptional children. Handicapping conditions, particularly those with no visible signs, may go on for years. Often they are the cause of serious learning and behavior problems.

Three types of program have been developed to meet the needs of these special groups.

1. *Cooperative.* The child carries on part of his work in the regular classroom but receives special help and/or instruction. For example, a speech therapist may take a child for instruction two periods a week.

2. *Segregated.* The child carries on his educational program in a special classroom. Many school systems maintain special rooms for children with health problems. Much attention is given to open-air classrooms, rest periods, and special lunches. Some schools have special rooms for children with poor hearing or faulty vision. Special rooms and special schools are sometimes provided for crippled children and the cerebral palsied, with furniture and equipment particularly suited to the needs of these children.

3. *Integrated.* The child in a rural area participates in the regular classroom and is also served by a visiting teacher. The recent trend is to segregate the mentally retarded and certain types of physically handicapped children, and to assimilate other types of deviants into regular classrooms whenever possible.

Many states require special credentials for teachers in these various fields. Anyone contemplating service in these areas should plan for special preparation. There is a great shortage of teachers equipped to teach these deviant groups of children who have more than their share of problems both emotional and physical. Teaching them can be a great challenge.

Promotion and Grades

The problem of promotion and grades was easily solved in the days when there was a fixed course of study for each grade. The teacher spent the year teaching it. At regular intervals she examined the children to find out how much of the subject matter they had memorized or otherwise learned. At the end of each month she sent home a report card expressing in percentages or letters how well each child was progressing in mastering the course of study. At the end of the year those who did not completely grasp the necessary subject matter failed, and the next year they went over it again in the same way in the hope that they would learn it on this second journey. That was elementary education during the early history of public education in America.

Today even in schools that do not consider themselves progressive the above type of education is not found. Gone are the midyear promotions that were necessary when the schools wanted to rush children through. Some elementary schools use no report cards. Children should be graded, if it is necessary to grade them, according to achievement on the basis of their individual possibilities or capacities.

Many schools today make an effort to keep children of the same social age together. Children seldom repeat a grade and are seldom given double promotions. This helps solve the problem of the misfit brilliant children who rush through the subject matter and soon find themselves in a group that they do not fit in physically or socially. On the other hand it keeps the lower grades free from "overgrown boys and girls who do not fit the seats." To sum up, few grades are repeated and few are skipped in the modern elementary school. Promotion each year is the accepted practice.

The function of the elementary school in America is to develop good citizens in a democracy. Democracy is a way of life. It is caught, not taught. If a child is to live successfully in a democratic society as an adult, he must begin by living in a democratic elementary school. There he learns the techniques of a democracy by living in an atmosphere in which the individual is important and each must share with others the responsibilities of group living.

The Expanding Curriculum of the Elementary School

The history of the American elementary school is one of growth in several dimensions. The elementary school has expanded not only in size and number to include practically all of the children in America but also in scope and nature of services rendered. The school of colonial America was established to teach reading. The modern elementary school not only teaches reading, writing, and arithmetic as well as other subjects but also provides health services, hot-lunch programs, guidance clinics, library facilities, and recreational programs and serves as a community activity center. The American public has demanded the continuance of many programs which were started on a trial basis. The kindergarten, the hot-lunch program, the guidance services are impressive evidence of this fact. The American public wants the best for its children.

Good schools are continually trying out new practices. For example, a few school systems have an outdoor education program as part of the regular school year, carried on in school camps. A great deal of emphasis is placed on conservation education and natural resources. Educators have discovered that learning is not restricted to the school classroom.

Another of the newer practices is the teaching of foreign language to elementary-school children. The major emphasis is on conversational ability and an increased understanding of the people who use the language. Most elementary schools are also teaching the "new" or "modern" mathematics, a program which will call for special preparation from the teacher.

THE ELEMENTARY SCHOOL TEACHER

Teaching in the elementary school is one of the most important positions in a school system. Here is congregated a cross-sectional representation of the community, and here the first phases of formal preparation for citizenship are begun. Much of what a person eventually becomes is determined during the years spanned by elementary education, and the classroom teacher, because she gives major direction to the pattern of living as far as the schooling is concerned, plays a prime role in determining children's attitudes. Because of the importance of these formative years, the attributes which elementary teachers must exhibit are demanding. The competent teacher of young children must be an intelligent, well-balanced individual with a functional cultural background and specific preparation for her job. She must also be aware of the great responsibility she has.

The required professional preparation for elementary teaching has become consistently more stringent in the past 50 years. Forty years ago the average elementary-school teacher was a graduate of a two-year normal school. Today most states require a minimum of four years of college education—divided among the areas of general education, professional education, and in some cases specialized work in a single academic discipline. Some states require a year of graduate study as a qualification for a permanent certificate, and several colleges and universities have structured their initial period of elementary-teacher preparation in terms of a five-year program. It has long been recognized that it is impossible to provide the comprehensive preparation necessary for modern teaching in four years.

The Five-Year Training Program

A typical five-year program of preparation for elementary-school teachers includes one year of graduate study. Students for the program are selected at the end of their sophomore year, and since there are usually more applications than there are places in the program, the students must be selected with some care. Such things as the ability to do university work as evidenced by grade-record, personality, ability to get along with people, experience with children, and other factors are taken into account in making the selection. In the program of studies shown in Table 4, beginning with the sophomore year an effort is made to combine a broad general education with the necessary professional preparation for teaching.

The question concerning the length of time a student should spend in preparation for teaching is difficult to answer. Certainly no one should teach who has not had at least four years of preparation, and perhaps five.

TABLE 4.   A SAMPLE FIVE-YEAR PROGRAM FOR ELEMENTARY TEACHERS

Sophomore		Junior		Senior		Graduate	
Subject	Hours	Subject	Hours	Subject	Hours	Subject	Hours
Sociology	5[a]	Educational Psychology	5	Educational Sociology	5	Student Teaching	24
						Curriculum	6
Introduction to Music	3	Child Psychology	4	Audio Visual Education	1		
Art	2	Observation in Elementary School	4	Curriculum	8	Guidance	3
General Psychology	5	School Camping	1	Electives		Electives	
Introduction to Education	3	Clinical Observation	3				
Political Science	5	Art in Elementary School	4				
Electives		Nursery School Practice	3				
		Elementary School Physical Education	4				
		Speech	3				
		Electives					

[a] All hours shown are "quarter" hours.

Although a five-year program of pre-service education for elementary teachers is highly desirable, most programs are four years in length. The following program is typical of these four-year programs.

A SAMPLE FOUR-YEAR CERTIFICATE PROGRAM FOR ELEMENTARY TEACHERS

I. General Education:
   A minimum of 60 semester hours in general education is required, distributed as follows:

A. Language Arts:
   Minimum requirement of 15 semester hours, distributed as follows:

Area	Minimum Hours
1. Written composition	5
2. Speech	3
3. Literature	3

B. Social Science:
   Minimum requirement of 12 semester hours exclusive of legally-required state History, distributed as follows:

Area	Minimum Hours
1. American History and Government	6
2. Sociology	3
3. Economics	3

   Note: State History requirement may be fulfilled by high school course (Grades 9–12) by college course, History 162, or by passing State examination.

C. Mathematics:
   Minimum requirement of 3 semester hours:

Area	3
1. Mathematics	Minimum Hours

D. Science:
   Minimum requirement of 12 semester hours, distributed as follows:

Area	Minimum Hours
1. Biological Science	3
2. Geography	3
3. Physical Science	3

E. Fine Arts:
   Minimum requirements of 4 semester hours from any one or more of the following areas, distributed as the student wishes:

Area	Minimum Hours
1. Music	
2. Art	
3. Drama	

F. Health and Physical Education:
   Minimum requirement of 5 semester hours, including 2 semester hours activity courses.

G. Humanities:
   Minimum requirement of 4 semester hours.

H. Foreign Languages ⎫
I. Practical Arts ⎬ :
   Minimum requirement of 4 semester hours if either is chosen to complete 60 hour requirement.

J. Psychology—which may include courses in child growth and development:
   Minimum requirement of 4 semester hours.

II. Specialized Subject Matter:
   Minimum requirement of 25 semester hours, distributed as follows:

Area	Minimum Hours
A. Music Education	2
B. Health, Physical Education and Recreation	2
C. Library Science	2
D. Children's Literature	3
E. Arts and Crafts in the Elementary School Curriculum	3
F. Reading and Language Arts in the Elementary School Curriculum	4
G. Social Studies in the Elementary School Curriculum	3
H. Science in the Elementary School Curriculum	2
I. Mathematics in the Elementary School Curriculum	2
J. Utilization of Audio Visual Materials	2

III. Professional Education:
   Minimum requirement of 21 semester hours, distributed as follows:

Area	Minimum Hours
A. The School in American Society	3
B. Child and Adolescent Psychology	3
C. Educational Psychology	3
D. Evaluation in the Elementary School Curriculum	2
E. Student Teaching	7
F. History and Philosophy of Education	3

IV. Area of Concentration:
   An area of concentration consisting of a minimum of 21 semester hours must be completed in one of the following areas: English, Social Studies, Science, Mathematics, Music, Art, Health and Physical Education, Foreign Language.

   At least 6 hours of the minor must be upper division work. A maximum of 10 hours from areas I and II above may be counted as part of the minor.

   Grade point requirement in area I is 2.3, based on 4.0 for an "A," and that for areas II and III is 2.5. Minimum hours for graduation will be 128 hours with at least 80 hours from general education and supporting subject matter fields.

RELATED READINGS

Goodlad, John I., and Robert H. Anderson, *The Nongraded Elementary School,* New York, Harcourt, Brace & World, 1962.

Herrick, Virgil E., and others, *The Elementary School*, Englewood Cliffs, N.J., Prentice-Hall, 1956.

Klausmeier, Herbert J., and others, *Teaching in the Elementary School*, New York, Harper & Row, 1956.

Lambert, Hazel M., *Elementary Education*, Washington, D.C., The Center for Applied Research, 1963.

Ragan, W.B., *Modern Elementary Curriculum: Revised Edition*, New York, Holt, Rinehart and Winston, 1960.

Warner, Ruby F., *Elementary School Teaching Practices*, Washington, D.C., The Center for Applied Research, 1962.

The main hall of the Boston Latin Grammar School, 1877. Among its students were Benjamin Franklin, John Hancock, Samuel Adams, Ralph Emerson, Cotton Mather, and Henry Beecher. Small wonder these schools were called the cradle of American democracy.

Below: America's first coeducational high school, Chicago, 1856. (*Chicago Historical Society*)

"Vocational education," *circa* 1874.

Under the careful supervision of their student teacher, these junior high school boys put the finishing touches on an ambitious group project. (*Illinois State University*)

Below: In September, 1910, all seventh grade pupils in Richmond, Indiana, were transferred to this building which was renamed Garfield Junior High School. Thus began what was probably America's first junior high school. (*Richmond Community Schools, Richmond, Indiana*)

The resources of the local community can often serve as "classrooms" for today's secondary schools. (*Board of Education, St. Louis*)

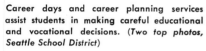

Career days and career planning services assist students in making careful educational and vocational decisions. (*Two top photos, Seattle School District*)

Above *right:* Pupils in this classroom study mathematics. They take the responsibility for checking and recording their own progress, and for choosing materials for study which are suited to their ability level.

Right: "Make a joyful noise and rejoice, oh my soul." In addition to their intrinsic values, experiences in art, music, and physical education bring a welcome variety to the school day. (*Board of Education, St. Louis*)

Chapter 9 / SECONDARY EDUCATION

FAITH IN OUR SCHOOLS

America's modern comprehensive secondary schools represent this nation's major educational contribution to civilization. Although many other countries provide some type of education beyond the elementary school, only the United States has undertaken to provide this amount of education for all youth. Our secondary schools serve pupils which represent all degrees of social, intellectual, and economic levels, and thus are uniquely a product of American, democratic thinking.

The faith which the people of the United States have in the value and necessity of education is epitomized in their continuing and increasing support of secondary schools, which enrolled at least 5,000,000 students in 1930, more than 9,500,000 in 1950, and on the basis of current elementary school populations will provide educational opportunity for approximately 19,000,-000 in 1970. It is not surprising that these schools have been characterized as "the people's college," that in most communities the secondary schools are among the most significant focal points of the community.

HISTORICAL BACKGROUND OF SECONDARY EDUCATION

To understand the American secondary school as it exists today it is necessary to examine the history of the development of secondary education. As in the case of the struggle to provide universal elementary education, the battle to establish and maintain the kind of secondary education imperative in a democracy has been long and sometimes bitter. Few people ever seriously doubted the value of secondary education, but many who admitted that a democracy demanded free, accessible elementary schools resisted the taxation which could provide secondary education on a similar basis. Therefore, free public education on the secondary level did not become an actuality until many years after it was achieved in the elementary school. The history of secondary education in the United States begins with the establishment of private, Latin grammar schools.

The Boston Latin Grammar School

The first secondary school in America was founded in Boston, Massachusetts, in 1635, only 15 years after the original settlement of the Massachusetts Bay Colony. As was true in the case of elementary schooling, the desire for improved religious education provided the impetus for the Boston Latin Grammar School. Not only did the Puritans intend that every man should read and interpret the Bible, but also they proposed a secondary school which would prepare boys for college and the theological education which would supply ministers for the community.

St. Paul's school, founded in England more than a century prior to the establishment of the Boston school, was the prototype of the early secondary schools in America. Such Latin schools were common in England and on the Continent in 1635. At first these schools were established for the purpose of teaching the reading and fluent use of the Latin language. Until well into the sixteenth century Latin was the common professional language, and mastery of Latin was a necessity to the educated and professional man. Later, as Latin became less functional, the teaching turned from a communicative approach to an emphasis on the mastery of Latin grammar for its supposed cultural and mind-training value. Few students ever mastered Latin as a language, or were even encouraged to do so. Nevertheless, Latin remained the cornerstone of the program in these schools, and the Boston Latin Grammar School continued to follow the precedent.

The curriculum of the Latin grammar school was extremely restricted, consisting mainly of Latin, Greek, and literature. The aims and objectives of the school were equally narrow. It was not a free public school, it was for boys only, its students were carefully selected from a list of applicants, and it catered to the intellectual and social elite. The Latin grammar schools were financed by tuition, donations, taxation, lotteries, legacies, and other means. They were in no way connected with the rapidly expanding concept of American democracy; on the contrary, they were faithful copies of the aristocratic society of Europe. Most of the teachers in these schools had prepared themselves in similar schools in England.

The Latin grammar schools were the only secondary schools in America for more than a century, a fact which is impressive evidence of their acceptance by most people. Yet, these schools had little influence in shaping the early development of the nation. As the years went by, they became more and more isolated from the important affairs of life, and eventually ceased to exist except in a few isolated instances.

The basic reason for the demise of the Latin grammar schools as a force in American education was their apparent inability or unwillingness to alter their philosophy or practices to fit the nation of which they were a part. They failed to make adjustments to changing social needs, and persisted with a narrow program when the developing country demanded that a much broader curriculum be offered to a far greater number of young people. Since they refused to yield to the new demands, they were gradually superseded by a new development in secondary education, the academy, which made a more liberal program available to a significantly larger segment of the population.

Franklin's Academy

The first academy was established in Philadelphia in 1749, largely through the efforts of Benjamin Franklin. This academy later became the College and Academy of Philadelphia, and still later the University of Pennsylvania.

Like many other colonial leaders, Franklin was distressed because education had been neglected in the colonies despite the fact that many colonists had been well-educated in Europe. Franklin was familiar with the system of academies of England. He knew much about their educational program and was determined to establish an academy in Philadelphia as early as 1743. It was his hope that Pennsylvania might take the lead in providing education for its people, and in addition to his interest in the academy he noted that Massachusetts, Connecticut, New Jersey, and Virginia had already established colleges. Undoubtedly the pressure of other important duties kept Franklin from effecting his educational plans for Pennsylvania earlier.

Franklin wrote in his diary, "I turned my thoughts again to the affair of establishing an academy. The first step I took was to associate in my design a number of active friends . . . the next was to write and publish a pamphlet, entitled 'Proposals Relating to the Education of Youth in Pennsylvania.' "[1]

His next move was to institute a subscription drive "for opening and supporting an academy." He asked the donors to pledge specific amounts per year for five years to assure the academy continuous support for its beginning years.

After the money had been pledged, the subscribers met and elected 24 of their number as trustees of the proposed academy. They appointed Benjamin Franklin and Mr. Francis, then Attorney General of Pennsylvania, to formulate the constitution for the government of the academy. Finally, the trustees hired masters, took over the building of the old "Charity School" which had been established in 1740, and elected Benjamin Franklin as the first president of the Academy, a position he held from 1749 until 1756.

Franklin's ideas of an academy included a highly definitive statement of the program of studies which seemed important to him:

As to their studies, it would be well if they could be taught everything that is useful and everything that is ornamental. But art is long and their time is short. It is therefore proposed that they learn those things that are likely to be most useful and most ornamental, regard being had to several professions for which they are intended.

All should be taught to write a fair hand, and swift, as that is useful to all. The academy should teach arithmetic, accounts, and some of the first principles of geometry and astronomy. Not only the skill but the habit of keeping accounts should be acquired by all as being necessary to all . . . the English language might be taught by grammar; in which some of our best writers, as Tillotson, Addison, Pope, Algernon, Sidney, Cato's Letters, etc. should be classics. The style principally to be cultivated being the clear and the concise. Reading should also be taught, and pronouncing, properly, distinctly, emphatically . . .[2]

Franklin also believed that much attention should be given to writing and public speaking, he was convinced of the importance of the teaching of history, and also believed that no one should be required to study Latin or Greek.

Franklin's active interest in the academy did not end when his term as president was finished. Many years later he wrote in his journal:

The trustees of the academy, after a while, were incorporated by a charter from the governor; their funds were increased by contributions in Britain and grants of land from the proprietaries, to which the Assembly has since made considerable addition; and thus was established the present University of Pennsylvania. I have continued as one of its trustees from the beginning, now near forty years, and have had the very great pleasure of seeing a number of the

---

[1] Carl Van Doren, *Benjamin Franklin*, New York, Viking, 1938, p. 187.
[2] *Ibid.*, pp. 190–191.

youth who have received their education in it, distinguished by their improved abilities, serviceable in public stations, and ornaments to their country.[3]

With Franklin's school as the prototype, academies spread rapidly, especially in the coastal states. New York, for example, had more than 300 of them by the middle of the nineteenth century.

The Curriculum of the Academy

As the number of academies increased, their curricular offerings expanded in the attempt to fill the needs of a changed social order—an objective which the Latin grammar schools were unable or unwilling to recognize. The academy was typically open to both sexes, and the program was planned for students who were not preparing for college as well as for those who were. In general this new school keyed its curriculum to the needs of the day, in protest against the rigid, classical, class-conscious program of the Latin grammar schools.

The basic language of the academies was English. The program of studies provided for many branches of English—among them grammar, composition, reading, writing, and speaking, as well as British and American literature. Penmanship, drawing, arithmetic, science, and modern foreign languages were also included in the curriculum, in addition to the college-preparatory centered subjects of the Latin grammar schools. Bookkeeping, navigation, the rudiments of vocational education, and other practical subjects were also offered by many academies because these protest schools attempted to be functional in their day.

The academy made at least three important contributions to American education. First, it served to popularize the idea of secondary education for a much larger section of the population, particularly for students who were not planning to go to college. Second, it provided secondary education for girls. Third, it established the concept that the secondary school should serve the needs of the public. The academy therefore enriched and extended the offerings of secondary education.

The academies, however, also had some characteristics which were inherently weakening. They were private schools, usually connected with a religious denomination. They were supported largely by tuition, and thus were expensive and catered chiefly to those who could pay the cost. Consequently they were not democratically orientated. Furthermore, most of them were so located that the students had to live at the school, thus increasing the expense.

These limitations, among others, made it impossible for the academies to expand sufficiently to meet the increasing educational demands which they themselves had fostered. It remained for free public high schools to make secondary education accessible to everyone.

[3] *Ibid.*, p. 196.

The Comprehensive Secondary School

The demand for a secondary school that would be within reach of every child as to both location and costs had become very insistent when the first public high school was established in Boston in 1821. This school, the English Classical High School, offered a curriculum which was in many respects patterned after that of the academy, but its program was related to practical life and the earning of a living and did not require college-preparatory courses. It is interesting to note, however, that it did not accept girls as students. It was not until 1856 that the first coeducational public high school was opened in Chicago.

Following the Civil War, public, tax-supported high schools spread rapidly, but not without vigorous opposition from the owners of private academies, religious groups that had hoped to dominate secondary education, and some taxpaying groups who objected to being assessed for secondary education. In many states the question of financing secondary education became a matter of litigation, usually ending in a supreme court ruling. The case which became most famous, and established the precedent, was one that originated in Kalamazoo, Michigan and ended in the supreme court of Michigan. The group bringing suit in Kalamazoo claimed that there was no legal basis for hiring a superintendent of schools and levying taxes to support a high school. The court's decision, made in 1847, included the following statement: "Neither in our state policy, in our constitution, or in our laws, do we find the primary school districts restricted in the branches of knowledge which their officers may cause to be taught, or to the grade of instruction that may be given."

The clarity and forcefulness of the Michigan decision proved to be decisive, and the "Kalamazoo Case" settled for all time the question of tax-supported public secondary schools. Junior and senior high schools are now considered an integral part of our basic educational structure, not a privilege of the few but the right of every boy and girl.

Types of Organization in the Secondary School

Secondary schools are organized in many different ways. The traditional form was a four-year high school that followed eight years of elementary school. This was the predominant pattern when most elementary pupils attended one-room rural schools and the preponderant number of high schools were located in villages. Beginning in 1910, with the advent of the junior high school movement, however, there has been a steady trend towards the reorganization of secondary education. Table 5 indicates this trend, and points up the fact that several types of organization are now used for secondary schools.

The trend towards reorganization is even more pronounced when viewed in terms of the numbers of pupils affected. Whereas almost all secondary

TABLE 5. NUMBER OF PUBLIC SECONDARY SCHOOLS BY TYPE, 1920–1959

	1919–1920		1951–1952		1958–1959	
	Number	%	Number	%	Number	%
Combined Jr.-Sr. High Schools (6–6)	828	5.8	8,591	36.2	10,130	41.9
Separate Jr. High Schools	55	.4	3,227	13.6	4,996	20.6
Senior High Schools (6–3–3)	15	.1	1,021	4.3	1,642	6.8
Reorganized 4-yr. High Schools (6–2–4)	7	.01	739	3.1	1,396	5.8
Unreorganized 4-yr. Trade Schools (8–4)	13,421	93.7	10,168	42.8	6,023	24.9
TOTAL	14,326	100.0	23,746	100.0	24,187	100.0

SOURCE: NASSP "Spotlight," National Association of Secondary School Principals, September–October, 1963, p. 2.

pupils were enrolled in traditional, four-year schools in 1910, by 1958–1959 reorganized schools (junior-senior high schools, separate junior, and separate senior high schools) enrolled 71.6 percent of the students in all types of secondary schools. Of the various systems of reorganization: the six-year junior-senior high school enrolled 3,536,921 pupils, or 32.0 percent; separate junior and separate senior high schools together enrolled 4,374,315 students, or 39.6 percent; while 10.8 percent, or 1,193,518 students were enrolled in four-year high schools which followed a separately organized two-year junior high school according to statistics published by the United States Office of Education.

THE JUNIOR HIGH SCHOOL

The junior high school is the most American part of our system of public education. With the exception of the junior high school, the United States has transplanted its school-types from the European nation where they originated. The kindergarten and the graduate school were begun in Germany, nursery schools were first established in France and England, and Comenius recognized the existence of elementary and high schools in his *Great Didactic*, written in the seventeenth century. Furthermore, the junior high school has no counterpart today, except in Canada where there has been a very recent trend towards the establishment of American-style schools for early adolescents.

Historical Background of the Junior High School

The junior high school did not grow out of the needs of public education as envisioned by superintendents or principals, nor was it proposed by school board members or demanded by school patrons. The junior high school emerged as a result of the reorganization of public education planned by several national committees under the leadership of University presidents.

The presidents who gave greatest impetus to the movement were Eliot of Harvard, Harper of Chicago, Butler of Columbia, Suzzallo of Washington, and Baker of Colorado, each of whom headed a committee that dealt with some phase of the reorganization of the public-school system.

During the last part of the nineteenth century higher education in America was influenced largely by German education. In fact, this influence extended through to the end of World War I. Before our own graduate schools had achieved the status which they have today, many college teachers, and a majority of college administrators, were graduates of German universities, and American higher education was measured in terms of a German standard.

Many university presidents, aware that in America boys and girls entered college when they were about two years older than was customary in Germany, sought to remedy the situation. It is interesting to note that in all of the material written at that time no one pointed out that the whole German education system was different from ours. Germany provided one school system that did not lead to college, and another one, for a selected few, that did. Whereas in Germany only a few young men were allowed the privilege of a university education, in America a single system of education permitted any boy with ability to go to college. Thus the American secondary schools served two purposes. Nevertheless, college administrators set about making the American secondary school better fit the German pattern of higher education.

Dr. Charles W. Eliot, President of Harvard University, was one of the first to become vocal concerning the length of time it took to prepare an American boy to enter college. He made two addresses before the Department of Superintendence of the National Education Association. The first address, made in 1888, was entitled "Can School Programs Be Shortened and Enriched?" The second address, in 1892, was entitled "Shortening and Enriching the Grammar School Course." It was Eliot's opinion that there was much waste of time in the elementary school, particularly in the last two grades (the seventh and eighth), and for this reason students entered high school and college two years later than necessary.

Two notable committees studied the questions raised by President Eliot. The Committee of Ten, under the chairmanship of Dr. Eliot, was appointed by the National Council on Education in 1892. This committee, whose purpose was to study the reorganization of secondary education to facilitate the economy of time, made its report in 1893. Several groups of experts, in various academic fields, assisted this committee. Each group advised that the subject matter in the field it represented should begin at an earlier point in the course of study. The Committee of Fifteen, appointed by the Department of Superintendents, submitted its report in 1895. This committee also decided that some of the secondary-school work might well begin at an earlier grade —for example, algebra and Latin in the seventh or eighth grade.

The National Education Association committee reported in 1899. This Committee on College Entrance Requirements expressed itself in favor of "a unified six-year high school course of study beginning with the seventh grade." It further said: "The most necessary and far-reaching reforms in secondary education must be begun in the seventh and eighth grades of our schools. Educators agreed that these grades must be enriched by eliminating non-essentials and adding new subjects formerly taught only in the high school.

"In our opinion these problems can be solved most quickly and surely by making the seventh and eighth grades part of the high school, and under the immediate direction of the high-school principal."

Thus the junior high school was proposed as a timesaver. The senior high school by moving some of its subjects down into the seventh and eighth grades could prepare students to enter college at an earlier age.

It is not possible in limited space to report the findings and opinions of the many committees that studied this problem. However, mention should be made of a report of a committee on the "Cultural Element and Economy of Time in Education" that was made by the chairman, President J. H. Baker of the University of Colorado. This report, presented at the annual meeting of the NEA in Cleveland in 1908, recommended a six-year elementary school and a six-year secondary school.

Economy of time was the watchword of all committees reporting on the problem of reorganization of our schools from 1890 to 1910 and even later. It was this demand for economy that led to the establishment of a six-year elementary school, and eventually to the junior high school. So far as can be determined in no instance did the establishment of the 6–3–3 plan of organization shorten the school period or enable students to enter college at an earlier age.

It is difficult to set the date or place of the beginning of the junior high school. During the first decade of this century numerous school systems experimented with various forms of this new school organization. Many cities claim the honor of having established the first junior high school. It may have been Berkeley, California, or Richmond, Indiana, or Saginaw, Michigan, or Los Angeles, California. The date is most often reported as 1910 and it is known that after 1910 there was a very rapid increase in the number of these schools, and the movement continued to gain momentum.

At first, junior high schools were established in many cities as an expedient in solving a serious housing problem. This accounted for their rapid development following World War I. The schools were crowded, and most school systems were badly in need of new buildings. The congestion in both elementary and secondary schools could be relieved by building junior high schools to take the top two grades from the elementary schools and the largest grade from the senior high schools.

The junior high school as merely an answer to building needs was not always a successful school. The seventh- and eighth-grade teachers were usually transferred from the elementary schools, as were also the teachers who taught the ninth grade in the senior high school. The program in such schools was usually made up of two years of elementary education using the textbooks, materials, teachers, and methods of the elementary school, to which was added a ninth grade using the subjects, textbooks, and methods of the senior high school. Such a hybrid had no chance for educational success. It was not until the junior high school developed a psychology, a philosophy, and a distinctive curriculum that it became educationally successful. Furthermore, in many cities the junior high school has never been a successful part of the school program because those who administer the schools have not attempted to make it the distinctive unit that it must be if it is to fulfill its educational mission. On the contrary, they have made out of it a little high school, even developing a senior high program of competitive athletics. To this is sometimes added the organizations and societies that are found in senior high schools, and the type of boy-girl parties that are common on the higher level. This is particularly true in cities where the superintendent of schools has had all of his teaching experience in a senior high school. If the school also has a principal and many teachers from high schools, even the program of studies and the methods of teaching may take on the pattern of the senior high school.

The Junior High School Pupil

The only legitimate purpose for a junior high school is to better serve early adolescent youth, usually spanning the ages of 12 to 14. These students are too mature for the elementary school with its maternalistic approach to education, and are not yet ready for senior high school with its more adult and sophisticated approach to learning. Because it was planned with a chronological orientation, the junior high school represented not only a new type of school but also instituted a drastic reversal in educational practice. The years when the junior high school was beginning was also the period when the fixed curriculum was in its ascendancy. Every school system prescribed in minute detail what was to be taught in each grade, and the child who could not master the required curriculum in one year was failed and required to repeat the grade the following year. This kind of educational planning made the age-range in the upper grades of the elementary school very great. It was not unusual to find young adults and pre-adolescent children in the same grade. Hence the proposal to create a new school for all pupils of seventh and eighth grade age which would offer them a differentiated curriculum based on their current growth status rather than on their success with previous school work was indeed revolutionary. Thus the junior high school was created first of all to provide a better educational opportunity for children at the upper elementary level.

The junior high school was also planned to benefit pupils of senior high school age. In 1910 only a small percentage of the potential group entered senior high school, and those who did were immediately subjected to a school which was a radical departure from earlier years. The familiar elementary pattern was gone, and the pupil studied isolated subjects under the direction of four or five different teachers. He missed the constant supervision of one teacher and the intimacy of one set of classmates. Thus many students became discouraged and dropped out of school during the first year of the four-year high school. The junior high school was established to eliminate the sudden transition and make for smoother articulation between elementary and secondary education.

The Junior High School Curriculum

The proper curriculum for early adolescent youth can be more readily planned in a junior high school than in an elementary or a senior high school. The typical junior high school curriculum is more challenging than that in the seventh and eighth grades of an eight-year elementary school, and more general in character than the program of the senior high school. The junior high school is primarily concerned with the problems of general education—with the education necessary for all individuals regardless of sex, nationality, or mental endowment. There are many broad and comprehensive courses often scheduled in longer blocks of time than are typically found in either the elementary school or the senior high school. In the seventh grade there is most often a high percentage of prescription; all the students are required to take certain core courses. These are in such general areas as social living, general science, practical arts, fine arts, music, and mathematics. As the student progresses through the junior high school, the percentage of prescription gradually decreases. Thus the school provides a type of curricular articulation between elementary education and the senior high school.

The junior high school has progressed much faster than the senior high school in developing a functional curriculum, largely because it is not dominated by college entrance requirements, a structure which has played a large role in setting the pattern of senior high school offerings and discouraged extensive thinking and experimentation.

Exploration is the key concept of the junior high school curriculum. The opportunity to explore many intellectual areas and have vital experience in fields which they will later study in greater detail is provided pupils at a most portentous time. The typical junior high school student is undergoing a growth cycle second in degree only to the growth in the first three years of life; in some cases the growth pattern seems almost to constitute a metamorphosis. It is logical to assume that these years of great physiological, social, and emotional change, when old interests and habits are being dropped and a rapid succession of new ones tested—some to be kept forever, others discarded almost immediately—make intellectual exploration especially sensible.

Because his classroom is equipped with television and an overhead projector, the lectures of this master teacher can be attended by many students simultaneously. (*Benjamin Franklin High School, Rochester, New York*)

Below: Producing the school annual utilizes student skills in writing, photography, salesmanship, typing, drawing and painting, editing, and using reproduction equipment. (*City School District, Rochester, New York*)

"Be it resolved that . . ." Students gain poise and diplomacy in debate team sessions. (*Seattle School District*)

Presentation of an operetta, a musical comedy, or an opera culminates the year's work in the fine arts curricula of many schools. (*Lincoln Public Schools, Lincoln, Nebraska*)

The students of this social studies research class have proven able and eager to discipline themselves in a rigorous study program. Some authorities believe that the senior high school student of the future will spend nearly one-half his time in individual and small-group discussion. (*Seattle School District*)

The good junior high school teaches many things well. It helps the early adolescent discover a great deal about himself and plan for his future. The field of the arts affords an excellent example. A junior high school should provide a wide range of experiences in both fine and practical arts using such media as wood, plastic, metal, oil paints, water color, pencil drawing, and even "tin" cans, string, old newspapers, and empty oatmeal containers. The general art program is not designed primarily to train the artist. Rather, its function is to give all pupils opportunity for creative expression and to introduce them to new and exciting segments of the arts, as well as to provide the "artist" a place to discover the fact that he does have special talent. The program in the senior high school art classes must obviously be built in terms of the experiences in the junior high school, and the majority of students in these advanced classes will have more than a general interest in art. However, the basic purpose of art in the junior high school is not one of preparation for senior high school art, it has intrinsic value for all.

Many junior high school educators have believed that a "core" or "unified studies" curriculum offers the most efficient approach to meeting the needs of early adolescent youth. One typical program is shown in Table 6.

The Junior High School Teacher

The junior high school demands a special type of teacher: one who is greatly interested in early adolescence and who has had a special type of preparation. He must be well-grounded in a diverse range of broad, subject matter fields, and have special professional education to work in this area. It is distressing to note that such preparation is extremely difficult to obtain.

TABLE 6. THE JUNIOR HIGH SCHOOL CURRICULUM

	Hours per week					
	7th Grade		8th Grade		9th Grade	
	1st	2nd	1st	2nd	1st	2nd
Subject	Sem.	Sem.	Sem.	Sem.	Sem.	Sem.
Unified studies (combining educational experiences in the language arts and social studies; including the time allotted for mathematics in grades 7 and 8)	15	15	15	15	10	10
Algebra	0	0	0	0	5	5
General Science and Health Education	3	3	3	3	(5)	(5)
General Art	2	2	2	2	(2)	(2)
Dramatics, Library	(2)	(3)	(3)	(2)	(2)	(2)
Homemaking or Industrial Arts	3	2	2	3	(5)	(5)
Physical Education	3	2	2	3	3	3
General Music	2	3	3	2	(2)	(2)
Instrumental Music	(2)	(3)	(3)	(2)	(2)	(2)
Electives for 9th Grade						
Business and Typing						
Industrial Arts						
Homemaking						
Language						
Latin						5	5
French						
Spanish						
Art						
Music						
Total hours per week per pupil	30	30	30	30	30	30

NOTE: Parentheses indicate that student may choose between two subjects that have the same number of hours.

It would seem that preparation for junior high is almost forgotten in the programs of teacher education. There has been little significant research concerned with the specific experiences of prospective junior high school teachers, but one fact is apparent—few colleges have teacher education programs designed for the preparation of junior high school teachers. A study of 65 major college and university catalogs made in 1950, repeated in 1954, and again in 1960, showed very little specific interest in this area. More significantly, perhaps, there was almost no change to be seen from one check to the next.

In an article published in the *School Review*, it was noted:

It is axiomatic that no school is stronger than its professional staff, and that the strength of the staff varies with the preparation of its members. Research into the amount and type of preparation that a junior high school teacher should have is lacking. Teacher-education institutions have done little toward setting up programs for preparing junior high school teachers. In fact the junior high school might well be described as "an orphan of education" or "a school without teachers." A study of college offerings reveals that teacher-education institutions appear to have forgotten the junior high school in their courses of study.[5]

Although few teacher education institutions have a special curriculum designed for the preparation of junior high school teachers, there are a number that offer a plan of academic preparation which meets the requirements of the teacher of young adolescents. In some schools this is called a "general secondary major," in which the student completes the equivalent of a minor in each of three or four different fields. This, together with the general and professional education requirements, helps insure the teacher a breadth of culture. The poorest possible preparation for teachers of a junior high school is a "strong" major in a narrow field coupled with a few hours of education and psychology. The best academic preparation is in broad fields of study such as the humanities, social studies, the arts, or the sciences.

Selective preparation for teaching in this field is important. A careful and extensive study of the psychology of adolescents, based on a more general knowledge of psychology is imperative. This study should include such significant areas as individual differences, the psychology of learning, motivation, mental hygiene, the giving and interpretation of tests, and the principles of guidance.

Finally, the junior high school teachers' professional preparation should include actual application of functional teaching methods to the subject matter and students of a school. The preservice laboratory experience of a prospective junior high school teacher takes place in a junior high school where he should gain an insight into the concept of the junior high school as a unique institution in American education.

Because of the nature of the educational pattern in the junior high school and the nature of the pupils, at least one-half of the professional staff of a junior high school should be male. Many junior high school programs place special emphasis on "club," "activity," or "interest" periods and these relatively informal contacts provide unique opportunity to build high moral ideals and foster good citizenship. The influence of a well-balanced, high-minded, vigorously masculine personality is never more contagious than at this time in the lives of young men when they are leaving childhood and constructing their own adult value systems. The presence of men as teachers is more vital in the junior high school than in elementary school or even in college, because junior high teachers—perhaps more than any other—teach much more than subject matter.

Advantages of the Junior High School

The first argument in favor of establishing the junior high school had to do with shortening the time necessary to complete the work of elementary and

[5] James E. Frasier, "The Professional Preparation of Junior High School Teachers," *The School Review*, December, 1954, p. 342.

secondary education. However, this reduction did not occur and the time required to finish high school is the same as it was before the development of the junior high school movement. As the junior high school has continued in its growth, however, other advantages have become apparent.

The greatest argument in favor of the junior high school is that it groups together students who are at once too old for the elementary school and too immature for senior high schools. It enables the school system to develop a unit that is particularly suited to the needs of early adolescence, and it makes possible the employment of teachers who are expert in dealing with children of this age.

Other advantages of the junior high school, some of which have been mentioned earlier, include:

1. Provision of a better transition from the elementary to the secondary school.
2. An improved guidance and counseling program. Since the pupils constitute a common age-group with similar problems, a guidance officer can specialize in the problems of early adolescence.
3. More efficient provision for special courses needing special and sometimes expensive equipment. In such fields as home economics, industrial arts, music, art, physical education and dramatics, a junior high school that has all the necessary equipment can teach pupils who would otherwise be scattered over a dozen elementary schools.
4. A better program of extracurricular activities. Inasmuch as the children are all in the same age-group, they have a similarity of purpose.
5. Newer curriculums and teaching methods. The junior high school is a unit of the school system that is not tied to tradition; hence it has been possible to experiment with new ideas.
6. Provision for individual differences because of the richness of curriculum.

The junior high school program also benefits both the elementary and senior high schools. It removes from the elementary school the older children who do not become an integrated part of the elementary school program. Similarly, the problems of conducting an acceptable senior high school is simplified by the omission of the ninth grade. Students who enter senior high school at the tenth grade level upon completion of a rich junior high school curriculum, have considerable experience that is similar to senior high school life. Furthermore, the records and diagnoses made by the junior high school are available. Therefore, such pupils are eminently better prepared to do senior high school work.

It should be noted that the junior high school program costs more than the usual elementary school program. The building itself costs more per pupil than does the elementary building, and special equipment for the special courses adds to the total cost. However, few educators doubt that the increased educational opportunities more than justify the additional cost.

With a well-planned building, adequate equipment, a well-stocked library, and sufficient studios, laboratories, offices and shops, together with specially prepared teachers, principal and guidance workers, all of whom understand the philosophy and psychology of the junior high school, this unit of the American school system is one of the bright spots in the educational picture. It is, without doubt, one of the most forward-looking developments in public education in the twentieth century.

THE SENIOR HIGH SCHOOL

In the traditional pattern of education which first grew up in America, grades nine, ten, eleven, and twelve constituted the senior high school. Since the movement toward reorganization, the ninth grade is more commonly a part of the junior high school, and secondary education for the majority of students begins in seventh grade and is characterized by either a six-year junior-senior high school or a three-year junior high school and a three-year senior high school. When the ninth grade is part of the senior high school in an 8–4 school system, and students enter directly from elementary school, the principal and teachers are confronted with a more difficult task in orienting the students to high school. The change in subject and methods of teaching is so radical that many students are not able to make the necessary adjustments. However, students who go from the junior high school into tenth grade seldom have as much difficulty in adjusting themselves to the senior high school environment.

The Senior High School Student

The senior high school was once a school for a highly selected group of students, as its program and methods of teaching reflected. In fact, until the turn of the present century, the senior high school was largely a college preparatory institution and made little pretense of being anything else. Three-fourths of the graduates went on to college, and the program of the senior high school at that time made little provision for terminal education. Later, however, this senior high school became a school for all youth. As a result, the enrollment has increased enormously in recent years, and only one in four enters college.

Many factors have contributed to the increased enrollment in secondary education besides the general increase in the population. Some of these factors are compulsory attendance laws, a better secondary school program, and an increase in the popularity of the senior high school as the school for all children of all people. There is no doubt that the secondary schools have grown tremendously. In 1880 there were approximately 111,000 students enrolled in American high schools. In 1950 the corresponding secondary school grades—9 through 12—enrolled approximately 5,700,000 pupils. This fiftyfold increase in secondary school enrollment in 70 years must be compared with a threefold increase in the total population during the same period. In each of the six decades preceding 1940, secondary school enrollments throughout the country nearly doubled. Nor has the growth ended. In the school year 1961–1962 almost 13,000,000 youths were enrolled in public secondary schools, and estimates of the future foresee a secondary school population of about 19,000,000 in 1970.

If the secondary schools are to provide education for all youth, the program obviously must be a varied one. The Latin grammar school with its fixed-in college entrance curriculum enrolled only a small percentage of the children of secondary school age. Its program was not important except to the few people who were interested in having their children go to school beyond the elementary level. The academy changed this situation very little, and by the time it was succeeded by the modern high school, the academy resembled the earlier Latin grammar school strikingly. It remained for the free public high school to present a comprehensive program.

The present-day senior high school has all types of students. Even those students who were never able to do acceptable work in elementary school or junior high school must be provided with classes within their capacity for as long as the compulsory attendance laws are operable; and classes for these students should have intrinsic value in preparing them to be citizens in a democracy and workers in a productive world.

The high school must also provide suitable courses for students who plan to go to college and later enter business or one of the professions.

Between the two extremes represented by these groups, there is a large population composed of the students who will drop out after a year or two of high school or who will graduate and not go on to college. The senior high school must offer them an acceptable program of general education and also education of a vocational nature. These students must be prepared to take their place in business and in industry upon graduation from senior high.

Thus, the secondary school must be suited to all types of students even though they differ in intelligence, maturity, interests, and social and economic background. The individual differences in the student body of the average senior high school are a great challenge to those who plan education on this level and also to those who plan and administer the guidance program. In an earlier discussion, we noted the importance of attention to individual guidance and a well-rounded testing program. Important, in any consideration of the senior high school, is recognition of the fact that a well-developed guidance and counseling program under the general direction of an expert in this field is imperative. Studying each pupil and then helping him to plan a school program and a life career to fit his possibilities is one of the most important tasks of the staff in a modern secondary school.

In the past, parents in general were satisfied to have their children complete the elementary school program and then quit school to go to work; but today most parents desire at least a secondary education for their children. The possession of a high school diploma has become a symbol of great importance to families in the low-income group. There are few occupational opportunities which do not require the completion of a high school education as prerequisite, and the high school education has been for some a means of attaining a higher social status. As more and more people move to the senior high school and go on to college, senior high school seems certain to become minimum education for everyone.

The Senior High School Curriculum

The status and importance of the curriculum in the American senior high school can best be understood when viewed against the background of two ideas mentioned previously. First, a society expresses itself through its social institutions—and modern secondary education is the major educational contribution of the United States. Secondly, any school can be viewed most validly in terms of its curriculum. Smith, Stanley, and Shores have noted:

> If any observer looks at the curriculum of the school in any society, he will find, either stated or implied, a set of educational objectives, a body of subject matter, a list of exercises or activities to be performed, and a way of determining whether or not the objectives have been reached by the students. . . . The objectives stressed will be those that reflect the controlling ideas and sentiments contained in the universals. The subject matter will tend to be that which is believed to embrace the most significant ideas and most generally used knowledges and skills. The way in which the learners are controlled will reflect the prevailing methods of social control of the society at large. As the instrument of society for the education of the young, the curriculum will reflect the ideals, knowledges, and skills that are believed to be significant, or that are related to the common activities of the members of society. The curriculum is, therefore, interwoven with the social fabric that sustains it.[6]

The Latin grammar school had a narrow classical curriculum, and the academy offered a broader one (in which some emphasis was placed on preparing students for living in their society and for earning a living) that was still restricted in terms of our modern thinking. The modern secondary school has attempted to develop its curriculum from these antecedents and from a knowledge of more current happenings. Even in its earliest times the modern high school presented a program designed to prepare the student for college at the same time it offered various curricula of a vocational and general nature. This type of comprehensive, multipurpose secondary school is still the most common in American education.

There is much discussion in the field of secondary education concerning the proper curriculum pattern for a secondary school. Some people have believed that there should be two kinds of high schools; the nonacademic school preparing its graduates for business, trade, and industry; the entirely academic school preparing its graduates for college. There was a time, par-

[6] Othanel B. Smith, William Stanley, and J. Harlan Shores, *Fundamentals of Curriculum Development,* New York, Harcourt, Brace & World, 1957, p. 8.

ticularly in the 1920s, when many cities in America built some vocational high schools and others designed for academic programs only. This is no longer the common pattern and practically all high schools now being built envision a complete educational program for students regardless of their vocational goals. In fact, the term most commonly used to describe today's senior high school is "the comprehensive senior high school."

As might be expected, the earliest of the modern high schools presented a program more closely related to earlier programs. The curriculum of a typical high school in 1850 included a group of isolated subjects, such as ancient history, Latin, algebra, and English Composition in the ninth grade. This pattern of isolated courses continued through the high school in a similar manner. The present-day high school presents in addition to the traditional program, such courses as social living, world problems, home and family relations. A smaller percentage of the high school graduates now go on to college; the actual number is greater, but the relative number is smaller. Therefore, present-day high school curricula must be planned with the knowledge that a varied program is demanded by varied pupils.

The vocational courses offered in senior high school and the number of students taking them have increased rapidly in recent years, largely because of the subsidies granted by the federal government. The vocational courses most commonly offered are in agriculture, home economics, and physics.

Education that is discontinued when a student leaves school is for the most part wasted effort. With this philosophy in mind, it is possible to evaluate most of the subjects offered in the senior high school. Literature should lead to better adult reading habits; science should develop a lifelong interest in scientific developments; social studies should lead to an interest in government and good citizenship. Art and music should develop a taste for the best in these fields; physical education and health courses should develop good habits of living and a healthful recreation pattern. This is one reason why such sports as volleyball, softball, badminton, golf, and tennis are of more ultimate value to a boy than is football or basketball.

The offering of courses in mathematics, usually thought of as part of the college curriculum, special programs for accelerated students in all areas, and greater flexibility is scheduled for students at both the top and the bottom of the ability scale.

Individual Differences in the Senior High School

In Chapter 8 there was a discussion of ability grouping in the elementary school. The problem of meeting individual differences is even greater in the secondary school. As students progress through the grades, the differences among them are magnified by the breadth and depth of the experiences they have had. Ability or homogeneous grouping was one of the solutions that was used to meet this problem. During the 1930s and '40s, there was a trend away from any kind of ability grouping on the grounds that it was an un-

democratic idea. Since the advent of the struggle for world supremacy between the United States and the USSR, however, a number of persons, both
lay and professional, questioned whether an ungrouped senior high school
would offer the proper kind of challenge to the superior student. These persons hold that the need for leadership, which a world crisis demands, makes
it necessary that more attention be given to the curriculum of the academically talented student. The current science and mathematics programs
have been especially criticized as has the small amount of foreign language
instruction offered by most school systems.

Undoubtedly some of the criticism is unjustified. A number of the most
vocal critics have based their statements on half-truths, and some of them
have not been intellectually honest. Anything as vital as the public schools
will always be subjected to attack by self-centered, unfair persons.

Current curricular and grouping practices have also been questioned by
intelligent, interested persons, however. Dr. James B. Conant, President
Emeritus of Harvard University, has published two reports that are more
likely to have a greater effect on the American junior and senior high school
of any of the more recent critical studies.

Dr. Conant, unlike many of the current writers, based his statement on
study and first-hand observation of the schools as well as upon a great deal
of experience in the field of education. His reports list a number of specific
recommendations for improving the comprehensive secondary school. Some
of the major ones listed in his discussion of the senior high school are:

1. Students' programs of study should be more individualized.
2. A greatly expanded counseling system is needed.
3. Special programs should be provided for such pupils as slow readers, gifted
   pupils, various vocational interest areas.
4. Grouping by ability in all required and in some elective subjects.
5. Five "solid" subjects is not too many for a majority of students.
6. A greatly reduced teaching-load for English teachers.
7. High school graduating classes of at least 100 pupils.

Dr. Conant has made a strong plea for a more academic orientation of
the American secondary schools. Many of his criticisms of the existing schools
are well-founded. Because of the relative moderation of these recommendations, and because of the reputation of Dr. Conant, these ideas are having
a noticeable effect especially in our senior high school programs.

There have also been other recommendations concerned with the ac-
celeration of the curriculum for superior high school students, and a number of interesting and significant changes have already been made. Some
high schools have made provision for students to complete the four-year
schedule in three years by carrying additional subjects each semester. Others
have chosen a program of enrichment whereby the student stays in the
junior-senior high school grades the usual six years but begins his advanced

science and mathematics courses in the junior high school grades. This allows him to have such courses as "college" algebra and trigonometry, fifth and sixth year foreign languages, and college-level biological or physical science before completing high school. Still other schools have decided to offer the traditional courses in their usual order and placement but have also attempted to achieve enrichment by broadening and deepening the content of the more traditional courses.

There are many other plans and even more variations on the basic ideas, but they all share a common objective—providing a special program for the superior student. It is too easy to forget, however, that a special program for one segment of the student body automatically sets up a different program for the rest of the student body. It is all too easy to lose interest in the needs of the great normal majority in an all-out program for a smaller number. This principle applies regardless of what group is singled out for special emphasis.

The American educational system rests on the premise that education is another of our unalienable rights and that public schools are bound legally and morally to serve all the children of all the people. Our honest and undoubtedly necessary effort to better serve the superior student must not be achieved at the expense of the other 90 percent of the students.

Any kind of grouping bears potential dangers as well as advantages. Grouping that is used for stratification of pupils or only as a measure to nullify the critics has no place in today's schools. It must be remembered, also, that no plan of grouping, heterogeneous or homogeneous, is the whole answer to the problem of meeting individual differences. This problem is entirely too complex for any unilateral situation to remedy it.

The Senior High School and the College

Near the end of the past century a committee on college entrance requirements presented a system of counting credits in the high school. At that time the high school was regarded as a school for certain selected youth who planned to go on to college and the committee developed the famous Carnegie unit for measuring the number of high school credits to be accepted by the college. This unit was defined as 120, 60-minute periods. Sixteen units were required for graduation from the four-year high school, and most colleges defined their entrance requirements as 15 or 16 units specifying that a certain number of these units were to be in English, science, mathematics, and other subjects. This system has continued and is still the dominant pattern for assaying the program of a secondary school.

The Carnegie unit, undoubtedly an important contribution in its day, has become a great drawback in the development of an adequate program of study at the secondary school level. It has had a tendency to put the high school program into a straight jacket, and the special subject matter requirements for college entrance have tended to freeze the high school into a pattern. Thus, the retardation of progress in changing the hig curriculum has been widespread. This is particularly true in t school. With a few students and four or five teachers, the high sc attempts to prepare a portion of its students for college soon discovers that the school week is scheduled with required courses and that there is no time left to schedule courses for the overwhelming majority who will not be going on to college.

An Eight-Year Study of the Senior High School and College

In 1930 the Progressive Education Association created a commission on the relation of high school and college to explore the possibilities of better coordination of the work of these two units. The commission established a program which involved 30 secondary schools of all types and sizes. The commission next secured the promise of a large number of colleges and universities to waive their usual pattern of entrance requirements to their liberal arts courses for the graduates of these 30 experimental groups. The program was carried on for eight years, long enough for the students to go through the experimental program in the secondary schools and to complete the usual four-year college curriculum. The 30 schools, freed from the necessity of following a pattern prescribed for admission to college, inaugurated new programs, no two of which were precisely alike. Some schools departed much further than others from the usual program, however all of them made many important changes.

Results of this study were both significant and far-reaching. The study established beyond doubt the falseness of the idea that a certain pattern of high school studies is necessary for successful work in college. Many of the 30 schools have continued the "core" courses they developed, and other high schools have followed their example.

It is interesting to note that some of our finest universities have had a list of required prerequisite subjects, whereas other equally fine schools have a long history of freedom in the matter of college entrance. In fact, some prescribe no special subjects for admission, and the record of the latter group is as admirable and as academic as that of the former.

Extracurricular Activities in the Senior High School

Of all phases of the modern secondary school, none has been as misunderstood as the extracurricular program. The lack of consensus regarding the place of this segment is attested to by the fact that it has been variously called "extracurricular," "cocurricular," and "extracurriculum." In this discussion, the term "extracurricular activities" will be used to denote any activities in a high school not resulting in credit toward graduation. Such a definition makes it possible to list a very large number of valuable activities in one category.

When the secondary school limited its function to a place where students accumulated graduation credits leading to college entrance, extracurricular activities played a very small part and the school authorities did everything possible to curtail or discontinue these. The present-day high school encourages such activities. Most authorities in secondary education view the extracurricular program as an important part of secondary education. In fact, many believe it constitutes the most valuable part of a school, particularly for the noncollege-bound student.

Every student preparing to teach in either junior or senior high school should make definite preparation in the field of extracurricular activities, for as a teacher he will have a part in such a program. These activities consist of such things as the high school newspaper and various other publications, including the *Annual,* special magazines, and handbook for students. All phases of student government are important extracurricular activities, and it is through student government that many of the other activities are controlled. In music there are such special activities as glee clubs, bands, chorus, orchestra, opera, and various other projects. However, in a large percentage of our high schools, all music activities are curricularized and take place during the regular school day. In some schools assemblies are extracurricular projects, whereas other staffs have seen the value of school assemblies when they are built on an educational basis and have made them part of the regular school program. In most schools the entire athletic program is extracurricular, as are all interschool contests and activities. In the interschool work we find teacher-coaches, and many of the other related activities must be taken care of by teachers. Other activities in this category include pep clubs, student attendants at out-of-town games, and the selling of tickets and advertising. Activities in the field of dramatics, debating, and public speaking are sometimes not on the regular school program. In addition to these activities, there are the special clubs such as the camera club, departmental club, and various special interest groups.

Every extracurricular activity has a teacher as a sponsor, and it is his duty to see that the activity is carried on in the best possible manner with an educational emphasis. To do this and still allow the students the maximum control calls for a skilled person who knows the activity and also knows how to work with the young people in a more informal unregimented program than the typical classroom. Therefore, it is important that prospective teachers learn some of the necessary techniques in working in the extracurricular program.

THE SENIOR HIGH SCHOOL PERSONNEL

The modern senior high school is a complex organization which demands the services of many women and men skilled in many fields. The most important staff members are the teachers, and what was said a few pages earlier regarding the junior high school teacher applies also to the senior high school teacher.

Anyone preparing to teach in a senior high school should be prepared to work in several different fields. Teachers often begin their teaching in a small high school where the limited number of teachers makes it necessary for each person to handle classes in a variety of fields. In a typical small school the science teacher may teach general science, biology, chemistry, and algebra. Although such an assignment is exceedingly demanding, there is a distinct advantage to the beginning teacher because it enables him to become familiar with a variety of subjects and gives him a chance to work with pupils on several levels. In this way he is able to see the total pattern of education and can try different fields and different ages before deciding specifically on his life's work. The teacher who begins his work in a large high school is more apt to teach several sections of the same course and in this case may only see part of the educational process that takes place in the secondary school. Such an assignment, however, does constitute a less demanding load than teaching several different classes on as many levels.

Regardless of the specific assignment which the beginning teacher has, it is a wise idea for him to offer a program of studies as general and as broad as possible. It should be further noted in this connection that there has been a movement in secondary schools in recent years to break down the subject matter barriers and to organize the materials of instruction into new and larger units. It is not unusual to find a large block made up of materials from social studies, English, and language arts. Such courses are usually referred to as "core courses." This term, however, is sometimes used to designate the various subjects that are required for graduation.

RECENT DEVELOPMENTS IN SECONDARY EDUCATION

It has been said that the only thing in American secondary education that is constant is the fact of change. Certainly this segment of the school system has undergone both evolutionary and revolutionary readjustment during its relatively short history. At least two of the current proposals for change demand attention here.

The first is commonly referred to as the "Trump Plan," although it is more descriptively known as the "Staff Utilization Studies of the National Association of Secondary School Principals." Dr. Lloyd Trump and his associates, working with a grant from the Ford Foundation, have made a number of interrelated suggestions for more efficient utilization of professional personnel, school building facilities, and pupil time.

Two of the more novel of their recommendations are especially significant. They have suggested that the proper perspective of the students time schedule would be 40 percent in large-group instruction, 20 percent in small-group discussion, and 40 percent in individual study. The recommendations for the teachers' time schedules are equally new. They suggest that teachers might be organized into "teams" consisting of one "master teacher," one or more teachers in the early years of their professional careers, and a number of teaching assistants, clerks, and other aides. The large-group instruction classes would be led by the master teacher who would present material to as many as 250 or more students simultaneously in a special lecture room. Small-group discussion would then be directed by all professional members of the team. Of all the suggestions and recommendations included in the Staff Utilization Studies, team teaching is the one which has received the most attention. Students who are interested in further study of this interesting innovation are directed to the reference on page 215 of this text.

The "Trump Plan" is being used in a number of schools today, and early analyses seem to show that student development is, at the least, not hampered by the changes and often is enhanced. It is also quite obvious that this plan allows the professional teacher time to do the things for which he received his professional training and relieves him from many of the routine tasks that are better accomplished by someone else.

The second interesting innovation in secondary education is the "nongraded secondary school." This plan, brought to its greatest current development by Frank Brown and his staff in Melbourne, Florida, is more recent than the "Trump" proposals, and thus less well-tested. In essence, this plan does away with the typical "grades" in the secondary school in a manner similar to that of the primary school approach discussed in Chapter 8. Many educators are studying this plan with great interest.

DEMOCRACY AND THE SENIOR HIGH SCHOOL

The American high school has a European background and came from a civilization that looked upon secondary education as the privilege of the few. It began in America as a class institution and not until the public high school came into being was secondary education looked upon as the democratic right of every child. Since the high school is a school for all children, it must serve the interests of the majority who do not go to college as well as for the minority who do. Democracy is not well served by establishing one school for the masses and another for the classes, one for the thinkers and another for the toilers. The modern high school provides valuable experiences for all types of students so they may develop into socially efficient individuals. In brief, high school students should have the opportunity to develop the knowledge and skills that will enable them to support themselves and to contribute to the welfare of society.

RELATED READINGS

Bent, Rudyard K., and Henry Kronenberg, *Principles of Secondary Education,* 4th ed., New York, McGraw-Hill, 1961.

Brown, B. Frank, *The Nongraded High School,* Englewood Cliffs, N.J., Prentice-Hall, 1963.

Conant, James B., *The American High School Today,* New York, McGraw-Hill, 1959.

——————, "Recommendations for Education in the Junior High School Years," Princeton, N.J., Educational Testing Service, 1960.

——————, *Slums and Suburbs,* New York, McGraw-Hill, 1961.

Shaplin, Judson, and Henry F. Olds, Jr., *Team Teaching,* New York, Harper & Row, 1964.

Trump, J. Lloyd, and Dorsey Baynham, *Guide to Better Schools: Focus on Change,* Chicago, Rand McNally, 1961.

Van Til, William, Gordon Vars, and John H. Lounsbury, *Modern Education for the Junior High School Years,* Indianapolis, Bobbs-Merrill, 1961.

The first buildings of the University of Pennsylvania. The building on the left was built when the school served as an academy. (*University of Pennsylvania News Bureau*)

Right: A student of the Lexington, Massachusetts, Normal School made this drawing about 1840. Normal schools were America's first institutions for teacher preparation. (*Courtesy Lexington Historical Society*)

Below: America's colleges and universities, unlike those in many countries, concern themselves with the student's social and emotional development as well as his intellectual growth. The student center of this university is evidence of such concern. (*University of South Florida*)

The community junior college is America's fastest growing educational institution. Closely tied to their communities, each serves the educational needs of young and old in beautiful, functional facilities such as this office of community services at Foothill College. (*Foothill College, Los Altos, California*)

Below: Observation of a master teacher at work affords the opportunity for prospective teachers to see educational theory translated into practice. (*Board of Education, St. Louis*)

Today's teacher education students have the opportunity for concentrated periods of professional laboratory experiences including observation, participation in limited teaching roles, student teaching, and full-time internships. (*University of Portland*)

Chapter 10 / HIGHER AND ADULT EDUCATION

THE DEVELOPMENT OF POST-SECONDARY SCHOOL EDUCATION

The development of the American educational system beyond the secondary school years presents a pattern similar to the growth of elementary and secondary education. Belief in democracy and in the imperative nature of education in a democracy led the United States to provide universal opportunity for formal education from nursery school through high school graduation. The extension of that belief led to the development of institutions of higher education and opportunity for adult training. Elementary and secondary education began as private schools for the few and evolved into tax-supported institutions for everyone. For education beyond the high school years the earliest schools were also private schools which catered to the few. Today institutions, both private and tax-supported, are providing higher education to an ever-increasing number of people.

Early Colleges

Nine colleges were established in the American colonies prior to the Revolutionary War, basically for the purpose of preparing young men for the ministry. The major religious sects of the day considered it necessary to establish their own individual schools. Harvard (1636), Yale (1701), and Dartmouth (1769) were founded by the Congregationalists. William and Mary (1693) and Kings College—later Columbia University (1754)—were established by the Episcopalians. Princeton (1746) was started by the Presbyterians, Brown University (1764) by the Baptists, and Rutgers (1766) by members of the Dutch Reformed Church. Of all the institutions of higher learning established during the colonial period, only one, the University of Pennsylvania (1755), was nonsectarian. It should be remembered, however, that it was established as an academy and that its purpose was to provide vocational training for secondary-school youth who were not planning to enter college. Only later did it become an institution of higher education. The University of Pennsylvania is also unique in the fact that it is the only state university which is not controlled by the state, for even though the state does contribute to the support of the school, it remains under private control.

The purpose of most colonial colleges was avowedly religious and followed the English traditions of Oxford and Cambridge to a considerable extent. The early Puritan settlers were anxious to build and maintain a high order of church leadership so that they might preserve the values of their various Protestant faiths. Such a belief was specifically expressed by the founders of Harvard College at the time of its origin, and more than one-half of its graduates during the seventeenth century were clergymen. Dartmouth College was established with a specifically missionary function: it was charged with the task of bringing Christianity to "the heathen red-man." Similar observations could be made in reference to the other colonial colleges. The social philosophy of colonial America was based on a discipline of learning that was deeply rooted in the Christian faith, and the colleges which these people established were of course rooted in the same value system. The inscription on the west gate of Harvard leaves no doubt about the religious implications of its founding:

After God has carried us safe to New England, and we had builded our houses, provided necessaries for our livelihood, rear'd convenient places for God's worship, and settled the Civil Government: One of the next things we longed for, and looked after was to advance Learning and perpetuate it to Posterity; dreading to leave an illiterate Ministry to the Churches when our present Ministers shall lie in the Dust.

The church influence on higher education dominated the scene during the seventeenth century and extended well into the eighteenth. Graduates of colleges in the eastern part of the United States were largely instrumental in establishing similar institutions in the middle and far western states. Ministers who graduated from Congregational colleges such as Harvard and Yale went west as missionaries. Many of them established congregations in the new territory, a process which was often followed by the opening of a college. Whitman, Olivet, Colorado College, and Pomona are examples of such a set of circumstances.

State support of higher education developed slowly. As late as the Civil War only 6.5 percent of all institutions of higher education in the United States were state-supported. The first state university to be chartered was in Georgia (1785), although some students believe that the University of North Carolina actually held university classes first. In any event the first state university was antedated by Harvard College by approximately a century and a half.

The early colleges in the United States took their educational pattern from similar institutions in Europe—as, indeed, did all early American education. The European-Americans who founded the United States were no further removed from their early cultural patterns when they established Harvard or William and Mary than when they settled "New" London, "New" York, or "New" Haven.

POPULARIZING HIGHER EDUCATION

A brief survey of the development and popularization of higher education in America can be made by reviewing the rapid changes which occurred during the nineteenth century, changes that led to the establishment of the remaining four major types of collegiate institutions which have supplemented the earlier private schools.

The Ordinance of 1787

Although enacted prior to the beginning of the nineteenth century, the first of the significant factors in the popularizing of higher education was The Ordinance of 1787. This law set apart specific sections of land in the Northwest Territory for the use of public schools, and every state admitted to the Union from that date onward received land for schools. Ohio University, founded in Athens in 1803, received the first land grant for higher education. With the exception of Maine, Texas, and West Virginia, every state admitted to the Union since 1800 has not received less than two townships for the purpose of founding a university, and the grants for institutions of higher learning under this law have aggregated more than a million acres. The availability of these land grants was, in the beginning, the main reason for establishing state universities, and as the country developed, these schools have become institutions of great size and influence in our nation.

The Dartmouth College Decision

In 1816 the New Hampshire legislature, assuming certain authority over Dartmouth College, passed a law which superimposed a board of overseers on the board of trustees of Dartmouth, designated the institution as Dartmouth University, and gave the governor-appointed overseers the power of veto over the college board. The college trustees carried the matter to the courts, and with Daniel Webster as attorney argued the case before the United States Supreme Court. In the now famous Dartmouth College case, the Supreme Court of the United States, in a decision written by Chief Justice Marshall, decided in favor of the college. The charter granted to Dartmouth College in 1769 was declared to be a contract and therefore not subject to change by the legislature without the consent of the trustees.

The Dartmouth College Decision was of obvious significance to the private colleges and universities of the United States, because it safeguarded such institutions and their endowments from interference by civil authorities and thus made possible the growth and integrity of the great private institutions. It also must be deemed highly significant in the development of the state university. When it became evident that the state could not assume authority over private colleges, the states began to establish their own universities and colleges, and a large number of major universities came into being as a consequence of this decision.

The Morrill Act

A third federal action, certainly of no less importance than the other two in the growth of the state university, was the Morrill Act of 1862, known also as the Land-Grant College Act. This action of massive land-grants to education for the support of collegiate training was taken because of a shortage of men prepared in military science, agriculture, and mechanics. These grants were eagerly used, some states founding new institutions, while others used their grants to enlarge and strengthen existing state colleges or universities. This act has proven to be one of the most potent forces in popularizing higher education.

The curriculums of these "A and M" colleges were originally planned in close relationship to the requirements of the law: courses in agriculture and mechanical arts. However, in more recent times, these schools have entered other fields, and the majority of them in reality have become universities. Departments and professors have been added in all the liberal arts fields, and some of the schools have established colleges of education, fine arts, business, law, and medicine.

In the southern states separate land-grant colleges were set up for Negro students. The land these states received from the federal government was divided, a part of it being set aside for separate schools for Negroes. In more recent years, these separate Negro colleges have been more closely integrated into state systems of higher education.

TEACHER EDUCATION

Under the impetus of early nineteenth-century movements towards increased educational opportunity at the elementary and secondary school levels, demands were felt for a systematic approach to teacher education. The first normal school (from the Latin *normalis*, meaning "model" or "pattern") in America was a private institution at Concord, Vermont, established in 1823 by the Reverend Samuel Hall. The first public normal school was founded in Lexington, Massachusetts, in 1839, beginning with one teacher and three pupils. These early teachers' schools were little better than high schools and served to train teachers for the growing grammar or elementary school demand. Despite generally low standards and poor leadership, the normal school idea received favorable public attention and the last half of the nineteenth century saw an expansion of teacher education with the extensive establishment of state teachers' colleges.

In the United States, during the last half of the eighteenth century and the first half of the nineteenth, a great deal was written about the need for schools to educate teachers. There were several attempts to establish private seminaries or normal schools, but those that were established survived for only a short time.

For several years prior to the establishment of the first normal school in 1839, a great many important men and women worked and wrote in this field. One of the best statements of the problem was made by Dr. William E. Channing in an address given in Boston on February 28, 1837. He advocated the establishment in Massachusetts of an institution for the professional preparation of teachers. He said in part:

We need an institution for the formation of better teachers; and until this step is taken, we can make no important progress. The most crying want in this commonwealth is the want of accomplished teachers. We boast of our schools; but our schools do comparatively little, for want of educated instructors. Without good teaching, a school is but a name. An institution for training men to train the young, would be a fountain of living waters, sending forth streams to refresh present and future ages. As yet, our legislators have denied to the poor and laboring classes this principal means of their elevation. We trust they will not always prove blind to the highest interest of the state.

We want better teachers, and more teachers, for all classes of society—for rich and poor, for children and adults. We want that the resources of the community should be directed to the procuring of better instructors, as its highest concern. One of the surest signs of the regeneration of society will be the elevation of the art of teaching to the highest rank in the community.

Nothing is more needed, than that men of superior gifts, and of benevolent spirit, should devote themselves to the instruction of the less enlightened classes in the great end of life—in the dignity of their nature—in their rights and duties —in the history, laws, and institutions of their country.

We want a class of liberal-minded instructors, whose vocation it shall be, to place the views of the most enlightened minds within the reach of a more and more extensive portion of their fellow-creatures.

We maintain that higher ability is required for the office of an educator of the young, than for that of a statesman.

We have said that it is the office of the teacher to call into vigorous action the mind of the child. He must do more. He must strive to create a thirst, an insatiable craving for knowledge, to give animation to study and make it a pleasure, and thus to communicate an impulse which will endure when the instructions of the school are closed.

The legislature of Massachusetts, in 1838, passed the first normal school act in the United States. It provided for the setting up of three normal schools in that state. These were the first public institutions for the education of teachers in our country. They were patterned largely after similar institutions in Germany that had been visited by some of our leading educators.

Schools of Education

Parallel with the development of teacher education in separate state institutions has gone the establishment of schools and colleges of education in the public and private universities. These schools went through the same general stages in their development. First normal departments were established in the universities. This was true in such universities as Michigan, Iowa, Missouri, Wyoming, and a number of others. Later the normal departments were extended and expended and schools of education resulted. From these beginnings teacher education rapidly expanded until the school of education has become the largest professional school in most universities having such a school.

Trends In Teacher Education

There are many important trends in teacher education both in teachers' colleges and in the schools of education in universities. The curricular trend is toward broader major fields of study and a greater emphasis on general education. In no field has the trend toward general education been more important than in the preparation of teachers. The professional curriculum gives much more emphasis to studying the growth and development of the individual child, and there is also much greater interest in studying society, particularly the community problems that involve children. In the field of student teaching there has been a rapid expansion of internships, under which students are sent to public school systems where they teach under supervision while still enrolled in college. The internship usually lasts for one college term. Students are not sent out as interns until they have had at least one term in the laboratory school on the campus where they have observed master teachers at work. There is much greater emphasis on teaching aids, particularly audio-visual aids.

The trend is toward the more careful selection of those who are to become teachers. Selection is not based, as it once was, on intelligence tests and school marks alone. Such attributes as mental stability, personality, and health are also considered important.

The college's interest in those it sends out to teach does not end when they have been graduated. Most institutions concerned with the education of teachers also do in-service work for and with teachers. This involves classes on the campus in the evening and on Saturday morning, and classes at more distant points where college teachers conduct in-service meetings and seminars.

THE "JUNIOR" OR COMMUNITY COLLEGE

The third major type of post-secondary school is the uniquely-American community college. This school, usually a two-year institution, typifies many attributes of the approach to education for which the United States educational system is noted. The junior or community college is most often built and maintained by local taxpayers, it serves students in an area which varies from a few blocks to a few miles away from the campus, it has a general education orientation with heavy emphasis on the "practical" and "useful," it has grown with remarkable speed, and its curriculum is continuously being re-examined and altered in terms of stated needs and interests of the community which it serves.

The first junior college was established just before the end of the century that saw such enormous expansion in higher education. The founding of state universities, women's colleges, teachers' colleges, and land-grant colleges was followed by the beginnings of the junior college.

William Rainey Harper, first president of the University of Chicago, is often referred to as the father of the junior college movement, he was its most active supporter. It was largely through his efforts that the first junior college, Lewis Institute, was established in Chicago in 1896. By 1900 there were eight private junior colleges. President Harper's report to the board of trustees of the University of Chicago in 1903 discussed the junior college movement in some detail. He pointed out many of the advantages that would result from the development of such colleges. The first public junior college was established in connection with the township high school at Joliet, Illinois, in 1902. It is still functioning.

Once begun, the junior-college movement rapidly gained momentum. Twenty-five of the colleges were organized during the first decade of the present century, many more have been established since then. In 1920, 34 of them joined in setting up the American Association of Junior Colleges. From that inauspicious beginning, the junior college has proved to be the fastest-growing of all American educational institutions, and there are now between 600 and 700 junior colleges in the United States. A majority of these are public junior colleges, or community colleges as they are often called. These public colleges receive well over 85 percent of the total junior college enrollment. There are about 275 privately supported junior colleges, most of them residential. The number of junior colleges is steadily growing, but the growth is not evenly distributed. California has the largest number. Many other states, though, are trying to catch up. Florida, Michigan, and Maryland are good examples of states that are moving towards the goal of locating a junior college within reach of nearly every student.

The rise in junior college enrollments, when compared with other areas of higher education, is marked. In the fall of 1962, junior colleges enrolled 6.6 percent more first-time students than at the opening of the school year in 1961. Four-year colleges enrolled .5 percent fewer students than before. Since 1961 enrollment in junior colleges has increased by 13.7 percent as compared with 7.2 percent in four-year institutions. For all institutions combined, the first-time opening enrollment has increased by 65 percent from 1954 to 1962, but in junior colleges the increase is over 100 percent. In addition, the junior colleges now enroll 25.2 percent of the total number of first-time degree students, whereas in 1954, junior colleges enrolled only 20.7 percent of the total. One out of every four students entering higher education now enrolls in a junior college. It is estimated that by 1975 one out of every two students will be attending a junior college.

Some of the key junior college states report individual statistics that show a surprising growth in enrollment for fall 1962 over the previous year. New York State reports an increase of 40 percent; Florida, 27.75 percent; Texas, 15.3 percent; Illinois, 13.5 percent; and California, 6 percent. Florida, one of the states with a mushrooming junior college system, reports that in Escambia County nine out of ten students beginning their college education enrolled in junior colleges. In Michigan, enrollments at the community colleges increased more than eight times in ten years, from 4,022 in 1951 to 32,987 in 1961.

Types of Programs in the Junior Colleges

Most junior colleges provide two types of programs: (1) the transfer or pre-professional curriculum, sometimes called the "university parallel curriculum," and (2) the technical-terminal or semiprofessional curriculum.

1. *Transfer curriculum.* This program is similar to courses of study of-

fered in four-year institutions during the freshman and sophomore years. If the student takes the prescribed number of courses and achieves the required level of work, he may transfer to a four-year college or university for the third and fourth years. According to numerous research-project findings, this transfer is usually accomplished successfully, especially if the student entering junior college has already chosen the institution to which he will go to complete his program. If such planning is done, work at the junior college can be effectively related to later work at the college of his choice. Studies show that the number of students taking two years at a junior college and then transferring is rapidly increasing.

2. *Technical-terminal curriculum.* This type of program is planned for the student who wants to complete his formal education at the end of two years. The program usually leads to an associate in arts or associate in science degree. The emphasis is on preparation for a specific vocation and the programs offered vary, depending on the aims of the institution and the needs of the student body. Many educators believe that the community junior college may provide the answer to the problem of training the many workers who will be needed in the technical and skilled occupations. Besides preparing the student for a vocation, the junior college usually takes some responsibility for providing courses that stimulate intellectual growth.

In addition to preparing students for transfer to higher institutions and for specific jobs, junior colleges serve other functions. They emphasize guidance and counseling services in educational, vocational, and personal areas. They also provide adult education courses for people who want to upgrade their skills or continue their education, and they give special services to the community. In fact, adult education, long a subsidiary function of the high school, has reached a level of great importance in the junior college.

LIBERAL ARTS COLLEGES AND "PROFESSIONAL" SCHOOLS

The first institutions of higher learning established in this country were four-year colleges. Most of these, as noted earlier in this chapter, were for the preparation of ministers for the various religious denominations. As time went by, some of them developed into universities and others became liberal arts colleges.

There are now a great many four-year liberal arts colleges in America. Although most of them were formerly controlled by religious groups, the trend has been away from church control. Hence today the majority of those that were once controlled by Protestant denominations are now under self-perpetuating boards of trustees.

The purpose of the liberal arts college is to complete the formal education of some of its students and to prepare others for later preprofessional work in a university.

The term "university" is used in this country in many different ways. Usually it connotes a group of colleges that function under a single charter or that were established by a single act of a legislature. The American university is usually a large institution, covering a great many fields. It generally includes a four-year liberal arts college. This may not be called a college, but nevertheless it offers four years of liberal arts work leading to a baccalaureate degree. There is also a graduate school with curricula leading to the master's and doctor's degrees, degrees which are usually bestowed in the same major fields as the bachelor's degree.

The greatest development in the university in the past century has occurred in the field of professional education. Beginning with the first medical school in 1765 and the first law school in 1779, schools or colleges have been developed in education, engineering, dentistry, divinity, forestry, and many other fields.

The first graduate school was opened in Johns Hopkins in 1876, but Yale granted the first Ph.D. Today graduate schools are an important part of our educational pattern; the development on this level has been especially rapid in the field of professional education. Several states now require one year of graduate work for secondary certification. Continued graduate study leading to a doctor's degree is necessary for holding important administrative positions or teaching in a college or university.

Trends in Higher Education

Higher education of some type is found in every civilization. Its aims and goals are derived from the philosophy of the social order of which it is a part. In a democracy, higher education must be keyed to the democratic ideal that guides the life patterns. If equal freedom and equal rights are to be achieved, the democratic system of higher education must develop equality for people regardless of sex, race, religious faith, or economic status. These things are fundamental to the realization of the best possible democratic state.

THE INDIVIDUAL STUDENT

The modern college devotes much attention to the individual student, but that has not always been true of colleges and universities in America. During the nineteenth century higher education in this country was under the influence of German universities. College presidents and professors were largely graduates of these universities, and they brought with them the philosophy and methods of higher education in Germany: the emphasis was on subject matter. The German professor lectured and gave examinations, and spent most of his time doing research. The university granted degrees but gave no attention to the individual student. It accepted no responsibility for his

If a Freshman couldn't spell his name when orientation week began, he certainly can after registration. Laborious as the process seems to students, the data on these cards form the basis for all placement, guidance, and transcript records so necessary for their own welfare. (*New Mexico State University*)

Left: The opportunity to serve as a biology technician under the guidance of a research scientist and professor at Argonne National Laboratory gives this student the chance to work with the most advanced theories in her field. (*William R. Simmons, Ford Foundation*)

Preparation for active leadership in a busy society includes many hours of solitary study and contemplation. (*Hendrix College, Conway, Arkansas*)

Left: According to one recent study, an average United States college student will spend 2000 hours in classes, seminars, and laboratories, and 7000 hours in extracurricular activities of one sort or another. All 9000 hours should contribute to his education in a positive way. (*Kalamazoo College, Kalamazoo, Michigan*)

housing, feeding, activities, or health. The relationship was purely intellectual.

Today it is recognized that the whole student comes to college. He is not just an intellect; he is a citizen in a democratic state. Since education is a process of developing a whole personality, colleges today are greatly concerned with their students' total life pattern.

This new concept of higher education has led to the formation of departments of student personnel. A student receives a great deal of personal attention; it often begins before he enters. He probably takes a battery of placement examinations as part of the entrance routine. When he arrives at college he is further examined and diagnosed so that his education can be planned to fit him as an individual. Most colleges also have an orientation program for freshmen, given sometimes the week before classes begin. This enables a student to become acquainted with the college and its program before he registers, and it enables his advisors to become acquainted with him so that they can work with him more intelligently.

Colleges no longer boast of the large percentage of freshmen they "flunk" and send home. When freshmen are carefully selected and advised by a functioning personnel department and when their teachers are interested in them as individuals, very few of them fail to become acceptable college students. The trend today is away from the mass handling of freshmen and toward more individualized guidance.

Better Provisions for Student Health

Some type of health program has been set up in all institutions of higher learning. Most colleges and universities accept complete responsibility for student health problems during the college course. This includes a careful physical examination as part of the entrance procedure. After the student has been admitted, he has the services of a group of doctors and nurses. Most institutions are equipped with the necessary laboratories for special tests, and many provide rest homes and hospitals. Necessary operations and hospital care are part of the services the student receives for the health fee he pays.

More Adequate Housing and Feeding Facilities

Most institutions of higher education accept the responsibility of housing and feeding their students. Hundreds of dormitories containing thousands of rooms have been built in recent years. Most of them have dining rooms in which the students eat. A satisfactory place to live, with well-planned meals, is conducive to better work on the part of students. These living halls also take care of much of the students' social life.

A generation or two ago few colleges accepted any responsibility for the lives of their students outside of the classroom. But following World War I, American colleges and universities discovered the student as an individual and began a program of out-of-class education. The provision of better housing and feeding facilities is one of the results of this discovery.

Better Extracurriculum Activities

Student unions, also a result of the discovery of the student as an individual, are the center of student life on most campuses. Most of them are given over entirely to social life; no classes are held in them. Provision is made for all types of recreation, and places to eat are commonly included. The unions make it possible for the campus to be the center of the students' lives.

The trend is toward more student government. Whereas, in days gone by, the students played at government, now they have a real part in the government of student affairs on the campus. Most colleges and universities are glad to turn over to them many problems concerning their campus activities. On most campuses the students publish their own papers, usually without faculty supervision. Student government does not typically extend to athletics, because such sports as football and basketball have become big business and are usually under a faculty committee.

GENERAL EDUCATION

The day of narrow specialization on the undergraduate level is definitely over, the trend being toward majors covering a wider area and toward courses of a more general nature. It is away from unrestricted free electives and toward a required pattern of general education, particularly in the lower division of the college.

Several very important studies have been made in the field of general education. The most extensive of these was the one sponsored and directed by the American Council on Education and made cooperatively by a group of colleges and universities from 1939 to 1944. The final report, published in four volumes by the Council, contains valuable information regarding general education on the college level. Another very valuable study was made by a faculty committee of Harvard University. This was a three-year study that covered both secondary and higher education. The results were published in 1945 by the university under the title *General Education in a Free Society*. This study, too, made a significant contribution to the field of general education.

The State University of Iowa has been a pioneer in the field of general education. Nine faculty members of the University, under the chairmanship of Dr. Earl J. McGrath, made a report, *Toward General Education*. Another pioneer was Dr. Malcolm MacLean, who when dean of the General College of the University of Minnesota did much experimental work in this field.

It would be difficult to name all outstanding colleges and universities in the field of general education because the movement is so widespread. It would be still more difficult to discover a college that has not been affected by the new trend.

It might be wise to define general education. Although there are as many definitions as there are writers in the field, we particularly like the short definition given by McGrath and his group: "General education, as we conceive it, is that which prepares the young for the common life of their time and their kind."[1]

PROBLEMS OF HIGHER EDUCATION

Even in the best of times the problems of higher education are legion. Obviously, we cannot discuss these in any number; however, two major problems facing colleges and universities will be mentioned. These problems are interrelated. Moreover, both are related to certain social issues.

The common background of the problems will be particularly evident when the current attacks on education are noted, for such attacks involve public schools as well as institutions of higher learning, and the various levels of education are not separable and self-contained. Damage to one part of the system necessarily impairs the total organism; education is not any more divisible than freedom or democracy.

Traditionalism and Experimentalism

Traditionalism and experimentalism represent two conflicting philosophies in the stream of American education. While the reverberations of this ideological struggle can be felt on all educational levels, the most articulate proponents of the two sides are to be found in our colleges and universities.

Traditionalists are characterized by a firm belief in the "great tradition," their emphasis is more on retrospect than prospect and they believe in a faculty psychology and the transfer of training. For them, the universe is fixed and essentially inalterable. Truth is similarly fixed and may be ascertained by the study of classics and by meditation. Generally, the traditionalists can trace their philosophical roots to the Middle Ages and Scholasticism. Because of their faith in pure intellect they insist that colleges should be free of the taint of the outside world. They believe that society should be ordered. In such an order, higher education would be the property of the intellectual elite.

The experimentalists, on the other hand, are typified by the accent they lay on the present. This does not mean that they wish to abandon the intellectual heritage, but rather that they are concerned with using it to comprehend and solve the pressing social problems of the modern world. Thus, the past is actively regarded as a problem-solving instrument, not just as some-

[1] Earl J. McGrath, et al., Toward General Education, New York, Macmillan, 1948, p. 9.

thing to be remembered. The experimentalists point out that faculty psychology has long since been proven invalid. In its place they put the psychology of the whole man—the man not as an isolated individual but as a living member of a social organism. They prefer scientific method to revealed truth, a fluid social order to a rigid one, the laboratory to the ivory tower. They are far more generous in estimating the number of persons who might benefit from a college education than the traditionalists.

In a controversy such as this, it is necessary for the individual to take sides. Having done so, one may proceed to set up his own position as "right" and that of the oppositions as "wrong." While many professors identify with the experimentalist position, whose position is thought to be the more congenial to our democratic pattern of living, it must be noted that the traditionalists have in many ways benefited higher education in America. They have helped to remind people of the richness of the cultural inheritance, they have helped to make it clear that scientism unguided by morality can be destructive as well as constructive, they have vigorously combated attacks on academic freedom as well as anti-intellectualism both inside and outside the university.

Many of the difficulties between the two factions are verbal rather than real. For example, both would agree that study of the past has intrinsic as well as instrumental value: the difference is one of emphasis. There are, of course, actual disagreements and these should not be minimized. In view of contemporary attacks on our colleges, however, it might be wise for the two groups to close ranks. Intellectual disputes, at least in their earlier stages, might better be aired within the profession than prematurely projected upon the public scene where they are easily seized upon by political opportunists and antidemocratic forces.

WHO SHOULD GO TO COLLEGE

This is a question of importance for two reasons. First, because human resources are most valuable. For the productivity and well-being of the nation, it is necessary that we develop fully the capacities of each citizen. Often this entails education beyond high school. Secondly, in America we believe in equality of educational opportunity. We do not feel that higher education should be the exclusive property of any class or group: instead, we hold forth the hope of college education for all those who are capable of benefiting from it.

The problem is to determine what percentage of the college-age population should go to college. Under the GI Bill of Rights fourteen billion dollars were spent in seven years to send eight million veterans to some type of school. A great many of these veterans attended colleges and universities. Generally, their records were excellent. Thus, we know that a larger percentage of our youth are capable of gaining from higher education than was formerly thought. Indeed, the President's Commission on Higher Education has concluded that "at least 49 per cent of our population has the mental ability to complete 14 years of schooling," while "at least 32 per cent of our population has the mental ability to complete an advanced liberal or specialized professional education."

The Commission on Financing Higher Education, in a slightly different estimate, believes that the top quarter of our youth in intellectual ability should have the opportunity of attending a four-year college. This means that about 453,000 additional students should be attending college at the present time. Locating and motivating these students constitutes a complex problem. Byron S. Hollinshead points out that while the problem of finance is also of concern, it is not insuperable.

We believe that all students in the upper quarter in ability of the age group should be given a certificate which so states and that society should find ways of financing those who want a college education if they need assistance. We are hazarding the guess that the average need will be around $500 and that therefore the costs would be approximately $226,000,000.

This seems like a large sum, and indeed it is. But when we consider the value of the human resources involved, the costs of their development seem small. Or if we compare this figure with the $60,000,000,000 needed to maintain the cold war in the fiscal year 1952–53, it amounts roughly to the expenses of the cold war for one and one-half days. Such an expenditure for developing academic talent on a national scale may be wiser, even for defense purposes, than any other expenditure we can make. Or if it be thought that such an expenditure would set an unwise precedent, we may compare it with the expenditure of $257,250,000 made by the Federal Government in fiscal 1951 to farmers as rewards for making soil improvements. Certainly the development of our human resources would seem to be as fully justified as the development of our soil resources.[2]

President Conant of Harvard, in his book *Education and Liberty*, says: "Something like 20 per cent of the American youth of college age attend a college or university full time for at least a year, while the maximum figure in any other English-speaking nation is not over 7 per cent."[3]

There are in our society forces of considerable magnitude that do not believe in proposals of this sort. They wish to diminish rather than increase the number of students who attend institutions of higher education. Because these forces are antidemocratic, they argue that college should be the exclusive property of a small group of from 2 to 5 percent of the college-age population. They think the English plan is more satisfactory than ours. They assume that this "aristocracy" will possess a corner on both wealth and

[2] Byron S. Hollinshead for the Commission on Financing Higher Education, *Who Should Go to College?*, New York, Columbia University Press, 1952, pp. 83–84.

[3] James Bryant Conant, *Education and Liberty*, Cambridge, Harvard University Press, 1953, p. 5.

intellect. Often these forces twist the arguments of traditionalists who are staunch defenders of democracy to support their own case. This is one of the most unfortunate aspects of the philosophy of traditionalism. While its sincere proponents wish a social order based on intellect, less principled persons use it to defend a rigid class society based on wealth and inheritance.

Nevertheless, the direction of the future is clear. Higher education must be extended to more and more persons. The necessity for such an extension is both practical and moral; it is the projection of democratic ideals into the field of the actual.

THE ATTACKS ON COLLEGES AND UNIVERSITIES

The attacks on our public schools have been accompanied by attacks on institutions of higher education. The attackers have been so vituperative that many unwary and uninformed persons have been led to believe that our universities are hotbeds of communism. Often a press overeager for news has taken up these charges. The results have been unfortunate. It has become common practice to depreciate intelligence and there has been a sharp curtailment of freedom of inquiry. Under such conditions, professors cannot do their best teaching and students are badly handicapped in their learning. If attacks and so-called loyalty oaths were successful in ferreting out communists, a case might be made for them. The fact is that they have been singularly unsuccessful.

The attack on universities is part of a larger movement which includes book-burning, the pillorying of the Protestant clergy, the fight against the public schools, and the stigmatizing of all liberals as subversives. This movement, or disease, is essentially anti-intellectual. It is born of hysteria, nurtured on fear, and married to distrust. It is opposed to the philosophy which is at the root of democratic government. Anti-intellectualism holds that man, at best ineffectual, is incapable of solving his own problems. Far from deserving freedom, he must be tightly constrained by repressive legislation and rigid class society. In such a society the people are uneducated because education itself is regarded as the exclusive possession of the elite. The marks of the average "good citizen" are ignorance, poverty, and subservience.

Those who believe in democracy hold that such anti-intellectualism is narrow and unlovely. They maintain our faith in freedom and intelligence, not out of any precious academicism, but out of the sure knowledge that they are the moral lifeblood of the community. Chief Justice Earl Warren has pointed up the value of intellectual freedom in the words: "Liberty—not communism—is the most contagious force in the world. It will permeate the Iron Curtain. It will eventually abide everywhere. For no people of any race will long remain slaves. Our strength is our diversity. Our power is in freedom of thought and of research."

RELATED READINGS

American Colleges and Universities, Washington, D.C., American Council on Education, 1960.

Brickman, William, and Stanley Lehrer, Eds., *A Century of Higher Education: Classical Citadel to Collegiate Colossus,* New York, Society for the Advancement of Education, 1962.

Higher Education in a Decade of Decision, Washington, D.C., National Education Association, 1957.

Knowles, Malcolm S., *The Adult Education Movement in the United States,* New York, Holt, Rinehart and Winston, 1962.

McConnell, T. R., *A General Pattern for American Public Higher Education,* New York, McGraw-Hill, 1962.

Sanford, Nevitt, Ed., *The American College,* New York, Wiley, 1962.

Thornton, James W., Jr., *The Community Junior College,* New York, Wiley, 1960.

PART III

The
Teacher
and
American
Education

INTRODUCTION

Parts I and II of this text were concerned with education as a necessary function of society, and with schools as the institutions society has established to educate its youth. The place of education and schools in our society was discussed in earlier chapters, and attention was then focused on the various levels of the American public school system and on some of the important problems they face. Because of the importance of education in any society, and especially due to its imperative nature in a democratic society, the study of education should be a valuable part of the general education of any college student. A nation looks to its college graduates for leadership not only in their chosen field of specialization but also as well-educated citizens. In the United States, schools play such a vital role that an educated citizenship needs more than a cursory knowledge of schools and education.

Throughout the book, and particularly in Part III, special emphasis is given to the study of education as a profession. In this aspect, we invite the reader to consider teaching as a life's work. Part III will consider the professional aspects of the job of teaching, and some of the outcomes of successful teaching. It also will be concerned with the past, present, recent, and probable future of our schools. Finally, it poses the question: "Shall I be a teacher?"

———————————————————

CRITICAL ISSUES
IN AMERICAN EDUCATION

Each of the statements below is representative of an opinion commonly held concerning American education today. Most of them indicate a definite position on issues that are closely related to the topics discussed in Part III of the text.

It is suggested that you follow the same procedure and use the same scale with these statements that you applied to the Critical Issues list preceding Chapter 1.

What's Your Opinion?

1. Although a teacher is a public servant, his conduct after school hours is his own private business.
2. The scholastic attainments of pupils as revealed by standardized tests constitute a reliable basis upon which to rate the teachers of those pupils.
3. It is misleading to believe that anyone is a born teacher.
4. In the ideal situation the learner is clay to be molded by the hands of the master potter, the teacher.
5. A teacher should be expected to follow such instructional procedures as are recommended by the author of the basic textbook.
6. A teacher should have his own philosophy of teaching and should select instructional procedures in terms of this philosophy.
7. A school should have a definite philosophy of instruction in all fields of work and should require all teachers to conform to this philosophy of instruction.
8. A teacher's value to a school should be judged by the success with which his pupils meet the requirements of the course.
9. A teacher should recognize that each subject has a special function that requires systematic study.
10. A teacher should select a minimum set of facts, principles, and concepts for drill to the point of effective mastery by all pupils, the fast as well as the slow.
11. The recent decisions of the United States Supreme Court concerning the use of prayers and Bible-reading in the public schools are indicative of the "Godlessness" of the American school system.
12. Most teacher education programs put excessive emphasis on "how to teach" and too little emphasis on "what to teach."
13. The right to strike for better pay, improved working conditions, and other benefits is not consistent with teachers' obligations to society.
14. It is time for teachers to stop pretending they have a profession, accept the philosophy of unionism, and make real gains for themselves.
15. No group in our society makes a greater contribution than do teachers.

A university supervisor and four student teachers discuss various methods of presenting subject matter. (*Drake University, Des Moines, Iowa*)

Left: This student, a member of the Future Teachers of America (FTA), is making plans with a teacher for the classroom work she will conduct. (*Sybil Shelton from Monkmeyer*)

That wonderful day when the student teacher's carefully planned lesson proceeds smoothly while both the cooperating teacher and university supervisor observe. (*University of Portland*)

Below: Members of the Student National Education Association (SNEA) hold local, regional, and national conferences to share ideas and to plan for the future. (*National Education Association*)

The national headquarters of the NEA, an imposing structure serving the largest professional organization in the world. (*National Education Association*)

The personal interview is the capstone of the process of securing a teaching position. Both the applicant and the employer profit. (*Hayes from Monkmeyer*)

Right: An in-service workshop is one of the most popular ways by which teachers remain abreast of new knowledge, methods, and materials. (*Lew Merrim from Monkmeyer*)

Chapter 11 / THE TEACHER AND THE TEACHING PROFESSION

WHAT MAKES AN OCCUPATION A PROFESSION?

A recent edition of an occupational index listed more than 20,000 different types of jobs that are held in the United States today. The fact that so many different skills and abilities are salable is a tribute to America's ingenuity and to its free economy. Each new technological advancement brings new job opportunities, and the list of occupations is constantly lengthening at an increasing rate. It surprises many to learn that more than one-half of the jobs currently held by Americans did not even exist 50 years ago. Many of the jobs, however, are familiar to everyone. The list includes such occupations as dentistry, day-laboring, farming, medicine, nursing, and, of course, teaching.

Most indexes have organized the list of jobs by classifying the types of work in terms of their relationship to each other. Although this may seem like a simple task, it certainly is not. If one should decide to group the occupations with which he is familiar under several headings, his first task would be to choose the categories to be used. A typical set of categories would be "Unskilled," "Semiskilled," "Skilled," "Commercial," and "Professional." There are also other headings that could be used, and some entirely different bases for classification that might be chosen. The one given above would serve especially well in considering the place of the teaching "profession" in the occupational world.

Many jobs would be easy to classify under the headings "Unskilled," "Semiskilled," "Skilled," "Commercial," "Professional." The day-laborer is almost always an unskilled worker, the master brick layer is certainly a skilled worker. Some occupations are obviously professional; the lawyer, the minister and the dentist are universally accepted as professionals.

Not all of the occupations listed in an index are as easy to classify as that of the day-laborer and lawyer. Although, at one time there were great differences among the various types of jobs which made the task of classification relatively easy, recent socioeconomic changes have obliterated older guide lines. At one time the man whose work was basically manual was commonly referred to as a "blue-collar" worker. His opposite was known as a "white-collar" worker, and the differences between the blue-collar job and the white-collar job, including, of course, the professions, were readily apparent. The white-collar worker had a larger salary, job security, a place of prestige in the community, and attractive working conditions and surroundings. These benefits were denied the blue-collared man. Such is not the case today. More and more of the benefits of a higher standard of living are now enjoyed by almost everyone. The United States has made great strides toward achieving economic equality just as it has sought political democracy. Therefore, the differences between the various types of jobs people hold are not obvious. More than surface attributes must be surveyed to understand correctly the nature of today's occupations.

One way of proceeding in a classification of jobs would be to list the characteristics of a type of job—the professional occupations for instance—and then check a particular one—teaching for example—against the list of characteristics. Such a procedure should provide evidence to help determine what constitutes the "ear-marks" which make a job a profession. One "professional" characteristic almost certain to be listed would be a relatively long period of formal pre-job preparation. Many professional workers are required to complete six years of pre-service education, some of them even more.

Two other characteristics of a profession are closely related to the long period of formal training required: one, there is a selective process with regard to persons seeking to enter the profession; two, the profession itself exercises a sizeable amount of control over entrance to practice. Not everyone who wishes to be a physician is admitted to medical school, various criteria must be met before the candidate is permitted to enter the school. And no one would argue that all students admitted to law school will automatically complete the course successfully. The control of entrance to the profession by the current members of the profession is just as certain. The typical profession also exercises control over the schools that desire to prepare new members of the profession. Accreditation by the American Medical Association is required for any college of medicine, and this accreditation is not easy to receive or retain; nor is the successful graduate of the accreditated professional school always admitted into the profession. The neophyte lawyer must pass the bar examinations and be admitted to practice by other lawyers after completion of his college education. Entrance into professional practice calls for the passing of many hurdles by the candidate, and the practicing professionals supervise and help shape the nature of the hurdles.

A code of ethics and a tradition of ethical practices are other attributes of a profession. All professions have codes of ethics, most professions have ways of enforcing these codes in practice. Everyone is familiar with the fact that the minister and the lawyer are required to live up to a code of ethical behavior if they are to be permitted, by the profession, to continue their work. Thus the profession itself maintains control over its members even after they have been admitted into the group.

Three other closely related characteristics are also typical of a profession. First, the basic purpose of the professional worker is to render service without regard for personal gain or self-aggrandizement. The services of any true profession are available to anyone, regardless of his ability to pay or his supposed stature in the community. Secondly, however, it is also true that the average annual income for the members of some professions is very high. Although their primary objective is to render service, and it is universally recognized that they do, many professional groups have a schedule of salaries and fees which assures their members a far-above-average personal salary. A third attribute probably is caused by one or both of the two just mentioned. Most professional workers enjoy a place of prestige and honor in their communities. It is doubtless true that the real worth of any person in any community is finally determined by the person himself and the service which he renders, but there is a general feeling that the professional worker is an especially valuable member of society.

It seems important to list two more attributes of a profession. One, professions tend to have strong professional organizations; two, persons who enter a profession intend to remain in the practice of it until retirement. At least two results of the strength of professional organizations have already been mentioned in the current discussion. It is through its organization that the medical profession accredits schools, admits doctors to practice in hospitals and clinics, and generally disciplines its membership. It is obvious that such an organization must be a strong one. It seems apparent, also, that no one would complete the strenuous screening, long preparation, and the neophyte period of an occupation if he intends to use it only as a stepping stone to something else. Tenure in the job is certainly an important earmark of the professional.

There are many other characteristics of professions which could be listed, and anyone interested in pursuing the task of determining what makes an occupation a profession should delve more deeply into the subject of professional attributes than can this limited discussion. The student who is interested in considering teaching as a life's work must also investigate the characteristics of the job of teaching and then compare these findings with the list of professional "earmarks" and then determine if teaching is, can become, or ought to be a profession.

THE OCCUPATION OF TEACHING

Before making plans to choose a teaching career the prospective candidate will want to know much about it: the legal requirements of entering the profession; the salary and other compensations to be expected; how to obtain a position; what the nature of the teaching contract will be; how permanent a position the teacher has; what steps, "hurdles" and requirements the college will require. He should consider the drawbacks of the job as well as its advantages. Teaching is not an easy way to make a living; the prospective teacher should not be naive about his choice.

Pre-Service Preparation

Most of the readers of this text are already involved in one of the earlier phases of a program of undergraduate, pre-service, teacher education. Although each college for teacher education constructs its own program, and it would be impossible to typify all of them in a single discussion, there is sufficient similarity among most programs to point up major characteristics, examine trends, and identify several important problems common to the pre-service education of most teachers.

A recent report[1] of the National Commission on Teacher Education and Professional Standards, commonly referred to as NC TEPS, outlined the sequential steps in the identification, admission, and retention of prospective teachers which are followed in most accredited teacher education programs and which are recommended as being excellent practice. Because of the

[1] Margaret Lindsey, Ed., *New Horizons for the Teaching Profession: A Report of the Task Force on New Horizon in Teacher Education and Professional Standards*, National Commission on Teacher Education and Professional Standards, National Education Association, Washington, D.C., 1961, pp. 161–204.

stature of this body, and because of the movement towards national accreditation of teacher education programs in accordance with its recommendations, NC TEPS is certain to have a great effect on teacher education in America. It is suggested by this group that the identification of prospective teachers be begun early, no later than in connection with the activities associated with regular institutional admission. Such specific orientation to teacher education might well include a special program of meetings and the administration of interest and aptitude batteries.

Such early identification of teacher education candidates permits intelligent scheduling-building in terms of student goals throughout the four-year undergraduate program. Such planning is especially important for teachers because a most vital segment of their education, the general education program, must begin with the start of the college career. "New Horizons for Teachers," a part of the NC TEPS task force report, emphasizes the place and importance of this program of preprofessional education. The group recommends that students who wish to become teachers begin their college study in a professional program of one or two years' duration:

> Such a program should provide not only a base for later study, but should also be designated to strengthen the selection program. General (or liberal) education with breadth and depth is essential to each student recommended for graduation from an institution, as well as for those preparing to teach. But for persons upon whom responsibility will lie for transmitting both knowledge and understanding of the various disciplines, their interrelatedness and the cultures from which they have evolved or towards which they are developing, it is imperative that learning be effective. Those who would become teachers may well be expected to demonstrate knowledge and understanding to a greater extent than that required of liberal arts graduates as a whole, and even to a greater extent than required of persons in the general education curricula prerequisite to admission to the professional sequences for some other fields of endeavor.[2]

Preprofessional, or general, education comprises the majority of the work of the first two collegiate years in almost all accredited teacher education programs. In many colleges the general education sequence must be completed by the end of the sophomore year, in others some general education continues into the upper division period in a continuously reducing amount. In either case, its importance is a matter of general agreement.

Following the period of major emphasis on preprofessional education, whatever the specifics might be, most accredited programs require the prospective teacher to meet the first of several screening devices which he must pass before graduation and certification. This first step is usually called "admission to teacher education," and most often it is required that formal application be made. At this time the candidate and the institution give careful attention to such factors as aptitude, interest in teaching, and the

---

[2] *Ibid.*, pp. 193–194.

choice of a specific teaching field. Minimum grade-average requirements, successful performance on standardized tests which cover the common branches of knowledge, acceptable scores on physical, psychological, and sociometric examinations, and a check on the students' ability in oral and written communication are common requirements for acceptance into the program of professional and specialized education.

The next major segment of the professional sequence of courses, admission to and retention in student teaching, also should require formal application. Admission to student teaching should be recognition of accomplishment by the student, signifying that he has completed prerequisites providing both breadth and depth in a general education program, knowledge in fields of specialization, and skill and knowledge through a professional sequence. Standards of performance required in all three areas should be sufficiently high to help insure that only persons of high caliber are admitted.

The period of student teaching must be preceded by opportunity for acquaintanceship with the normal behavior patterns of children in formal and informal situations, and by additional observations of children in the classroom. Actual teaching experiences should be interspersed with additional observations designed to help the student gain knowledge and skill in terms of specific problems, with opportunities for the student to acquaint himself with a school as a functioning organism and with student-teacher-cooperating teacher-college supervisor conferences designed to help the student develop his strengths and overcome his problems.

The last of the three "check points" commonly found in forward-looking programs of teacher education occurs at the time of graduation and certification. "New Horizons" includes the following statement:

If institutions are to be accredited for the purpose of preparing teachers, each institution should also be charged with the responsibility not only of vouching for the quantity and kind of preparation of its graduates, but also for the professional quality of the candidate for the teaching certificate. The institution's recommendation or denial of recommendation for a legal license to teach must therefore be based on careful assessment of the various measures and judgments made during the period of selection and preparation that are applicable in determining whether or not a candidate should be admitted to professional practice.[3]

The diploma and the teaching certificate, then, mark the end of the pre-service preparation of most teachers, although there is a recent trend toward a five-year program of pre-service preparation which includes an extended period of internship taken after initial licensing. In any case it is the teaching certificate, sometimes called teaching credential or teachers' license, and not the possession of a college degree which permits a person to teach in a public school.

[3] *Ibid.*, pp. 197–198.

THE TEACHING CERTIFICATE

Today every public school teacher must have a certificate, but such was not always the case. In the early days of this country no certificates were required; anyone who could get a job was allowed to teach. Later, certificates were granted by local school authorities. If a teacher applied for a position in a school, the members of the school board might give him an oral examination to convince themselves that he was qualified to teach. Still later, teaching certificates were issued on the basis of successful completion of a test. Teachers' examinations were given at regular intervals by county superintendents of schools or by local school boards because these officials had a legal right to grant certificates.

Today most certificates to teach are granted by state departments of education, although some state colleges still have the power to grant them. The trend during the first half of this century has been toward centralizing the certification function in the state department of education. Very few counties or local school districts now have the authority to issue certificates, and the right to certificate has also largely passed from the colleges and the county school authorities. As noted earlier most certificates are now granted upon the recommendation of the faculty of the college or university where the teacher received his education. The state, through the state department of education, sets the standards and the schools of education fulfill them.

Although at one time most credentials were granted for life, certificates are now usually granted for a definite period of time. They may be renewed when the holder has taught a certain length of time with success, or has taken certain additional courses, or both.

Certificates are more specific in some states than in others. In fact they have become very specialized in some states, where the department of education must grant a great variety of certificates. In California the state department now issues 59 different kinds of certificates for teachers, but the state of Washington has eliminated all special certificates for different subjects, levels, and types of children and has only one credential. A certificated teacher in Washington may teach any grade or subject or type of children on the common credential. Most states still issue certificates that are good only at certain levels, in certain subject fields, or for certain special types of children: one certificate is good only in the primary grades; another licenses the holder to teach science in the high school; still another may be good only for teachers of the blind. Certificates to teach art, music, physical education, or agriculture are common.

In some states a teacher must take an oath of allegiance to the United States to get credentials to teach. In most states he must pass a physical examination. Often he must pass an examination on the Constitution of the United States and on the history of the state in which he is to teach. Most states provide for the revocation of certificates upon the presentation of evidence that the holder is unfit to teach.

Reciprocity in Teacher Certification

For many years teaching certificates have provided a typical example of the fact that education in the United States is a state function. Issued by the various state departments of education, the teaching certificate has been valid only in the state of issuance although a great deal of similarity in the requirements of the various states has existed. Most states have a list of specific requirements for the certificate which apply to all applicants and which bear little functional relationship to teacher competence. Oklahoma, for example, has long required all persons to have completed a three-semester-hour course in American History, a three-hour course in American government, a two-semester-hour course in Oklahoma history (unless the course was taken in high school), and an organized study of the Oklahoma School Code, before they will issue a Standard Teaching Certificate. Other states also have had similar special laws, and the effect of them has obviated the possibility of anyone who received his preparation in another state—regardless of how well prepared he might be to teach in his field—obtaining standard certification. Recently, however, there has been a trend towards reciprocity in teacher certification which most students of the field favor.

In 1954 a new accrediting agency for teacher education, the National Council for the Accreditation of Teacher Education (NCATE), was established. This organization was novel in that it was nation-wide in scope; previous to 1954 all teacher-education accreditation was done on a state and regional basis. NCATE has made significant progress in the relatively short period of time since its inception, and appears to be gaining the respect of the teaching profession as few organizations have. The importance attached to the work of NCATE is indicated by the fact that more than 340 teacher education institutions are now accredited by it, and that these schools produce more than 70 percent of the nation's supply of new teachers each year. Furthermore, and perhaps of even greater significance, 29 states and the District of Columbia recognize, for the purposes of reciprocity, graduates of teacher education programs in NCATE-accredited colleges and universities. In other words, these schools' graduates will not be penalized by having to take the additional courses to qualify themselves after crossing a state line into one of these 27 states.

Copies of the most recent list of NCATE-accredited institutions and information concerning the states which offer reciprocity can be obtained by writing to the National Commission on Teacher Education and Professional Standards, NEA, 1201 Sixteenth Street, N.W., Washington 6, D.C. Any student who is obtaining his teacher preparation in one state and hopes to teach in another would be well advised to seek such information.

OBTAINING A TEACHING POSITION

One group of the "earmarks" of a profession listed earlier in this discussion was the existence of a selective process with regard to persons seeking to enter the profession. It was noted that this selective process operates not only during the time of pre-service preparation but also bridges the gap between the pre- and in-service period. In teaching, the requirements for the certification represent one "screen" which is found at this point in a professional career. The process of obtaining a teaching position is another occurrence which comes near the close of pre-service preparation and helps to denote the beginning of the active professional career, but the extent to which this is a selective process varies with the individual student, his teaching field, and the school systems to which he makes application.

Most professional openings in education are filled through college or university placement bureaus, although some state education associations maintain placement offices, state employment services sometimes handle teaching jobs, and a number of commercial teacher placement agencies also exist. Prospective teachers should always register with the placement bureaus at their own college regardless of wherever else they also might choose to register. Almost without exception, any opening that exists will be reported to all agencies—college, state, commercial—at the same time. It is also interesting to note that, while a minimum registration fee represents the total cost to the student for any position filled through his university placement service, all commercial agencies and some other bureaus charge the teacher a percentage of his first year's salary as a fee for their services. Wherever the student does register, the process to be completed is very similar. He will be required to present a transcript of his college work, give information concerning his interests, work experience, health, and other information of importance, and a list of persons who he knows will write letters of recommendation for him. The student whose professional papers show generally good grades, a record of active college life, evidence of radiant health, and favorable letters of recommendation from persons whose opinion is respected is in a strong position to obtain a desirable job.

The element of selection also operates in relation to the supply and demand which exists in the various teaching fields. Persons who are prepared to teach in an area where the demand exceeds the supply are in a position to choose placement from a number of openings, and the hiring official might be inclined to accept minimum preparation in these fields. It would be wise for the student who is engaged in an early stage of his teacher education to consult the factual information available on teacher supply and demand which is published by both the United States Office of Education and the National Education Association.

Finally, some school systems are able to screen candidates much more closely than others. The school system with a high scale of salaries, attractive working and living conditions, and the reputation of an outstanding educational program always has many candidates from which to choose even in fields where the national supply is short. Because these systems often maintain a continuing list of candidates in whom they are interested and fill openings from this list rather than instituting a new search every time they need a teacher, it is best for the interested person to make application and to keep his papers up to date with those of the school system.

TEACHERS IN SERVICE

After graduation, certification, and attaining the first position, the teacher moves from the pre- to the in-service facet of his professional career. As noted above, there is a great deal of similarity among the many accredited teacher education programs at the undergraduate level, thus the professional orientation of pre-service programs tends to be similar for most persons. No such situation of similarity exists at the in-service level. It is possible, however, to identify some trends and draw some generalizations which apply to the in-service career of most teachers.

The Salary Schedule

There was a time when teachers were paid only what the schools had to pay to keep a staff, and when each teacher was placed in the awkward position of having to "bargain" with the administration and school board each year to determine the size of his salary. Today, however, almost all school systems have a salary schedule which shows the beginning teacher not only what his first-year salary will be but also what he may expect for the future.

The salary schedule shown in Table 7 is typical of the one found in city school systems.

The three classes refer to the educational background of the teacher, and the steps down the left side are years of teaching experience. Most teachers' salaries are determined by these two criteria—education and experience, although the proportionate weight given varies from one school system to another and some schools give more "credit" for experience in other schools and military experience than do others.

This schedule is also typical in that it is a "single salary schedule," which means that no distinction is made between elementary or secondary teachers with regard to pay, nor between men and women teachers. The last three steps on the schedule, those marked PGI or Professional Growth Increments, are paid only to carefully selected teachers whose work merits this additional money.

The practice of merit rating, accompanied with additional pay, is a relatively recent one and is highly controversial. Teachers' groups and associations have generally taken a stand in opposition to this practice, while school

TABLE 7. A TYPICAL SALARY SCHEDULE

Years	Bachelor's Degree	Master's Degree	Post-Master's Degree
1	$4800	$5100	
2	4950	5250	
3	5100	5400	($250 above equivalent
4	5250	5550	MA schedule for com-
5	5400	5700	pletion of a "6-year"
6	5700	6000	program)
7	5925	6225	
8	6150	6450	
9	6375	6675	
10	6600	6900	($500 above equivalent
11	6825	7125	MA schedule for posses-
12	7050	7350	sion of Ed.D or Ph.D.
13	7275	7575	degree)
14	7500	7800	
15	n.a.[d]	8025	
Professional Growth Increments		1 8500	1 $250 above base
		2 8750	2 $500 above base
		3 9000	3 $750 above base

[d] Not available.

board groups and many school administrators tend to favor it. The state of Utah has recently adopted a state-wide salary schedule which is based on the merit principle, and is typical of these kinds of schedules. All teachers may expect some relatively automatic pay raises, but in order to achieve the higher levels of pay a teacher must be adjudged superior. In Utah the decision of the administrators determines who receives merit rating, in other places a committee of teachers, administrators, and, sometimes, lay persons make the determination. Whether or not this trend towards merit rating and pay grows, it seems obvious that teachers' salaries will continue the general rise they have had for the last fifteen years. In the short period of time between 1949 and 1961 the average salary paid to instructional staff members in the public schools rose from $3010 to $5716,[4] a significant rise which becomes even more meaningful when it is remembered that the 1949 salary represented a 50 percent increase over the salaries paid ten years earlier.

The salary schedule item of greatest interest to beginning teachers is the beginning salary. For many years teachers were paid very low salaries, but today teaching is becoming a well-paid profession, although salaries vary greatly from state to state and from district to district within each state. For the school year 1963–1964 the beginning salary for the inexperienced teacher with minimum preparation in Los Angeles, $5300; in Washington, D.C.,

[4] *Financing the Public Schools—1960–1970,* Special Project on School Finance, National Education Association, Washington, D.C., 1961, p. 64.

By virtue of this vote in September, 1962, Local 2 of the American Federation of Teachers (New York City) approved the contract negotiations by which all New York teachers were bound. (*The American Teacher Magazine*)

Below: Teachers' associations offer numerous special service benefits for teachers including group insurance and purchasing plans, travel tours, retirement homes, and placement service. (*California Teachers Association, Southern Section*)

Below: The European tour taken by these teachers, here visiting Venice, affords the opportunity to combine professional advancement with a vacation. Hundreds of students will gain from their experiences. (*American Express Company*)

This teacher, whose job rights are protected by good tenure laws, brings the benefits of his long years of experience to a "Great Books" discussion. (*Detroit Public Schools*)

$5000; in Omaha, Nebraska, $5000; in New York City, $5300; in Cleveland, Ohio, $5000; and in Dade County (Miami), Florida, $4750.[5] Many smaller school districts pay a much lower beginning salary, but the cost of living is usually less.

The number and size of guaranteed increments are of greater importance than the beginning salary; the maximum salary is the one which the teacher will have for many years, the minimum is temporary. As in the case of beginning salaries, the pattern of maximum salaries varies greatly. However, there are a number of school systems in the United States today where the regular classroom teacher can look forward to a maximum salary of more than $8,500 if he has a master's degree—certainly a minimum preparation for the career teacher, and more than $10,000 if he holds the doctorate. With or without the special merit rating, teachers do not get their annual increments merely because they have served time. In most schools an attempt is made to evaluate the work of the teacher, and promotion comes only to those who are doing an acceptable job. Many teachers are dropped at the end of each year.

How is this evaluation made? Usually some kind of measuring instrument is used, its type varying from one school system to another. However, the instruments have much in common. A typical one is reproduced in Appendix A. Careful study of it will point up many important facets of the professional competencies demanded of teachers.

TEACHER TENURE

Tenure is more important than salary to many teachers. A teacher wishes to know what salary he will receive but he wishes also to know how permanent his position will be.

Organized teachers have for years been much interested in tenure laws. The National Education Association has had tenure as one plank of its platform as far back as 1887. The "Proceedings" of the Association for that year, carried a committee report urging that the subject of teacher tenure be given publicity in the hopes that states would pass tenure laws. In 1915 the Association passed a resolution expressing itself in favor of tenure for teachers.

What is meant by teacher tenure?

This expression usually refers to the permanence of a teacher's position after a period of probation. A teacher may receive one-year contracts for three years and then become a permanent member of the teaching staff. It is difficult to discharge a teacher who has tenure.

At the present time 38 states have tenure laws. Some of the laws are very good, some are very poor. Before planning to teach in a certain state it is

[5] Salaries quoted here are quoted from *Research Bulletin,* vol. 41, no. 3, Research Division, National Education Association, Washington, D.C., 1963, pp. 80–81.

wise to check its tenure laws. In some states tenure laws protect incompetent teachers as well as the competent ones. The difficulty of writing a law that will protect the competent teacher without protecting the inefficient is great.

OTHER COMPENSATIONS

Teaching has a great many compensations. First there is the life of the teacher. He does not deal in his day's work with people who are old, disillusioned, ill, or psychopathic. When he meets his class in the morning he is surrounded by youth and enthusiasm. Each day's work is an adventure; each class is a challenge.

The vacations are another attraction. They can be used for study, work experiences, or recreation. A larger percentage of teachers travel in America and Europe than is true of any other group. Whereas the average American businessman works in the same place at the same job all year, this is not true of a teacher. Many young people choose teaching because of the added freedom this occupation gives them.

Another compensation that comes from teaching is the satisfaction of doing a job that is very important. When the teacher has taught for a great many years, he will constantly meet men and women who have gone far and done much and who will tell him that he had a great part in making them what they are. There is no feeling in the world like that of knowing that you have helped to build a life. If you are a good teacher you will have many such experiences.

Another compensation of teaching is the usual annuity which he gets when he finishes his active work. Annuities are available in most of our states. It is impossible to explain here all the different pension systems. Most pensions are state-wide, that is, they are paid not by the local school district in which the recipient was teaching when he completed his work, but by a state pension system. In general, they provide for teacher contribution, a small percentage being deducted from the teacher's salary each month. Systems vary widely as to the length of service necessary before retirement, the amount paid, and other regulations. Many of them provide for payment in case of permanent disability.

Some school systems and most colleges provide for sabbatical leaves. A teacher is given every seventh year, at half salary, for travel, study, or a similar purpose. Many schools also cooperate with other schools both here and in Europe in exchanging teachers for a year. Schools also vary widely in paying for sick leave. A large number of them have plans providing for group insurance, hospitalization, and medical fees.

PROFESSIONAL ORGANIZATIONS

As noted earlier, all professions, including teaching, have professional organizations and those who are professional-minded will become members of some of these organizations. Of course, no teacher belongs to all of them, for many of them are for specialized groups, as for instance the National Art Education Association, which is made up of art teachers.

There are some general education organizations. Chief among them is the National Education Association.

THE NATIONAL EDUCATION ASSOCIATION

In 1857, in Philadelphia, a small group of interested educators organized the National Teachers Association. Its name was changed to the National Education Association in 1871. In 1906 the Congress passed a bill, signed by President Theodore Roosevelt, which incorporated the organization as the "National Education Association of the United States." In 1920 the Association provided for democratic representation by setting up a governing body known as the representative assembly. Each member of the Association has a voice in electing delegates who formulate the policies of the Association and direct its management.

The National Education Association has headquarters in Washington, D.C., where it owns its own building. The Association employs a permanent secretary and a large staff of assistants. Its annual budget is in excess of two million dollars. Its membership is about half a million. All members of the National Education Association receive the monthly magazine, the *NEA Journal.*

The purpose of the National Education Association, as expressed in its charter, is "To elevate the character and advance the interests of the profession of teaching and to promote the cause of popular education in the United States." The best statement of the purposes of the Association is to be found in the 21 goals of the Victory Action Program adopted by the representative assembly in 1946.

1. Active democratic local education associations in every community, including an FTA chapter in every college which prepares teachers, affiliated with the state and national associations.
2. A strong and effective state education association in every state.
3. A larger and more aggressive national education association.
4. Unified dues—local, state, and national—collected by the local.
5. A membership enrollment of at least 90 percent in local, state, and national professional organizations.
6. Unified committees—the chairmen of local and state committees serving as advisory members of corresponding national committees.
7. A professionally prepared and competent teacher in every classroom.
8. A professionally prepared and competent principal at the head of each school.
9. A professionally prepared and competent administrator at the head of each school system.
10. A strong, adequately-staffed state department of education in each state and a more adequate federal education agency.

11. A professional salary for all members of the profession, adjusted to the increased cost of living.
12. Professional security for teachers and administrators guaranteed by effective tenure legislation.
13. Retirement income for old age and disability.
14. Cumulative sabbatical and sick leave.
15. Reasonable class size and equitable distribution of the teaching load.
16. Informed lay support of public education at local, state, and national levels.
17. Units of school administration large enough to provide for efficient operation, with special attention to the needs of rural areas and stronger state and local boards of education.
18. Adequate educational opportunity for every child irrespective of race, creed, color, or residence.
19. The equalization and expansion of educational opportunity including needed state and national financing.
20. A safe, healthful, and wholesome community environment for every child.
21. An effective and adequately financed United Nations Educational, Scientific and Cultural Organization.[6]

All education associations in the United States, unlike those in some other countries, are voluntary. In eight of the ten provinces of Canada membership in the teachers' association is compulsory. The fees are set with the approval of the Minister of Education and are deducted from the teachers' salary and paid to the association.

Each Canadian association is a body corporate, and the members are disciplined by the association. In the United States if a teacher is guilty of conduct unbecoming a teacher, or if he is an incompetent teacher, he is disciplined by the board of education. In many states the action of the board is subject to court action. The teacher tenure laws of all states are enforced by the courts.

In Canada the association disciplines its own members. A teacher who is accused of conduct unbecoming a teacher or who is incompetent is tried by a committee of teachers appointed by the association. The findings of the committee are final.

THE AMERICAN FEDERATION OF TEACHERS

As its name suggests, the American Federation of Teachers is a labor organization affiliated with the American Federation of Labor. It was organized in 1916, and it publishes *The American Teacher*. According to its president, it differs in four important respects from other national organizations of teachers:

1. It is affiliated with organized labor.
2. It is controlled entirely by classroom teachers.

[6] W. Ashby Lyle, "The National Education Association," *Phi Delta Kappan,* November, 1949, pp. 101–102.

3. It is an organization of action rather than words.
4. It is intensely interested in social and economic reform.[7]

The point most stressed by the Federation is that it is controlled entirely by classroom teachers because its members feel that too often other educational organizations are dominated by administrators.

Is the teacher a laborer or a member of a profession? This seems to be the main question on which the Federation and other organizations differ. This is a question which each teacher must answer for himself. He should approach the subject without prejudice, make a careful study of the literature, talk with teachers in whom he has confidence, and examine the advantages of the various organizations.

STATE AND LOCAL ORGANIZATIONS

Every state has some type of state educational organization. Usually it roughly parallels the National Education Association. Such organizations vary in their legal setup, their purposes and their organization, but they are always interested in everything that promotes the welfare of education and the teachers in the state. Educational Conventions are customary in most states. Some states hold a state-wide meeting, but other states are broken up into districts, with separate meetings in each district. These associations are also active in all the educational programs of their state, and usually sponsor and uphold legislation in education.

Most teachers belong to a state organization. The membership fee usually covers admission to the association's annual convention. It also covers a subscription to the monthly magazine published by the association. Many associations have other services for the teachers. One common one is a teacher's placement bureau, through which many teachers get their positions. It is also common for such an association to have a health plan, covering hospitalization, doctors' fees, and even a stipend to be paid during illness.

The California Teachers' Association maintains a purchasing bureau. The teacher wishing to buy almost any standard article, such as a television set, typewriter, radio, or piece of furniture, can get it at a substantial savings through the Association's purchasing department. Some other associations also have this type of service. Automobile insurance can be bought through many state associations at a reduced price. A student may write to the state association of the state in which he plans to teach and find out about it.

Most school districts have local education or teachers' associations. In many states these are affiliated with the state association. A great many districts provide for overall membership dues, whereby a teacher may join the local, state, and national organizations by the payment of a combined fee.

[7] John M. Eklund, "The American Federation of Teachers," *Phi Delta Kappan,* October, 1949, p. 66.

The FTA and the SNEA

Two organizations for students who are considering entering teaching have become important factors in professionalizing the occupation: the Future Teachers of America for high school pupils and the Student National Education Association for college-age students. Both organizations serve to orientate prospective teachers to the role and importance of teaching and teachers. FTA members often assist elementary and junior high school teachers as they work with pupils, and thus become better acquainted with the teaching job. Each member takes a pledge which is as follows:

The good teacher requires:

Physical Vitality—I will try to keep my body well and strong.

Mental Vigor—I will study daily to keep my mind active and alert.

Moral Discrimination—I will seek to know the right and live by it.

Wholesome Personality—I will cultivate in myself good will, friendliness, poise, upright bearing and careful speech.

Helpfulness—I will learn the art of helping others by doing helpful things daily in school and home.

Knowledge—I will fill my mind with worth-while thoughts by observing the beautiful world around me, by reading the best books, and by association with the best companions.

Leadership—I will make my influence count on the side of right, avoiding habits that weaken and destroy.

These things I will do now that I may be worthy of the high office of teacher.[8]

The Student NEA has adopted the following set of purposes:

1. To develop among college students preparing to be teachers an understanding of the teaching profession through participation in the work of local, state, and national education associations.

2. To acquaint students preparing to teach with the history, ethics, organizations, policies, and programs of local, state, and national education associations.

3. To interest capable young men and women in education as a life-long career and to encourage careful selection of persons admitted to approved programs of teacher education.

4. To give students preparing to teach practical experience in working with local, state, and national education associations on problems of the profession and society.[9]

Although only recently separated from the older FTA organization, the SNEA has grown at an impressive rate. Total individual membership was

[8] *Future Teachers of America Handbook,* Future Teachers of America, Washington, D.C., 1954, p. 133.

[9] *SNEA Handbook,* Student National Education Association, Washington, D.C., 1960, p. 126.

more than 50,000 in 1960, and more than 750 chapters of the organization are now in existence.

A CODE OF ETHICS

Every profession has its code of ethics. The American Medical Association adopted its first code more than a century ago, and to be in good standing with his medical society a doctor must live up to the provisions of the code of ethics. Many codes of ethics also have been written for teachers—the earliest ones for state teachers' associations. Since 1896, when a code of ethics was adopted by the teachers of Georgia, most of the other state associations have also adopted codes.

The Representative Assembly of the National Education Association adopted a new code of ethics statement at their 1963 meeting in Detroit. Because it will doubtless become the best-known and most widely used of all such statements, it is presented in Appendix B.

WHAT DOES A TEACHER DO?

What kind of a job is teaching? Is it as simple as it looks in a classroom where a capable teacher is working with an interested group of boys and girls? To answer these questions it is necessary to analyze the work of the teacher in terms of how much time he spends, how he uses his time, and what functions he performs.

Many studies have been made in an attempt to answer these questions, and they can be divided into two major categories—quantitative and qualitative. The first group of studies have attempted to ascertain the amount of time spent on the various duties which are part of the teacher's job.

A recent study pointed out that teachers, like most other professional workers, go far beyond the traditional 40-hour work week to meet the demands of their job. A scientifically selected sample of the nation's public school teaching population was asked to give their best judgment of the time spent in an average week on each of 17 activities other than classroom teaching in addition to assessing the time allotted to classroom instruction. According to this study the average teacher devotes 47.3 hours per week to the duties required in connection to his work, including more than 20 hours in addition to classroom instruction. Some of the specific tasks and the time which they require are shown in the charts below.

Other studies have attempted to assess the job of the teacher in terms of more general, qualitative terms. One such study was done by a committee formed by the National Commission on Teacher Education and Professional Standards of the National Education Association. Reporting in 1954, the committee reached the following significant conclusions:

How the Elementary-School Teacher Divides the Week*

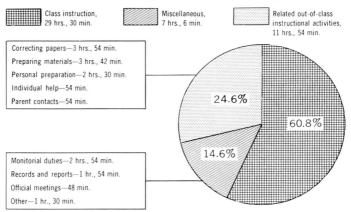

Class instruction, 29 hrs., 30 min.

Miscellaneous, 7 hrs., 6 min.

Related out-of-class instructional activities, 11 hrs., 54 min.

Correcting papers—3 hrs., 54 min.
Preparing materials—3 hrs., 42 min.
Personal preparation—2 hrs., 30 min.
Individual help—54 min.
Parent contacts—54 min.

Monitorial duties—2 hrs., 54 min.
Records and reports—1 hr., 54 min.
Official meetings—48 min.
Other—1 hr., 30 min.

24.6%

60.8%

14.6%

(Average work week of 48 hours, 30 minutes)

How the High-School Teacher Divides the Week*

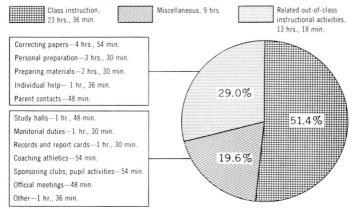

Class instruction, 23 hrs., 36 min.

Miscellaneous, 9 hrs.

Related out-of-class instructional activities, 13 hrs., 18 min.

Correcting papers—4 hrs., 54 min.
Personal preparation—3 hrs., 30 min.
Preparing materials—2 hrs., 30 min.
Individual help— 1 hr., 36 min.
Parent contacts—48 min.

Study halls—1 hr., 48 min.
Monitorial duties—1 hr., 30 min.
Records and report cards—1 hr., 30 min.
Coaching athletics—54 min.
Sponsoring clubs, pupil activities—54 min.
Official meetings—48 min.
Other—1 hr., 36 min.

29.0%

51.4%

19.6%

(Average work week of 45 hours, 54 minutes)

*"The National Education Association Research Bulletin," October, 1962, Vol. 40, No. 3., Research Division of the NEA, Washington, D.C.

Roles of the Teacher in Promoting Pupil Growth

1. Director of Learning.   The responsibility of the teacher for classroom instruction is widely recognized, but narrowly understood. Two major types of school activities are especially suitable for group situations: those designed to develop essential outcomes in groups with common needs, such as the common learnings and skill in the fundamental processes; and those that are inherently group experiences. Among the latter are cooperative projects in problem solving, planning, and other situations designed to develop attitudes and techniques for democratic living.

2. Counselor and Guidance Worker.   Many of the problems and needs of the pupil require individual pupil-teacher relationship. This necessity is recognized to some extent in the school system by the provision for special personnel staff and facilities. Yet, in actual practice, this function demands the manpower of the entire staff. The problems of the individual pupil are a responsibility primarily of the teacher.

3. Member of the School Community.   The classroom constitutes a small, homogeneous community. The school as a whole constitutes a larger and for some purposes a more effective one. It becomes the responsibility of the teachers working with administrators and with one another to provide an articulated sequence of learning activities in the over-all school program to develop the skills and attitudes of citizenship and for meeting the developmental needs of youth.

Liaison Roles of the Teacher

4. Mediator of the Culture.   The effective member of society must share in the cultural heritage. This is variously interpreted to include its values and behavioral controls, the great disciplines and sciences, and the techniques of democratic living. The function of the school is to draw on this cultural heritage, incorporating it in the curriculum, so as to provide the appropriate scope and sequence of experiences for learning.

The teacher is the official licensed link between adult society and its on-coming members. The efficiency of the school is measured, in the last analysis, by the success with which its product can meet the responsibilities of membership in organized society. The expert mediator of the culture is a teacher who is skilled in interpreting the social and physical environment, and preparing the pupil to utilize the fields of subject matter in solving his life's problems.

5. A Link with the Community.   Here the profession has a two-fold function: The first is to secure community cooperation to provide for a systematic induction of the on-coming member into organized adult society—a responsibility analogous to that of the teacher education institution to the student teacher. The second is to participate with the public informulation of goals, and in appraisal of the school program in terms of the goals.

6. Member of the Profession.   A member of any profession shares in its over-all responsibilities to society, to be discharged individually or as part of an organized group. Important among these are those that contribute to developing a more adequate system of public education, with improved staff, facilities, and program. These responsibilities of the profession, in practice, are, for the most part, carried out by organizations within the profession, some with general over-all responsibilities, others with highly specialized interests. What can be accomplished in any of them, however, depends on the competence, understanding, and participation of the teacher.[10]

Obviously, the concept of a teacher as one whose duties are limited to "holding class," "hearing lessons," "keeping discipline" is far too limited. Like the school system of which he is the keystone, the teacher has relationships which transcend the bounds of his classroom and school building. It is also apparent that the complex roles of a teacher cannot best be accomplished by his own efforts. As a counselor and guidance worker, the class-room teacher can be most effective as he utilizes resource persons such as counselors, physicians, and psychologists. As a member of the school community and a link with the larger community, his relationship is one which is shared with many others and he functions best as part of a cooperative effort.

It is the first-mentioned of the roles of a teacher—a director of learning—that demands the first attention of a teacher, however. As noted earlier, the teaching-learning situation is the area where the professional skill of the teacher becomes imperative. Regardless of whatever else the teacher may do, his major contribution to his pupils and his school system lies in the area of the direction of learning, and if the teacher is a successful director of learning, certain outcomes will be achieved.

SOME OUTCOMES OF SUCCESSFUL TEACHING

The purpose of the teaching process is to make certain desirable changes in the lives of children, changes involving growth and development in such attributes as knowledge, habits, skills, ideals, attitudes, and appreciation. The teacher, as a director of learning, is successful only when he helps effect these desirable changes. If growth is not promoted and if the changes are not desirable, then the teaching has failed.

Education is worth precisely the difference it makes in the activities of the individual being educated. Some of these differences can be measured and evaluated, the most important ones cannot. It is easy to measure reading speed, the number of words a child can spell, or his accuracy in adding or multiplying. It is not easy to measure his growth in honesty, fair-mindedness, appreciation, and ideals.

Some desirable outcomes of teaching are: to fix facts, form habits, produce skills, develop the thinking process, build character and ideals, and give the student an appreciation of the good and beautiful.

There was a time when the teacher planned each lesson to do just one

[10] *Factors in Teaching Competence,* National Commission on Teacher Education and Professional Standards, National Education Association, Washington, D.C., 1954, p. 4.

thing. At eight o'clock he taught a drill lesson to fix the facts, and at nine an appreciation lesson. Each hour was dedicated to one type of lesson, but teaching and learning are not so simple and a modern teacher never teaches a "pure type" lesson. Ideals may be inculcated as the teacher drills his students in spelling; appreciation may be developed in any type of class. No present-day teacher says, "This hour I'll build character," for he knows that character is built in all sorts of situations in all types of teaching.

In spite of the fact that teachers do not "parcel out the ends" of education by teaching each hour to achieve a single outcome, they are well aware that the outcome desired has much to do with the method they select.

Teaching to Fix Facts and Form Habits

Every teacher at some time must teach to fix facts and form desirable habits. Lessons so taught are usually called "drill lessons." This method is one of the oldest forms of teaching. The school teachers of a few generations ago were largely drillmasters who "kept school" with the aid of a "hickory stick" and drilled their pupils on all types of subject matter. Most textbooks were written for drill teaching: the children memorized the multiplication tables, the names of generals and battles, long lists of dates; they repeated poetry in unison and memorized jingles about the Presidents and the months of the year; they memorized paragraphs about the boundaries of the states and their capitals; they learned to spell by continuous oral repetition.

There is no need to argue against the concept of teaching that reduces everything to repetition and drill because such teaching is not common today. However, there are many things that should be taught by the drill method—things that do not involve thinking and for which only one answer is possible. Two times two must always equal four; a word is always spelled the same. Teachers use the drill method only with subject matter which should become so fixed in the minds of pupils that the response to a stimulus is immediate and correct. The teacher should not drill children in literature, art, music, history, or geography; he does drill them in arithmetic combinations, handwriting, spelling, and other subjects involving simple skills that do not require thought but must become automatic.

Teaching to Encourage Thinking

Teaching to develop thought processes is the opposite of teaching to fix automatic responses. The drill lesson deals with facts and skills that should be reduced to an automatic basis. The teaching of thinking involves the recognition of problems, the collecting of data, the weighing of evidence, the making of hypotheses, and the testing of conclusions.

Education is a process whereby experiences are continuously remade and given a richer and fuller meaning. Thinking is the process whereby old experiences take on new meanings. Unless new facts are presented in such a way as to enrich one's past experiences, the process of learning becomes formal and disconnected from life. Learning without thinking becomes mere memorization. A pupil can "recite" accurately without understanding what he is saying, which is why it is easy to mistake verbalism for thinking.

Teaching that involves thinking was once divided into two processes: "inductive" teaching, in which the pupil attempted to solve a problem by collecting data and making a generalization, and "deductive" teaching, in which the pupils began with generalizations and applied them to certain individual facts. Today no teacher attempts to separate the two processes; for to say that a thinking process is purely inductive or deductive is to oversimplify. Most thinking involves both processes.

In learning to think their way through problems, children should attempt to solve their own problems and not the problems posed by the teacher or the textbook—if the problem is not real, the thinking process will not be genuine.

The weak point in teaching to encourage thinking is usually the teacher's failure to recognize that an individual is being educated only when he plans, purposes, executes, judges, generalizes, tests, and applies for himself. It is too easy to confuse "education" and "training." We *train* horses, dogs, and children by the drill process; no thinking is needed. We *educate* by the thinking process.

Teaching for Character Development

One of the major purposes of education is the building of character. It is not enough that boys and girls learn facts and develop the techniques of solving problems; they must also learn to live as good citizens in their homes and communities.

Character is developed as a by-product of all life activities, therefore, the school, the home, the church, and the community all contribute to the development of the ideals that direct conduct. Within these agencies such things as the radio, television, comic strips, playmates, books, and newspapers play an important part. Anything that influences the direction in which the child grows contributes to character formation.

What is the school's role in character education? In the early American schools character education was taught by the direct method. In other words, children were taught character formation much as they were taught reading or geography. They memorized "memory gems" with moral implications. Their writing lessons were entirely given over to writing concepts again and again. The old *New England Primer* consisted almost entirely of moral and religious lessons. Most of the other early textbooks were loaded with the literature of morality. Thus the children learned the rules of morality. It did not always follow, however, that they developed into moral adults.

Other countries have long histories of teaching morals and character by the direct method. Both France and Japan have for many years used the direct teaching of character. The plan involves special textbooks and courses of study and is pursued for many periods and for many years, but the results have not been satisfactory. Educators in general doubt the possibility of teaching character directly. Children do not become honest by writing "Honesty is the best policy" 100 times.

A moral person is one who has had to exercise moral judgment in many situations. The modern school knows that only indirectly can it produce adults who will act in a moral way at all times. This kind of education is not easy to achieve, nor are the results quickly evident. Some critics of schools today complain because young people seem to have too much freedom. However, it is only as children learn how to use this freedom, to make correct judgments among competing alternatives, to resist temptation, that they grow up to be the kind of citizens a democracy needs. For this reason the modern school is organized as a democratic group. The authority of adults is respected, and children's rights and privileges are respected also. Young people are given many opportunities to participate in making decisions, planning activities, and evaluating behavior. In this way character education does take place.

Character education is a continuous process. It is constantly taking place in the relationship between the teacher and his pupils. Whenever a child faces a problem and works out an honest and correct solution, he is building character. Whenever children work cooperatively on a common problem, they are learning to live together. They are building character.

Teaching to Develop Appreciation

Education not only enables one to avoid error, to discover truth, and to think straight; it also develops the ability to appreciate and enjoy. Hence teachers not only fix facts, form habits, develop the ability to think, build character; they are also interested in the pupil's growth in the field of appreciation. It is not enough for a man to be able to earn a living; he should also be able to appreciate and enjoy life. The ability to enjoy a beautiful picture, a worthwhile drama, a symphony concert, an opera, tasteful clothing, a well-designed and artistically decorated house, well-made furniture, or a beautiful automobile is a valuable product of education. Part of each teacher's time should be spent in developing appreciation in his students.

As in the development of character, it is difficult to develop any kind of appreciation by direct methods. The best lessons are taught incidentally. A teacher cannot give his pupils one list of books "to appreciate," and another list that they must not appreciate! One of the best ways to teach children to appreciate good books is to have such books available on a special shelf where any pupil may borrow them. Leaving good books around children who have leisure time is a fine way to introduce them to good literature.

Schools have tried for generations to teach the love of good books by requiring every student to read a prescribed list of books. Many of these books are available in one large volume. In general this type of teaching has been a failure. Generations of reading *The Lady of the Lake, The Scarlet Letter,* and *The Merchant of Venice* have resulted in a reading public that bothers with little except current fiction and popular magazines. Clearly, appreciation is not taught directly or on the command of the teacher; it is a subtle attribute that must be taught indirectly and with great skill.

The pupil's attitude is the basic consideration in appreciation, and he must be appealed to through many avenues. For example, in the field of art, paintings are only one of the types of objects of appreciation. The modern art department allows children to express their artistry in various ways. Painting, sculpture, modeling, woodworking, carving, printing, leather tooling, bookbinding, etching, linoleum block making, weaving, designing, and pottery and jewelry making are all types of creative art and avenues of appreciation.

IS TEACHING A PROFESSION?

There are a great many more attributes of teaching as an occupation than can be included in one brief discussion. However, on the basis of those characteristics which have been covered, it should be possible to again ask the question introduced earlier—"Is teaching a profession?" Therefore, it seems logical to review the list of "earmarks" of professions, this time in comparison with the job teaching.

The first professional attribute in the earlier list had to do with the relatively long period of formal pre-service preparation which is a universal attribute of professions. What about teaching? If one compares the necessary minimum preparation of the physician or the lawyer with that of the classroom teacher, teaching certainly cannot be termed professional. In some states elementary classroom teachers can still begin their work with less than a baccalaureate degree. However, when it is remembered that many states now require graduate work as a prerequisite for standard certification, teaching compares more favorably. The trend towards requiring significantly more pre-service preparation of teachers is very evident. In Oklahoma, for example, whereas 25 years ago a majority of classroom teachers did not have a bachelor's degree, more than 99 percent of today's teachers have such a degree and the majority have a master's degree. In many school systems in the United States a significant number of classroom teachers now hold an earned doctor's degree.

A similar situation of comparability exists with respect to admission to colleges of education, progress through the preparation program, and qualification for certification. The "standards" for becoming a teacher may not be as high as that for the prospective brain surgeon, but today's teacher has certainly successfully passed more screening devices than his normal-school-graduate-counterpart of a few years ago.

Several teachers' codes of ethics were presented in this chapter, and the great majority of teachers welcome the opportunity to meet these standards of behavior. In the matter of ethics teaching compared very favorably.

Teaching also qualifies as a service-giving job. No one primarily interested in personal gain or self-aggrandizement would remain a teacher for long if, indeed, they ever did enter the field of work.

Education does not compare quite so favorably on several of the other characteristics. The practicing educator has little or no control over schools of education because teaching lacks the attribute of a profession, i.e., the power of its professional organizations. Specific accreditation of these colleges is often done by state legislatures or state boards of education. The permit to practice—the certificate or credential—is usually issued by a state legislature. There have been very few instances when a person's right to teach was removed by his peers on the basis of his denial of or refusal to live up to a code of ethics. Nor has the teaching profession been able to set a schedule of salaries and fees which assure its members of a salary comparable to that of the engineer or the physician.

In terms of standing in the community, many teachers are among the most respected persons in any town, and are as well salaried. But the tenure of teachers is not as long as many other professions.

Therefore, it seems necessary to decide that teaching is not now a profession of full status in most places in the United States. Yet, when we think of the great progress that teachers and the teaching profession have made in a relatively short time compared to much older occupations such as law and medicine, it seems possible to conclude that teaching is in the process of becoming a profession.

RELATED READINGS

Lieberman, Myron, *Education as a Profession,* New York, Prentice-Hall, 1956.
———, *The Future of Public Education,* Chicago, University of Chicago Press, 1960.
Lindsey, Margaret, Ed., *New Horizons for the Teaching Profession,* Washington, D.C., National Commission on Teacher Education and Professional Standards, National Education Association, 1961.
National Commission on Teacher Education and Professional Standards, *The Education of Teachers: New Perspectives,* Washington, D.C., The National Education Association, 1958.
———, *Moving from Ideas to Action, Official report of the 1962 Regional TEPS Conferences,* Washington, D.C., The National Education Association, 1962.

In a friendly atmosphere the high school psychologist tests a brilliant pupil. Identifying and enhancing individual differences is a cooperative effort of teachers, counselors, and psychologists. (*Bloom from Monkmeyer*)

Below left: A university representative talks with students who are completing a non-teacher education degree about one of the new fifth-year programs leading to a Master of Arts in Teaching degree. (*Roy Stevens, Ford Foundation*)

Selective admission and retention in teacher education programs offer the best single means of upgrading the profession. These policies also necessitate extensive testing and counseling of prospective teachers. (*New Mexico State University*)

Below: Not only play; these students and their active teacher are doing their version of an Indian Summer Dance. (*Strickler from Monkmeyer*)

American Education Week Open House is one of the best-attended of all parent meetings. (*Eva Luoma from Monkmeyer*)

Teaching requires vitality and stamina. The teacher, too, has taken the five-mile hike. (*Photos above and right, Wide World*)

"The first duty of government, and the surest evidence of good government, is the encouragement of education . . . I consider the system of our common schools as the palladium of our freedom . . ."; Governor De Witt Clinton.

Chapter 12 / **SHALL I BE A TEACHER?**

CHOOSING A LIFE'S WORK

One of the most important decisions anyone ever makes is deciding what he will select as a life's work. No one can really make this decision for anyone else, and the entire life of an individual will be affected by the choice he makes. A few people seem to be able to make an early choice of their vocation and never deviate from it: they are in the minority. Studies have shown that many college Freshmen and Sophomores are undecided in their vocational plans. Some college students have a tentative goal in mind, but they have never given serious thought as to the reasons for their choice, or whether or not they could become qualified for success in the field. Still others know the general field which holds the greatest appeal for them, but are undecided regarding the specific position within the area for which they are most interested in preparing. Finally, some people never really choose a vocation. They drift from one job to another until the choice is made by default; usually by a set of extraneous circumstances. Few people can afford such a luxury, and the wise college student makes an intelligent decision concerning his vocational choice (a choice based on evidence which he has gathered).

This chapter invites the student to consider teaching as a career choice. Evidence will be provided to help make an intelligent decision, and some significant questions will be discussed. The qualities needed for success in teaching will be considered as well as some of the positions available in the teaching profession and what is expected from the teaching profession and our teachers.

The various studies and statements which will be noted should help a student gain an insight into teaching as a career possibility. At least one observation is pertinent immediately—the requirements for success in teaching are rigorous and demanding. Many vital areas are included. The teaching profession demands the best from the right kind of people because society expects a great deal from its teachers.

The following story may help with a career choice regardless of what the final decision may be. It shows how one young man, who eventually had a long and distinguished career in education (which included being president of Teachers College, Columbia University) made an intelligent decision concerning teaching. Perhaps his experience will give some guidance concerning the technique of making an intelligent choice.

I was 18 years old and ending my sophomore year in college when I went to my father for advice with a problem I had not been able to solve.

"What career do you think I should choose?" I asked.

My father was then head of Teachers College at Columbia University. He was a great and wise teacher. He proved it with his answer.

"That you must decide for yourself," he said. "The important thing is to take a good long look—from the inside. Then make up your mind."

The next day he gave me a handful of letters of introduction. During that summer I talked with many leaders in various professions—a doctor, a lawyer, the head of a big New York department store, a banker, a broker, and the editor of a powerful newspaper. Each was enthusiastic about the rewards of his own career because each had chosen the work for which he was best suited.

I also talked with men on my father's staff.

At the end of the summer my way was clear. I knew beyond a shadow of a doubt that I wanted to be a teacher.

It is a choice I have never regretted.

To me, teaching is the most challenging, exciting, rewarding career a young man or woman can choose, and its satisfactions are many.

It brings dignity of position in the community. It often gives the security of steady employment and of pension.

It provides more than a comfortable income for the ambitious student who plans a career in education, with the care and determination demanded for success in any profession.

It brings another and very important reward—the sense of doing a job that is meaningful and important.[1]

MAKING AN INTELLIGENT DECISION

Most of the students who use this book are taking a course in a sequence designed to prepare teachers. How much serious thought have you given concerning teaching as a career? Do you wish to be a teacher?

Some of the questions you might ask yourself are:

1. Is the work particularly interesting to me?
2. What kind of activities does it require?
3. What kind of living does it provide?
4. Is the work important?
5. What kinds of positions are there in the teaching profession?
6. What are the chances for advancement?
7. What are the necessary qualifications for success in teaching?
8. Do I have the necessary qualities for success?

There are also many other questions you will probably want to ask and answer. Some of your queries will depend on your own interests and abilities and what you want from life. Only you can ask yourself all the proper questions. Only you can provide many of the answers.

WHAT QUALITIES DOES A SUCCESSFUL TEACHER NEED?

Regardless of what other questions you may have asked, to make an intelligent choice concerning teaching it will be necessary to learn the personal qualities the successful teacher usually possesses. Over a thousand studies have been made and reported concerning the personal qualities needed for success in teaching, and it is impossible to discuss all of them. It seems important, however, to examine the findings of some of the most significant. In general the other studies came to similar conclusions.

Some Important Qualities as Set Forth by
A National Survey Commission

In 1938 the American Council on Education organized a Commission on Teacher Education. The purpose of the commission was to make a comprehensive study of the problems of teacher education. The findings of the

[1] William F. Russell, while president of Teachers College, Columbia University, wrote this for the New York Life Insurance Company. It is quoted with their permission.

commission have been published in several volumes. "Teachers for Our Times," one of these volumes, is in part given over to qualities needed in teachers. The qualities discussed are: (1) respect for personality, (2) community-mindedness, (3) rational behavior, (4) skill in cooperation, (5) increasing knowledge, (6) skill in mediating knowledge, (7) friendliness with children, (8) understanding children, (9) social understanding and behavior, (10) good citizenship in the school as society, (11) skill in evaluation, and (12) faith in the worth of teaching.

It is not possible to present in detail the discussions of the Commission. Students will find reading the whole volume well worth while; the following quotations are from it.

It is of basic importance that teachers should be good specimens of our culture. They should be devoted to the ideals that characterize the American people at their best. They should serve these ideals effectively. Thus teachers for our times should believe in freedom and the worth of each growing personality, in responsible citizenship and the worth of a genuine community, and in reasoned action as the surest means of meeting our problems and improving our lives together.[2]

But while a friendly attitude towards children is basic to excellence in teaching, it is not, by itself, enough. It needs to be supported by understanding and insight respecting human growth and development. Good judgment regarding the needs of children at different stages, their readiness for particular kinds of learning, and the ways whereby they may most effectively be helped may sometimes seem intuitive. But the biological, psychological, and social sciences offer an increasing store of tested knowledge bearing on these matters with which good teachers need to be familiar.[3]

No one doubts the importance, in a teacher, of general and specialized knowledge of the sort that is customarily thought of when the term "subject matter" is used. Children are inquisitive about the world in which they find themselves. They want to know and to be able to do. It is essential that they should have expert help in satisfying their interests and inquiries. Moreover the social situation, at any time, puts a premium on certain kinds of knowledge, a widespread grasp of which is prerequisite to social advance. Well informed teachers are called for at every school level. Scholarly resources are particularly important in our complex and changing times. The subjects of the arts and letters, of the natural social sciences, and of philosophy all bear on the needs of our society, of our children, and of the teachers themselves. Teachers need vital and extended instruction in these subjects.[4]

Good teachers must always vary as to the pattern of qualities that accounts for the excellence of each. Good teachers, in other words, are never exactly alike, and any notion that uniformity should be sought after in their education is unrealistic and dangerous. A relative weakness in certain respects can be tolerated when there are compensating strengths elsewhere. It is the balance of qualities that

[2] *Teachers for Our Times,* American Council on Education, Commission on Teacher Education, Washington, D.C., 1944, p. 156.
[3] *Ibid.,* p. 166.
[4] *Ibid.,* p. 163.

counts. Moreover excellence is not a static concept: it is not something that can be attained once and forever. Not only may present weaknesses be repaired in a measure through effort, but present strengths must be cultivated if they are not to decay. In a changing world excellence cannot maintain itself if growth does not continue.[5]

Some Important Qualities as Set Forth by Superintendents of Schools

When the student completes his professional preparation for teaching he probably will be interviewed by a number of superintendents of schools or their agents. It should be of interest to know what a superintendent is looking for and expecting to find in teachers.

He usually begins by looking over the college record of various applicants. What, specifically, is he looking for?

1. *College courses.* The superintendent wants to know the candidate's general pattern of college courses. Most superintendents want teachers with a broad educational background, best described as general education. Most colleges that prepare teachers do provide much in the field of general education. Students become familiar with the sciences, social studies, humanities, and other fields of general interest, in courses usually taken in the lower division of the college by all students. General education usually precedes professional education in the teacher's preparation.

The superintendent is also interested in the courses the candidate has taken in the field in which he desires to teach, and looks with great care at the record of work done in the major and minor fields. He is interested in the quality of work done, but even more interested in its spread. The superintendent is not, in general, looking for teachers who are narrow specialists. There was a time when an employing officer looked with favor upon a teacher with a high concentration in a major field, but this is seldom true today. A teacher who is adequately qualified in a wide area is preferred to one who must work with one restricted subject. A teacher who is prepared and certificated to teach in all fields of the social studies is preferred to one who has a large concentration in history and no work in sociology, economics, or political science. The same thing is true in other fields. However, do not conclude that superintendents do not desire adequate academic preparation in each field.

In the third place, the superintendent is interested in teachers who have had adequate professional preparation. This should include comprehensive knowledge of the child to be taught. It also involves knowledge of the community in which the school is located. But most of all, the superintendent is looking for teachers who can live with children and do a good job of teaching. He therefore wants to see the record the candidate made in his student teaching. When possible he wishes to talk with the supervisor under whom

---

[5] *Ibid.,* p. 173.

the student did his teaching. In general, he looks upon the student teaching record as the most important information he can get from college records.

The superintendent begins his consideration of potential candidates by making a study of these three areas of college preparation—general education, academic preparation in teaching fields, and professional courses.

2. Education other than college courses. The superintendent of schools always wants to find teachers who have many abilities and interests, so he looks well into the extracurricular pattern of a student's college life. If a candidate has been active in student affairs, it is put down to his credit. If he has held an elective office in student government, he is more attractive as a potential teacher. If he has been active in dramatics, debating, athletics, journalism or any other "out-of-class" activity, the possibility of employment is increased. If he has a hobby such as photography, aviation, or travel, the superintendent wants to know about it. A superintendent likes to employ teachers who have had experience in the fields that parallel the work in the public schools. If candidates are qualified Boy Scout leaders, or have worked with Campfire Girls or some other organization, as teachers they will be able to help with these activities.

3. Some personal qualifications. A superintendent of schools always desires to interview a potential teacher before employment. He already knows about the candidate's college preparation, and he also knows about the extracurricular activities. He wishes now to check on some personal qualifications. What is he looking for? He is very much interested in personality. During the interview he notes such things as posture, the way the candidate sits, walks, and gets up from a chair. He notes the way he dresses. In general, superintendents like good taste in dress; they are not interested in "freakish" hairdos or clothes. They are also interested in how well the candidate talks—the kind of voice and the quality of English spoken.

Probably more than anything else, the average superintendent is interested in the total personality of the student. He looks for teachers who seem intelligent, friendly, interesting, and who are healthy. No superintendent likes a "masculine" woman or an "effeminate" man.

A superintendent also attempts to discover the interests of a candidate. He wants to know what he reads; what kind of shows he likes; if he is interested in music; if he ever takes part in politics. If he discovers that a candidate is excited about horse races and slot machines and does not care for books or music, he has a way of losing interest in him as a potential teacher.

4. Some other requirements. It is impossible to cover in detail all the qualities asked for by individual superintendents. However, the following are typical. They want teachers who can work with others, who have a wholesome social outlook, who can adjust their personal habits to fit the standards of the community. They want teachers who are interested in doing a good job, who are willing and eager to undertake an assignment that calls for extra time, who have open minds, who take constructive criticism and welcome supervision. They are interested in potential teachers who ask intelligent questions during an interview, who want to know about the future of the position as well as the beginning salary. Above all, they want teachers who cooperate, who can handle a group of children without difficulty, and who show sympathy and kindness in dealing with children. They want teachers who have a desire for professional growth and who are constantly attempting to better themselves. All superintendents want teachers who have community interests. They don't like teachers who live in another community and commute. They want teachers who support community affairs and take an active part in community life as all good citizens should.

Some Important Qualities as Set Forth by A Committee of Educators

In March, 1948, a meeting was called in Chicago by the Department of Higher Education of the National Education Association. The subject under discussion was "Current Trends in Higher Education." The educators attending the conference were divided into groups for the study of special problems. One group, under the chairmanship of S. M. Brownell, at that time President of State Teachers College, New Haven, Connecticut, dealt with the problem "General Education for Prospective Teachers." The report of this group was written by Warren C. Lovinger; part of it is concerned with a "Portrait of a Teacher," which reads as follows:

What, then, are the characteristics which a teacher should possess?

As an individual the teacher should be a well-adjusted person who is able to realize the maximum of personal satisfaction from life and to contribute to the fullest extent of his capabilities toward the improvement of the society in which he lives. He has the same responsibilities and obligations as those which society places upon all other persons. For example, he must be able to participate in social groups of varying sizes and kinds from the small simple organization of the family to the large complex organization of government; he must have a satisfactory degree of competence in acquiring and using wealth; he must be able to communicate ideas; and, in general, he must be able to manage his own affairs in everyday life.

As a member of his profession the teacher should be an enlightened person of high ideals who possesses a thorough mastery of subject matter in the area of his specialization as well as understanding and appreciation of relationships between that subject matter and the whole broad field of human knowledge, attitudes, and behavior. It is equally as necessary that he be highly skilled in the techniques of teaching and have a thorough understanding of the learning processes. His interest in children or young people of the age-level with which he works must be great, and he must be willing so accept a major share of responsibility in the induction of all youth into society.

In his entirety the teacher should represent the best possible blend of fine personal qualities and professional skill.[6]

[6] *Current Trends in Higher Education,* Department of Higher Education, National Education Association, Washington, D.C., 1948, p. 93.

Some Important Qualities as Set Forth by
A Teachers College President

Dr. William F. Russell, while president of Teachers College, Columbia University, wrote for the New York Life Insurance Company the following statement concerning teaching.

How can you tell if your child will be a happy and successful teacher?

1. Does he like to study? A good teacher does not stand still. He has a natural curiosity and scholarship that makes him keep pace with all aspects of our changing world, as well as those of his own speciality.

2. Is he interested in other people, particularly in young people? If he is, association with the wonderful zest of the young will keep him young all his life. Too many people go into teaching in a negative way because it is the line of least resistance for them. These become the misfits who give the least and get the least, like the teacher who never married, "because I loathe kids, and they loathe me." If your child is strongly egocentric, teaching is not for him.

3. Is he adaptable? Does he know how to play on a team? A good teacher must be able to work with others. He must have tact and imagination and a strong sense of fair play in order to be useful to pupils from all levels of society and to take his own important place in the adult life of his community.

4. Does your child have strong health and nerves? Teaching is a complicated, demanding process. It takes great skill, concentration and self-discipline. It is not for the physically or emotionally weak.

5. Has your child good character, morals and manners? Remember that teachers deal not only with reading, writing, and arithmetic. He sets standards. He forms tastes. He needs to be a moral, decent, thoroughly trustworthy person, himself, if he is to be trusted with the guidance of the young.

6. Does your child believe in the brotherhood of man and the fatherhood of God? Without these two beliefs, he will miss the truest satisfaction of teaching. Every good teacher has a sense of "cause" and of service. It is a little more than ordinary public spirit. It is rather more a faith in human perfectibility. For instance, the Nazis were enormously effective teachers, but I would not call them good teachers—because they lacked those two faiths.

If your child has these qualifications, teaching will bring him a comfortable, secure, endlessly interesting life, an assured place in his community and best of all, the knowledge that his time on earth has been turned to useful account beyond the power of any man to estimate.

In the words of Henry Adams, "A teacher affects eternity. He can never tell where his influence stops."[7]

THESE FIVE THINGS ARE IMPORTANT

There are some things a teacher needs that are not taught in colleges of education. These are the things that make up the teacher as a person. One should be sure of them before beginning to make preparation for teaching.

[7] Quoted with the permission of the New York Life Insurance Company.

A teacher must have physical health, mental health and intelligence, personality, character, and a good general educational background.

The Importance of Physical Health

Teaching is hard work. Only those who are physically strong should attempt it.

The type of individual who has frequent headaches, tired spells, recurring colds, and other conditions that reduce his vitality, should not try to teach. Perhaps it is better to say that these conditions must be removed before one begins teaching. Children must not be in contact with teachers who have frequent infections, in fact, in most school systems a teacher is not allowed to be with children when he has a cold or any other illness that might be passed on to them.

It is difficult to get a teaching certificate or a teaching position without undergoing a careful physical examination. It will be a waste of effort to study education and prepare for teaching if the student is not sure he can pass the necessary physical examination for a certificate and a teaching position. The teacher must have excellent health—not just enough vitality to get by, but an abundance of energy.

The Importance of Intelligence and Mental Health

Of equal importance with physical health are intelligence and mental health. The fact that the reader has been graduated from high school and admitted to college is some evidence that he has the necessary general intelligence to become a teacher. If his college record is above average, that is also an indication. However, it must be noted that a high level of general intelligence is required to master the necessary subject matter and make the technical preparation needed for teaching.

Teachers sometimes fail because of lack of mental balance or emotional stability. A teacher faces situations every day that demand mental balance and emotional stability. How he meets such situations often determines his success or failure. Records show that more teachers fail because of poor mental health than because of poor physical health. Teaching is a demanding occupation. The teacher is in an important position every minute of the day. His reactions to problem situations are of the greatest importance.

A love of children is a necessary prerequisite for the well-adjusted teacher. No one should attempt to teach who does not get the greatest satisfaction out of associations with children. A dedicated teacher is closely tied to the group of children with whom he is associated.

To be certain he has a love of children the prospective teacher should associate with them, play with them, and live with them before he begins serious preparation for teaching. A position as camp counselor or playground worker, or any job that puts one into intimate contact with children is often helpful. Many colleges of education require work with groups of children as a part of the program of teacher education. Each student must spend at least one college term with a group of children. Working with Sunday School classes, Scouts, Campfire Girls, children's camps, or any other organized group provides the necessary experience. In this way a student soon learns whether he loves children or just tolerates them.

Self-control is a very necessary virtue. Enthusiasm for the work to be done helps in the development of good teaching situations in the school. The teacher who is cheerful, happy, good-natured, never irritated or upset has a much greater chance of success. The emotionally unstable or the mentally ill person has no business working with children and will have little success. So look well into your mental well-being.

Dr. William C. Menninger, one of America's most eminent authorities in mental health, wrote an article that was concerned with the mental health of school teachers. Here is some of it:

> Although there is no sure-fire method for the prevention of personality maladjustment, most people can maintain good mental health. Mental health depends not on being free of problems but on facing and solving them.
>
> The most important factor in your personal happiness and effectiveness is your ability to get along well with other people. This ability really depends on whether you can love and are loved more than you hate. And by love we mean family affection and friendship, as well as love of husband or wife. Difficulties and unhappiness almost always are related to the fact that one does not give and receive enough love to balance hate.
>
> To be mentally healthy, and to help children attain good mental health, you must get satisfaction from life. Satisfactions come from filling your personal needs, from making wishes come true. You can get satisfaction from creating a beautiful product, from carrying out a plan, doing a worthwhile job, or working toward an important goal.
>
> The amount of satisfaction you get from life depends largely on your own ingenuity and self-sufficiency. People who wait for life to supply their satisfaction usually find boredom instead.[8]

The Importance of Personality

Personality is closely related to physical and mental health. It is an extremely important consideration in teaching. Every request for a recommendation carries a question concerning personality. Some personalities are not adapted to teaching. Some people who would make good doctors would not make good teachers; some who would make good farmers would not succeed as engineers; others might be excellent ministers but would make poor merchants. It takes certain kinds of personalities to make good in different vocations. It is also important to note that teaching positions do not all demand the same type of personality. The personality necessary for a successful first-grade teacher would be very different from that of a

[8] William C. Menninger, "Self-Understanding for Teachers," *Journal of the National Education Association,* September, 1953, p. 333.

Who could possibly resist being charmed by this group? Who would even try? Certainly not this teacher or student teacher. Sharing the boundless joy of living so typical of boys and girls is one of the best reasons for teaching. (*National Education Association*)

Right: Thirty-three teachers worked to renovate this city's fourteen elementary schools, making extra money for themselves and saving the school system money. (*Wide World*)

The relationship between this girl and her student teacher is obviously deeply satisfying to both. (*Illinois State University*)

teacher of research problems in a graduate school of physics. There is no "teacher type" personality.

Do not make the mistake of thinking that you must be an extrovert to be a successful teacher. That is far from true. It would be wise to discuss this matter with your teacher or someone else who knows you well and also knows the kind of personality that is best for teaching. It should be said, however, that no teacher has the type of personality that is usually pictured in the movies or the comic strips as typical of teachers. That kind of teacher became passé a great many years ago.

The Importance of Moral Character

The world in general agrees that a teacher must be a moral person. There was a time when the teacher's life was very much restricted by school boards, and a generation ago many school districts would not allow a teacher to dance, play cards, go to the theater, or smoke. Teachers were required to attend church on Sunday. Such restrictions are no longer found in teachers' contracts. Usually the teacher as a person is able to live an ordinary unrestricted life.

There are things, however, that a teacher should not do if he is to be a moral person. Perhaps it would be more exact to say that he should observe the mores of the society he serves as a teacher. It is easy to agree that a teacher should not gamble, steal, lie, cheat, or use profane language. This, however, is true for all people in a decent society. A doctor, lawyer, or priest should not do these things either.

A teacher is with children all day. Many of the habits children develop are habits practiced by the teacher. To be a good example, a teacher should speak correct English, should dress with care, should not do any of the things associated with an immoral person. Because many children live in homes that are on a low moral plane, and never go to church, most of their decent habits must come from the school and from the teacher. This is a teacher's great responsibility.

The Importance of General Education

If one has the necessary intelligence, physical and mental health, personality, and character to make a success of teaching he is ready to go on with his preparation.

In most cases your education for teaching will be begun long before specific professional preparation is started, for the first thing you will need is a good general education. Teaching demands wide cultural education. The narrow specialist is not the best candidate; to know political history and nothing of the humanities is one-sided; to know the social studies and not the sciences is a mistake. Education should be as broad and as well-rounded as possible, even for the person who plans to teach elementary children. The term, "general education," as used here, can be defined in many ways; for our purposes it can be thought of as the kind of education that is needed by all people and it includes not just facts but relationships and meanings as well.

THE SUPPLY OF AND DEMAND FOR TEACHERS

Teaching is the largest of the professions, both in terms of the numbers involved and the breadth of their distribution. Instructional staff members in the United States total more than one and one-half million, and it should be noted that this does not include noncertified personnel such as cafeteria workers, custodians, and bus drivers. No other profession involves nearly as many workers as this. Slightly more than one-half of this number are elementary school teachers, approximately one-third are high school classroom teachers. It is interesting to note, also, that the average age of public school teachers is about 41 years; of superintendents, about 52 years; and the average age of beginning teachers, about 24.

Because the mandatory retirement age in most school systems is between 65 and 70, and many teachers do teach until retirement, a "typical" school system will thus include professional workers varying in age from 24 to 65. It will have one principal for each 18 teachers, and about three times as many elementary school teachers as secondary school teachers. Men will comprise 29 percent of the total instructional staff.

Even though there are more certified teachers today than ever before, the profession is in need of additional workers. In some teaching fields the supply of teachers now surpasses the demand, but in most areas the supply and demand of teachers is relatively equal and there are other areas where the demand far outstrips the supply. Anyone considering the teaching profession should check the specific data for the areas of his interest in the section of the country in which he hopes to be employed. Although teachers in some fields, notably foreign languages, school librarianships, and candidates prepared in "modern" mathematics are universally in short supply, the supply and demand situation varies significantly from place to place.

Regardless of local situations, however, the need for new teachers remains generally high. As of September, 1963, approximately 115,000 teachers were needed to replace those leaving the profession the year before; 55,000 more to serve increased enrollments; 25,000 to relieve overcrowding and half-day sessions; 20,000 to give instruction and services not then provided; and 40,000 to replace teachers certified with less than acceptable minimum qualifications. Thus in 1963 the National Education Association noted a need of 255,000 additional teachers to provide an educational program to meet today's needs, and the one and one-half million workers that teaching now attracts will prove totally inadequate in the decade ahead because each succeeding year will bring larger enrollments and demands for increased services.

Tomorrow's Schools Today

PAYNE ELEMENTARY SCHOOLS GO ON SPLIT-DAY SCHEDULE
ENROLLMENT UP AGAIN THIS YEAR

"Only A Stop-Gap Measure"—RICHARDSON

This headline from the *Payne Daily Dispatch,* and others like it, have appeared in too many newspapers in the past ten years. They stand as evidence that such things as split-day schedules, pupil-teacher ratios of 35:1 and more, conversion of auditoriums and gymnasiums into classrooms, and the erection of temporary, substandard buildings have been taking place all over the country. Pupils, teachers, and administrators have had to make many compromises with their usual ideas of adequacy in space, facilities and equipment. As the subheading implies, Payne's Superintendent of Schools, Dr. Richardson, is not pleased with his own decision. The emergency measure was necessitated by the conditions which exist.

Why was such a drastic step necessary? Has the community of Payne been negligent in its support of the school system? Is there an explanation for these temporary measures?

The major factor which has caused the "stop-gap" measures to be necessary is obvious. Anyone who has read a newspaper or a magazine in the recent past is aware that our schools—public and private; elementary, secondary and college—are overcrowded, and this overcrowding does have an explanation that is not simple and yet is sufficient.

School enrollments in Payne have grown with amazing speed! Few communities have been able to keep pace with their expanding enrollments. As a typical community in the United States, Payne had a school plant which was adequate to house the students in 1940, but was far too small only a few years later. Payne did not construct any school buildings from 1941–1945—the period of World War II. During those years the shortage of building materials limited major construction to projects which were directly related to the war effort, and shortly after the war Payne's school enrollments began to climb very rapidly. Thus, Payne, like many communities, was caught short. And the problems of "catching-up" are not easy to solve.

Today's record-breaking school enrollments all over the country are the results of a high birth rate a few years ago. In fact, the birth rate in the United States has confounded all predictions. In 1940, a relatively normal year, the number of births in the United States was approximately 2,500,000. It was expected that the number of births, which was quite small during World War II (as it always is during a major war) would rise rapidly immediately following the war, and then go back to a more normal amount within a few years. Such was not the case. The birth rate rose immediately after the war, as predicted. But it continued to rise, and, in 1957, went to a record-breaking 4,300,000, an increase of approximately 75 percent! Since 1957, the birth rate has declined somewhat, but it remains well above the 1940 level. Because today's births are school population in a few years, our schools can expect large enrollments for many years to come.

More Growth Ahead

Englehardt, Englehardt, Leggett and Correll, a firm of educational consultants in the determination of educational plant needs and the planning of school buildings, published a report in 1958 which summarized the facts of school enrollments for the period 1944–1958, and made some significant predictions which have proved accurate for the period 1958–1963.

Public school enrollment has been climbing steadily since 1944 when it numbered 23,266,000 pupils. Estimates for the year 1958–59 exceed 34,000,000 and by 1964 we may expect about 40,000,000 boys and girls.

If your community follows the national average, your first grade enrollments this year, 1958–59, will increase about 2 per cent over 1957–58 figures, and this rate of increase will continue year by year through 1962. In contrast, grade seven may jump 13 per cent in 1958–59 and almost 17 per cent in 1959–60.

Enrollment increases will continue at all levels for a number of years. As shown in the following table, increases in the elementary grades are slowing down but increases in the secondary grades are gaining momentum. This growth will be reflected at the college level, with continuing increases in the years ahead and a sharp rise following 1963–64.[9]

PERCENTAGE INCREASES IN PUBLIC SCHOOLS SINCE 1944

School Unit	1951–1957	1958–1964
Elementary Schools (grades 1–6)	27	11
Junior High Schools (grades 7–9)	20	25
Senior High Schools (grades 10–12)	22	26

When school enrollment predictions are projected from the present time to 1980, the figures are even more startling. It is probable that public school enrollments for grades kindergarten through six, which in 1950 stood at 15,178,000, and was approximately 32 million in 1960, will exceed 48,000,000 by 1980. Even more marked will be the increases in public secondary school enrollments—grades seven through twelve. In 1950 there were 9,650,000 in these grades; the enrollment for 1964 is estimated at 15,000,000 and should reach 17,500,000 by 1980.[10]

[9] N. L. Englehardt, Jr., *Estimates of Future Enrollments*, New York, Englehardt, Englehardt, Leggett and Correll, 1958, p. 1.
[10] "Projected School Enrollment," *Road Maps of Industry*, no. 1338, The National Industrial Conference Board, New York, August 18, 1961.

The impact of these data is being felt everywhere today. The recent past history of most school systems has been drastically changed by these enrollment figures, and the next ten to twenty years promise to be repetitions of the past and present. In view of the fact that school enrollments have virtually exploded on our schools and their facilities, it is amazing that communities have done as well as they have in meeting the problems.

Growth Brings "Growing Pains"

The early chapters of this writing discussed the relationship between one school system and its community and between the American public school system and our democratic society. It was pointed out that any social institution, a system of schools for example, is established by society, grows and flourishes so long as it receives continued support from the society which established it, and passes into oblivion if it ceases to be functional in its society. It was also noted that societies are dynamic in character and that social institutions tend to be static by comparison. People tend to look upon our social institutions as protectors of the heritage and expect the institution to remind society of its ancient values and honored traditions. The backward-looking nature of these tasks which our institutions have been given make it doubly hard for them also to keep pace with changing society. A democratic society does tend to change by evolution rather than by revolution, however, and the American public school system has the chance to carry out its ambiguous task looking both forward and backward with the real probability of survival.

The change in a democracy tends to be steady, but it is usually so slow that the institutions and even the society itself are not aware of the change as it is happening. During times of little stress and little noticeable change in our society, institutions tend to go along a rather smooth path—for most of the time society ignores its institutions. During times of great stress and much change in society, however, institutions tend to be examined with much severity, and the apathy which characterizes the relationship during more normal times, has proved to be the best possible breeding-ground for scathing criticism when the status quo is disrupted. As a result of these periods of stress, a readjustment takes place between society and its institutions.

Certainly the past few years have been times of great stress and much change, both to society in general and to schools specifically. A series of world-wide wars, the race into outer space, and monumental efforts to attain universal peace have presented American society with its greatest challenge. Not only have schools had a central place in attempting these tasks but the pressures have occurred during the period of tremendous growth noted above. Thus, the demands created by great numerical growth have been matched by the need for a new assessment by schools of their proper function in society. Because of this, education is news. Schools are as vital as tomorrow's headlines, and these periods of change always cause "growing pains."

Meeting the Challenge of Change

Most communities have risen to the challenge, and are protecting the future of their schools. Like mythical Payne, many towns have had to use emergency measures and less-than-standard buildings and equipment at times, but real progress is also being made. New buildings, higher teachers' salaries, new equipment and facilities are being provided at an increasing rate.

Louis Cassels, religion and educational columnist for United Press International, summarized information concerning some of the things which were done in the decade of the 1950s—a period of particular stress. He noted that no nation in the history of the world had ever expanded its public educational facilities as much as did the United States during the decade of the 1950s when more than 600,000 new classrooms were built and nearly 500,000 employees added to the instructional staff. He also pointed out that the average annual salary for the instructional staff, which was $3,010 in 1949–1950, increased by 71 percent to $5,160 in 1959–1960. Recent figures from the National Education Association estimate that teachers' salaries for the school year 1962–1963 averaged approximately $5747.

Real progress has been made even in terms of the greatly expanded student populations mentioned earlier. In the 1949–1951 school year, the average current expenditure per student was $210.34 a year. During the 1959–1960 academic year it was $390.00, and estimates of the per pupil expenditure for the 1963–1964 school year run as high as $650.00 not including costs for new buildings.

Yes, America's investment in public education, while still far short of what most educational authorities consider necessary, has increased enormously during recent years. We do have faith in our American public school system. And, as in years past, we are proving it. There is no reason to doubt that the future can show even greater gains.

WHAT WE EXPECT FROM OUR TEACHERS

The first topic discussed in this book was, "What We Expect From Our Schools." Many students are surprised when they begin to consider the implications of that idea—the fact is, that as a society we demand a great deal from our schools. No country in history has made schools more available to all of its citizens than has the United States; and no country ever expected so much from its schools. We look to our schools to provide instruction in the so-called "fundamentals," of course. Also, however, we expect our schools to be concerned with the total development of their students. Social, emotional, physical, and moral and spiritual growth are considered by many to be logical areas of concern for the public schools, in addition to the academic development for which schools are held basically responsible. Because we expect so much from our schools, it is only logical that we also expect a great deal from our teachers.

First, we expect our teachers to possess the personal qualities already discussed. These qualities are important bases for success. However, they are no guarantee of success; they are only a starting place. We expect our teachers to be the right "kind" of person, but we also expect much more.

Most important, we expect our teachers to be qualified professional workers, thoroughly prepared for their jobs. To meet this requirement a person must demonstrate a high level of ability in at least three areas. He should possess: (1) intellectual curiosity and competence, (2) technical professional skill and competence, and (3) competence in building a well-integrated personality.

Intellectual Curiosity and Competence

1. The competent teacher thoroughly understands his teaching field of specialization and stimulates students to learn in that area. He knows both the technical phases and practical applications of the field, he knows the interesting and challenging phases of the field and develops in his pupils an enthusiasm for learning more about the field.

2. The competent teacher also has a broad knowledge in more general fields, and is able to make clear the applications and relationships between his special fields of specialization and more general fields of study.

3. The competent teacher uses effectively the fundamental media of communication and thinking. He uses good oral and written English, handles tools of computation effectively, and reads with ease and understanding. He is skilled in the use of libraries and library tools.

4. The competent teacher maintains an active interest in events which affect the community, the nation and the world. He reads and listens with discrimination to reports of current happenings, and is able to relate the present and the past.

5. The competent teacher develops an intelligent social philosophy. He understands the basic implications of American Democracy and works constructively for its continuous improvement. He makes education functional as a means of helping students understand human experience and their responsibilities in maintaining and strengthening our American heritage.

Technical Professional Skills and Competence

1. The competent teacher teaches in accordance with what is known about human growth and development. He recognizes the fact that children are developing organisms and recognizes and provides for individual difference in learners.

2. The competent teachers teaches with regard to the nature of the learning process. He knows and utilizes the principles of educational psychology.

3. The competent teacher selects, organizes, and executes techniques of instruction suitable to the needs of pupils. He locates, selects and organizes interesting and pertinent teaching material, uses the resources of the community. He provides pupils with purposeful activities.

4. The competent teacher uses a variety of techniques in helping students carry out the learning process.

5. The competent teacher is acquainted with the significant research that has been done in his area of teaching, and utilizes the methods of conducting educational research in solving his own educational problems.

6. The competent teacher advises and uses desirable means of evaluation of the progress of students.

7. The competent teacher develops a wide range of interests in desirable activities and has the ability to stimulate students in engaging in such activities.

8. The competent teacher understands and cooperates in the operation and administration of the school. He knows the larger relationships and responsibilities of his job, and works for the betterment of the school and the profession.

Competence in Building a Well-Integrated Personality

1. The competent teacher formulates an ever-growing philosophy of life. He builds a value system which is high and functional.

2. The competent teacher develops and maintains his own physical and mental health. He recognizes the importance of a sound mind in a strong body, and develops a variety of challenging, worthwhile activities outside his job.

3. The competent teacher develops and maintains highly satisfying human relationships. He works well with others.

4. The competent teacher develops a variety of personal skills. He has internal confidence, he faces reality, he takes criticism objectively, he analyzes his own attitudes and beliefs. He is able to withhold judgment, and can change his own views in the light of new evidence.

Although this listing included a large number of skills and competencies, it should not be considered as comprehensive. The attributes that have been noted here are only typical of the things which we demand from our teachers. It is necessary to conclude that, just as we demand a great deal from our schools, we also expect a great deal from our teachers.

Do I Measure Up?

Many professions have an oath which outlines some of the responsibilities and the highest goals of the group. One well-known oath for teachers is John Ecklund's "Loyalty Oath for Teachers" which says:

I pledge myself to the unceasing search for truth, to the increasing of the general human welfare, and to the full emancipation of the individual child. I will constantly seek to serve the basic tenets of democracy, knowing that democracy is a way of life, not a static credo, and that the democratic way of life is served best through the challenge of social and economic problems yet unmet or unconquered. The hysteria of fear or prejudice shall not enter my classroom. In my day-to-day duties I will strive to keep alive the optimism of youth, positively directed and tempered by the experiences of human kind as I have found them. My classroom shall be the shrine of the dignity and worth of each child; their confidences shall be inviolate; their growth and development the motive of my job. This to the end that voluntary discipline and interest may supersede external control in our individual and collective search for the good life.

The teaching profession is worthy of your most thoughtful consideration. There is a great demand for well-prepared teachers. Teaching offers rich rewards to the person who understands and appreciates the importance of a teacher. No job available offers greater opportunity for service to society. Can you meet the high standards? Do you measure up to them?

RELATED READINGS

Conant, James Bryan, *The Education of American Teachers*, New York, McGraw-Hill, 1963.

Hodenfield, G. K., and T. M. Stinett, *The Education of Teachers*, Englewood Cliffs, N.J., Prentice-Hall, 1961.

Lieberman, Myron, *Education as a Profession*, Englewood Cliffs, N.J., Prentice-Hall, 1956.

Teachers for Tomorrow, New York, The Fund for the Advancement of Education, 1955.

Wynn, D. Richard, *Careers in Education*, New York, McGraw-Hill, 1960.

Appendixes

Appendix A **/ APPRAISAL OF TEACHER SERVICE***

Name...School...

Grades or Subjects...Date...

Instructions

The standards of excellence enumerated in this form are descriptive of the highly superior teacher. The **Appraisal of Teacher Service** is to be carried on with reference to those standards.

Five areas of service are to be considered. A general statement introduces each section, followed by a series of substatements to help the evaluator determine to what degree a teacher meets the standards described. This judgment constitutes the summary score for each area.

A five-point numerical scale will be used in scoring, with 1 designating highly superior service; 5, unsatisfactory service; and the numbers 2, 3, and 4, intermediate degrees of excellence.

Early in the school year the principal will explain the evaluative procedure to his teachers and will emphasize the constructive point of view which prompts it. He will stress its value in establishing a record of the professional growth and in-service attainments of the individual teacher.

SUMMARY

Area	Score
I. Personal Qualities	....
II. Teacher-Pupil Relationships	....
III. Classroom Teaching	....
IV. Out-of-Class Responsibilities	....
V. Professional Relationships	....

Comments

....

....

....

....

....

....

....

I have read this report and discussed its content with my evaluator.

....
Signature of Evaluator

....
Signature of Teacher

....
Position of Evaluator

* From the Omaha Public Schools, Omaha, Nebraska; used by permission.

Circle the number that best describes the individual in terms of the superior qualities described below.

I. PERSONAL QUALITIES   Summary Score 1 2 3 4 5

The personal characteristics and attitudes of a teacher make him what he is and influence all that he does. Usually, the excellent teacher possesses the following qualities:

Characteristic Outlook   1 2 3 4 5

He has faith in people. He is cheerful, optimistic, and enthusiastic. He sees the humor in a situation and does not take himself too seriously.

Sympathetic Understanding   1 2 3 4 5

He is approachable, friendly, and sincere in his dealings with people. His interest in the problems of others springs from a desire to be helpful rather than from personal curiosity.

Emotional Stability   1 2 3 4 5

He customarily acts with poise, mature judgment, and self-control. He responds judiciously to criticism.

Judgment and Tact   1 2 3 4 5

He shows insight and sensitivity to the probable outcomes of what he does and says and makes decisions accordingly. He works among teachers and pupils without creating resentment. He promotes understanding rather than antagonism by sensing the right thing to do and say.

Adaptability and Resourcefulness   1 2 3 4 5

He adjusts himself well to most situations and makes good use of the resources at his disposal. He approaches his work with initiative and imagination.

Cooperation and Dependability   1 2 3 4 5

He works well with others. Whether leader or follower, he carries his full share of responsibility. He is reliable and finishes what he begins.

Health   1 2 3 4 5

He has the stamina to meet the daily obligations of school life. He exhibits vitality and energy.

Speech   1 2 3 4 5

He uses good English and expresses his thoughts clearly and appropriately. His voice is agreeable and well modulated.

Appearance   1 2 3 4 5

He is well-groomed and suitably dressed. He makes a good impression.

II. TEACHER-PUPIL RELATIONSHIPS   Summary Score 1 2 3 4 5

A cooperative working relationship between pupils and teacher is fundamental to all good teaching. Such a relationship is founded on a genuine liking for children and young people, a belief in their capacities for growth, and a sympathetic understanding of their developmental needs. The end to be desired is a feeling of mutual respect and interest between pupil and teacher. In such an atmosphere learning flourishes, and mutual satisfaction results. The excellent teacher usually achieves the following:

Classroom Atmosphere   1 2 3 4 5

On the part of both teacher and pupils there is marked evidence of cooperation, respect, courtesy, and willingness to work. A friendly atmosphere prevails.

290

Personal Relationships

1 2 3 4 5

The teacher is interested in his pupils and shows an understanding of their problems. He is considerate of their rights and is fair in his judgment.

Pupil Freedom and Control

1 2 3 4 5

The pupils have freedom of action in proportion to their demonstrated ability to use their privileges wisely. Pupil responsibility and respect for authority develop under the teacher's guidance. Few instances of friction arise.

III. CLASSROOM TEACHING

Summary Score 1 2 3 4 5

Exceptional teaching ability is evidenced by the methods used in motivating learning, in presenting subject matter, and in adapting instructional materials to the needs of particular groups and individuals. The excellent teacher is usually able to provide the following experiences for his pupils:

Rich Content

1 2 3 4 5

He has a sound, growing knowledge of his subject, the result of a broad cultural and professional background. He draws upon the pupils' knowledge of the subject as well as the resources of the school and community.

Effective Use of Content, Materials, and Method

1 2 3 4 5

Planning and preparation: Keeping his aims in mind he carefully selects and organizes subject matter. He adapts method, motivation, and materials to the needs of his class, recognizing differing degrees of ability among the pupils. He plans for the intelligent use of such aids as exhibits, models, slides, films, radio, maps, references, field trips, radio, television, and excursions.

Presentation and development: He skillfully draws upon pupil interest as a motivating force to direct his teaching. He encourages all pupils to participate actively. He invites discussion. He encourages reflective, critical thinking. He commends pupils for noteworthy accomplishment and avoids embarrassing either class or individual by the use of sarcasm. He uses repetition and summation techniques effectively. Assignments are clear, motivating, and related to pupil ability.

Follow-up: He keeps adequate records of pupil achievement. He knows the available test materials and services and makes intelligent use of them. He vitalizes his reviews and drills. He is skillful in evaluating his pupils. He encourages each pupil to view his personal accomplishment in relation to his own ability.

Outcomes

1 2 3 4 5

Growth and responsibility: Under his supervision, pupils grow in the ability to use freedom wisely. They learn to give and take direction, to cooperate, to assume responsibility, and to act independently at appropriate times.

Growth in knowledge and skills: He works with pupils so that each grows to the best of his ability toward the mastery of fundamental learning.

Growth of attitudes, habits, and appreciations: He encourages and develops in pupils respect for authority and appreciation of school, home, community, and nation.

Special Needs

1 2 3 4 5

He is alert in his classroom to symptoms of disease, malnutrition, emotional disturbances, and to defects in eyes, ears, teeth, and speech. He refers cases needing special attention to other staff members, e. g., nurse, speech specialist, psychologist, adviser.

Attention to Essential Details

1 2 3 4 5

He handles routine matters efficiently, using pupil assistance whenever appropriate. He pays adequate attention to proper ventilation, seating, and lighting. He is prompt, careful, and accurate in making the reports and records required of him.

IV. OUT-OF-CLASS RESPONSIBILITIES Summary Score 1 2 3 4 5

Good teaching goes beyond the class period and the regular program. Pupils who have been absent need extra help. Many need personal counseling. School activities require teacher leadership. The excellent teacher usually helps the pupils and his school in the following ways:

Subject Matter Problems 1 2 3 4 5

He is willing to give extra time and help to pupils who have real needs. He gives pupils a fair chance to make up work. He reteaches when necessary. He takes advantage of informal opportunities to enrich the class program.

Personal Problems 1 2 3 4 5

Pupils come to him for help. When his own knowledge and experience are inadequate to satisfy their needs, he enlists the aid of others. He respects the trust pupils place in him.

School Activities 1 2 3 4 5

He recognizes that school activities expand the interests of pupils and form a normal part of the school program. He encourages pupils to join school-approved groups for purposes suited to their needs and interests. He cautions them to observe a proper balance between out-of-class activities and class work. He guides and assists.

V. PROFESSIONAL RELATIONSHIPS Summary Score 1 2 3 4 5

The excellent teacher recognizes his responsibilities to education in general and is constant in his loyalty and service to its many causes.

Total School Program 1 2 3 4 5

He sees his own work and subject in fair relationship to the whole school program. He assists actively with after-school activities and evening functions.

He is willing to serve on committees. Through discussion, research, and experiment, he shares the task of finding solutions for administrative problems.

Fellow Teachers 1 2 3 4 5

He works cooperatively with the school staff. He is friendly and courteous and shows willingness to help teachers new to the school. He recognizes and appreciates the good work of his associates.

Parents and Community 1 2 3 4 5

Recognizing that schools belong to the community, he does what he can to build community understanding and good will. He welcomes the natural interest of parents in their children's welfare. He treats visitors courteously, helps them understand the school program, and invites their cooperation. He stresses accomplishments, not failures, of pupils.

Teaching as a Profession 1 2 3 4 5

He has a deep and enthusiastic interest in teaching, believes in its worth, and encourages promising people to enter the profession. He reads and studies in his own and related fields, keeps himself informed of recent developments, and adapts his teaching to changing conditions and needs.

Appendix B / THE CODE OF ETHICS*
OF THE EDUCATION PROFESSION

PREAMBLE

We, professional educators of the United States of America, affirm our belief in the worth and dignity of man. We recognize the supreme importance of the pursuit of truth, the encouragement of scholarship, and the promotion of democratic citizenship. We regard as essential to these goals the protection of freedom to learn and to teach and the guarantee of equal educational opportunity for all.

* As developed by the National Education Association.

We affirm and accept our responsibility to practice our profession according to the highest ethical standards.

We acknowledge the magnitude of the profession we have chosen, and engage ourselves, individually and collectively, to judge our colleagues and to be judged by them in accordance with the applicable provisions of this code.

PRINCIPLE I
Commitment to the Student

We measure success by the progress of each student toward achievement of his maximum potential. We therefore work to stimulate the spirit of inquiry, the acquisition of knowledge and understanding, and the thoughtful formulation of worthy goals. We recognize the importance of cooperative relationships with other community institutions, especially the home.

In fulfilling our obligations to the student, we—

1. Deal justly and considerately with each student.
2. Encourage the student to study varying points of view and respect his right to form his own judgment.
3. Withhold confidential information about a student or his home unless we deem that its release serves professional purposes, benefits the student, or is required by law.
4. Make discreet use of available information about the student.
5. Conduct conferences with or concerning students in an appropriate place and manner.
6. Refrain from commenting unprofessionally about a student or his home.
7. Avoid exploiting our professional relationship with any student.
8. Tutor only in accordance with officially approved policies.
9. Inform appropriate individuals and agencies of the student's educational needs and assist in providing an understanding of his educational experiences.
10. Seek constantly to improve learning facilities and opportunities.

PRINCIPLE II
Commitment to the Community

We believe that patriotism in its highest form requires dedication to the principles of our democratic heritage. We share with all other citizens the responsibility for the development of sound public policy. As educators, we are particularly accountable for participating in the development of educational programs and policies and for interpreting them to the public.

In fulfilling our obligations to the student, we—

1. Share the responsibility for improving the educational opportunities for all.
2. Recognize that each educational institution may have a person authorized to interpret its official policies.
3. Acknowledge the right and responsibility of the public to participate in the formulation of educational policy.
4. Evaluate through appropriate professional procedures conditions within a dis-

trict or institution of learning, make known serious deficiencies, and take any action deemed necessary and proper.

5. Use educational facilities for intended purposes consistent with applicable policy, law, and regulation.
6. Assume full political and citizenship responsibilities, but refrain from exploiting the institutional privileges of our professional positions to promote political candidates or partisan activities.
7. Protect the educational program against undesirable infringement.

PRINCIPLE III
Commitment to the Profession

We believe that the quality of the services of the education profession directly influences the future of the nation and its citizens. We therefore exert every effort to raise educational standards, to improve our service, to promote a climate in which the exercise of professional judgment is encouraged, and to achieve conditions which attract persons worthy of the trust to careers in education. Aware of the value of united effort, we contribute actively to the support, planning, and programs of our professional organizations.

In fulfilling our obligations to the profession, we—

1. Recognize that a profession must accept responsibility for the conduct of its members and understand that our own conduct may be regarded as representative.
2. Participate and conduct ourselves in a responsible manner in the development and implementation of policies affecting education.
3. Cooperate in the selective recruitment of prospective teachers and in the orientation of student teachers, interns, and those colleagues new to their positions.
4. Accord just and equitable treatment to all members of the profession in the exercise of their professional rights and responsibilities, and support them when unjustly accused or mistreated.
5. Refrain from assigning professional duties to non-professional personnel when such assignment is not in the best interest of the student.
6. Provide, upon request, a statement of specific reason from administrative recommendations that lead to the denial of increments, significant changes in employment, or termination of employment.
7. Refrain from exerting undue influence based on the authority of our positions in the determination of professional decisions by colleagues.
8. Keep the trust under which confidential information is exchanged.
9. Make appropriate use of time granted for professional purposes.
10. Interpret and use the writings of others and the findings of educational research with intellectual honesty.
11. Maintain our integrity when dissenting by basing our public criticism of education on valid assumptions as established by careful evaluation of facts or hypotheses.
12. Represent honestly our professional qualifications and identify ourselves only with reputable educational institutions.

13. Respond accurately to requests for evaluations of colleagues seeking professional positions.
14. Provide applicants seeking information about a position with an honest description of the assignment, the conditions of work, and related matters.

PRINCIPLE IV
Commitment to Professional Employment Practices

We regard the employment agreement as a solemn pledge to be executed both in spirit and in fact in a manner consistent with the highest ideals of professional service. Sound professional personnel relationships with governing boards are built upon personal integrity, dignity, and mutual respect.

In fulfilling our obligations to professional employment practices, we—

1. Apply for or offer a position on the basis of professional and legal qualifications.
2. Apply for a specific position only when it is known to be vacant and refrain from such practices as underbidding or commenting adversely about other candidates.
3. Fill no vacancy except where the terms, conditions, policies, and practices permit the exercise of our professional judgment and skill, and where a climate conducive to professional service exists.
4. Adhere to the conditions of a contract or to the terms of an appointment until either has been terminated legally or by mutual consent.
5. Give prompt notice of any change in availability of service, in status of applications, or in change in position.
6. Conduct professional business through the recognized educational and professional channels.
7. Accept no gratuities or gifts of significance that might influence our judgment in the exercise of our professional duties.
8. Engage in no outside employment that will impair the effectiveness of our professional service and permit no commercial exploitation of our professional position.

Indexes

INDEX OF NAMES

INDEX OF SUBJECTS